Practical SharePoint 2013 Enterprise Content Management

Steve Goodyear

Practical SharePoint 2013 Enterprise Content Management

ISBN-13 (pbk): 978-1-4302-6169-8

ISBN-13 (electronic): 978-1-4302-6170-4

Trademarked names, logos, and images may appear in this book. Rather than use a trademark symbol with every occurrence of a trademarked name, logo, or image we use the names, logos, and images only in an editorial fashion and to the benefit of the trademark owner, with no intention of infringement of the trademark.

The use in this publication of trade names, trademarks, service marks, and similar terms, even if they are not identified as such, is not to be taken as an expression of opinion as to whether or not they are subject to proprietary rights.

While the advice and information in this book are believed to be true and accurate at the date of publication, neither the authors nor the editors nor the publisher can accept any legal responsibility for any errors or omissions that may be made. The publisher makes no warranty, express or implied, with respect to the material contained herein.

President and Publisher: Paul Manning
Lead Editor: Jon Hassell
Developmental Editor: Douglas Pundick
Technical Reviewer: Zach Millis
Editorial Board: Steve Anglin, Mark Beckner, Ewan Buckingham, Gary Cornell, Louise Corrigan, Morgan Ertel, Jonathan Gennick, Jonathan Hassell, Robert Hutchinson, Michelle Lowman, James Markham, Matthew Moodie, Jeff Olson, Jeffrey Pepper, Douglas Pundick, Ben Renow-Clarke, Dominic Shakeshaft, Gwenan Spearing, Matt Wade, Tom Welsh
Coordinating Editor: Anamika Panchoo
Copy Editor: Kimberly Burton-Weisman
Compositor: SPi Global
Indexer: SPi Global
Cover Designer: Anna Ishchenko

Distributed to the book trade worldwide by Springer Science+Business Media New York, 233 Spring Street, 6th Floor, New York, NY 10013. Phone 1-800-SPRINGER, fax (201) 348-4505, e-mail orders-ny@springer-sbm.com, or visit www.springeronline.com. Apress Media, LLC is a California LLC and the sole member (owner) is Springer Science + Business Media Finance Inc (SSBM Finance Inc). SSBM Finance Inc is a Delaware corporation.

For information on translations, please e-mail rights@apress.com, or visit www.apress.com.

Apress and friends of ED books may be purchased in bulk for academic, corporate, or promotional use. eBook versions and licenses are also available for most titles. For more information, reference our Special Bulk Sales–eBook Licensing web page at www.apress.com/bulk-sales.

Any source code or other supplementary materials referenced by the author in this text is available to readers at www.apress.com. For detailed information about how to locate your book's source code, go to www.apress.com/source-code/.

To all my fellow SharePoint worker bees feeling overwhelmed by swarms of information.
I have some of the honey you need to organize your hive right here, my friends.

Contents at a Glance

Contents

About the Author

Steve Goodyear hs an author and a SharePoint expert living in Vancouver, Canada, where he writes and works as a consultant and solution architect. He is also the author of *Practical SharePoint 2013 Governance* (Apress, 2013).

Previously, he worked for Microsoft as an Enterprise Consultant engaging as a SharePoint specialist with Microsoft's largest enterprise and government customers around North America to design technology solutions for their most challenging business problems. Before joining Microsoft, Steve was also a Software Engineer and Technical Lead at Electronic Arts. At the time of this writing, Steve worked as a Principal Consultant for DevFacto Technologies.

Steve is a Microsoft Certified Trainer and he holds several Microsoft Certified Professional (MCP) certifications, including: SharePoint Administration and Development on each version of SharePoint from 2003 to 2013, SQL Server Administration and Development, and ASP.NET Development. He loves writing about technology to share ideas that inform, entertain, and inspire readers.

You can send Steve a tweet @SteveGoodyear on Twitter or you can read more of his tips and insights on his SharePoint blog at http://stevegoodyear.wordpress.com. You can also connect with Steve on LinkedIn at www.linkedin.com/in/stevegoodyear.

Microsoft
C E R T I F I E D
Trainer

Microsoft
C E R T I F I E D
IT Professional

Microsoft
C E R T I F I E D
Professional Developer

About the Technical Reviewer

Zach Millis works as a Senior Consultant for imason inc., where he specializes in SharePoint infrastructure and long-term sustainability for imason solutions. His experience includes working for some of Canada's top SharePoint services firms and advising some of Canada's largest corporations on their SharePoint operations. Zach's latest infrastructure projects have included his consulting on SharePoint 2013 implementations on-premises and in the cloud, Office 365 deployments, and exploring Windows Azure Infrastructure as a Service platform for SharePoint 2013 web sites.

Originally from Madison, Wisconsin, Zach's infrastructure skills have taken him across the United States, New Zealand, and Canada, to his new home of Toronto, Ontario. Zach holds several Microsoft Certified Professional (MCP) certifications, including: Microsoft Certified Systems Administrator; SharePoint 2010 Administrator; Enterprise Desktop Administrator on Windows 7; Enterprise Desktop Support Technician on Windows Vista and Windows 7; SharePoint 2007 and 2010 Configuration; and Windows 7 Configuration.

You can connect with Zach on LinkedIn at www.linkedin.com/in/zacharymillis, and read his blog posts on www.imason.com.

Microsoft
C E R T I F I E D
Solutions Associate

Microsoft
C E R T I F I E D
IT Professional

Microsoft
C E R T I F I E D
Technology Specialist

Acknowledgments

I would like to express many thanks to all my family and friends who offer their constant encouragement and ongoing support. I am a lucky guy to have so many wonderful and inspiring people in my life.

A huge thanks and kudos to my editing team at Apress for joining me for a second time on this book: Jon Hassell, Ana Panchoo, Douglas Pundick—each of whom are a pleasure to work with and learn from. Thanks to everyone supporting my title behind the scenes at Apress who I did not get a chance to meet, and to the production team at SPi. Thanks to my copyeditor, Kimberly Burton-Weisman, for having such an eye for detail and for working hard to give my text a final polish.

Thanks also to my technical reviewer, my good friend Zach Millis, for joining me again on our second book project together, for lending his expertise, and for his hard work providing me with feedback. Thank you all for helping me make a quality book!

Introduction

This book takes you through how to analyze and plan enterprise content management (ECM) solutions for an effective and end-to-end information design built in SharePoint 2013 and based on your organization's needs and business requirements.

My primary focus as I wrote this book was to guide you through analyzing business processes and requirements to design an ECM solution rather than simply deploying technology. Technology plays a part, and I guide you through the steps you need to deploy and configure relevant aspects of SharePoint, but I also move beyond surveying the product features to consider the underlying business needs that drive decisions in your solution design.

Throughout this book, you will receive expert guidance on how to manage your information life cycle—from identifying and understanding your organization's information, to creating and collaborating on your transitory content, to capturing and controlling your records. This book walks you through each phase to guide you with your ECM strategy, from content creation and discovery to retention and disposition, and it gives you the basis to design and implement your ECM solution.

After reading this book, you will know how to

- Apply a content life cycle model to analyze and understand your organization's information.

- Plan and configure your SharePoint 2013 enterprise eDiscovery portal and manage your discovery cases.

- Design your file plan with content routing rules for your SharePoint records repository.

- Design solutions to interface and integrate with external records management systems.

- Design content types and implement an enterprise content type hub to categorize and organize your information.

- Identify your organization's information security requirements.

Who This Book is For

Practical SharePoint 2013 Enterprise Content Management is for you if you are a SharePoint architect, administrator, consultant, or project manager and you implement SharePoint solutions that relate to one or more aspects of the information life cycle involved with ECM.

This book is also for you if you are an enterprise architect or a records manager and you want to learn how ECM fits in SharePoint. This book is definitely for you if you want to analyze, design, and implement an ECM solution on SharePoint 2013.

I wrote this book in a conversational manner to share my ECM knowledge and experiences with you as a peer.

How This Book Is Organized

This book organizes enterprise content management topics by phase in the information life cycle. I choose to organize the book in this way to help you apply the appropriate SharePoint 2013 features to meet your needs, depending on which stage of the information life cycle you are addressing.

I broke the book into the following four parts:

- **Part I** focuses on information management concepts and the content life cycle in general. Chapters in this part discuss enterprise content management in general along with the content life cycle model I use to analyze content and its life cycle within an organization.

- **Part II** focuses on transitory content where users create or capture information. Chapters in this part discuss collaborative and web content, as well as information management features such as content types.

- **Part III** focuses on content discovery and how to connect users with the organization's knowledge. Chapters in this part discuss enterprise search, social computing, eDiscovery, and securing content.

- **Part IV** focuses on official records and records management. Chapters in this part discuss designing a file plan and then applying it to a records repository, creating content retention and disposition policies, and integrating with external records management systems.

I tried to reference other chapters anywhere I mention something that I describe in greater detail elsewhere in the book, whether it occurs earlier or later. In this way, I hope to accommodate any readers who read the book out of order or who are only interested in particular sections. Of course, you can also read the book in order, cover to cover.

▓ **Note**   As you read, please do let me know if you have any feedback on the book. I would love to hear from you! Please send me a tweet @SteveGoodyear on Twitter to share any of your feedback or thoughts.

■ ■ ■

PART 1

Planning and Analyzing Your Information Life Cycle

Enterprise content management is a complex topic and it may feel overwhelming when you look at its vastness and intricacies. It may even lead to a feeling of project paralysis of sorts, a bewilderment of where to start—stalling the project before it even takes shape. When challenges feel too large with too many dependencies, I find the best approach is to simplify the challenge and break it down into manageable, achievable parts. In my first pass at simplifying enterprise content management (ECM), I divided this book into four main parts, and then I further divided each part into four chapters, laying an approach for where to start and how to progress through your ECM initiative, starting with establishing foundational knowledge and a process to analyze your content.

The chapters in this first part look at how to plan and analyze the information life cycle within your organization, setting the foundation to understand ECM concepts in general, as well as your enterprise content's life cycle specifically, both of which the rest of the book will build upon. I start by describing enterprise content management concepts to establish a shared understanding, and then I introduce the content life cycle model I use in this book to analyze content and its relation to the organization. From there, I provide an overview of Microsoft SharePoint 2013 and its ECM features, and then I describe how to analyze your information life cycle. Finally, I guide you through how to take your content analysis and design your information architecture.

As you begin, I find it helps to create a roadmap to approach your enterprise content management solution design; a roadmap with a series of phases culminating into the entire scope of the ECM solution but divided into manageable and discrete iterative stages. You can use such a roadmap to plan an iterative approach that will eventually address your ECM needs, all through a series of smaller and focused project iterations. Your first iteration should be to understand enterprise content management itself, which is where I begin.

■ ■ ■

CHAPTER 1

Overview of Enterprise Content Management

Learn the rules like a pro, so you can break them like an artist.

—Pablo Picasso

What is enterprise content management? In this chapter, I provide an overview of enterprise content management (ECM) to provide you with a basis of ECM concepts that the rest of the book references and builds upon. I also introduce a model illustrating the life cycle of a piece of content that I use throughout this book to relate the different aspects of enterprise content management in the context of an information life cycle within an organization. From there, I discuss the difference between transitory content vs. official records as I relate each to the life cycle of content within your organization. Finally, I consider some of the costs and value associated with an enterprise content management solution.

After reading this chapter, you will know how to

- Describe enterprise content management concepts.

- Explain the difference between transitory content and official records.

- Understand and apply the content life cycle model.

- Describe the costs and value associated with an ECM solution.

- Plan your approach to an ECM project.

Understanding the Value of Enterprise Content Management

An enterprise content management program delivers long-term value because it brings together information within the organization, facilitating the organization to function and operate rather than waste inefficiencies tracking down content or basing decisions on outdated or missing information. To achieve this, ECM enables collaboration and enterprise search, simplifies administration and management, systematizes policies and processes, and automates the retention and disposition of individual pieces of content.

Enterprise content management also standardizes content repositories, organizing several well-known locations for particular types of content, easing the management burden by centralizing the administration. This helps users find relevant content based on relevant locations, but it also helps protect and secure content by having policies cascade down through an area, ensuring that the right permissions are set for a given type of content, and minimizing the risk of a security gap due to incorrect or incomplete security access controls on a piece of content.

The automation in an ECM system provides further ongoing value, reducing time lags associated with waiting for human input, and eliminating labor costs accompanying human involvement. This system automation helps reduce errors, particularly those due to human error, as it validates input and processes workflows according to predefined steps and rules. Automation also helps maintain your content by automating its cleanup.

Cleanup of content is not usually a high priority for users, especially with their more pressing priorities in their job functions. As such, the majority of manual content cleanup usually coincides with deploying new system or upgrading to a newer version. Your first wave of value with a new ECM implementation can come from the content cleanup as you reorganize some content and dispose of other content. Your subsequent waves of value come from any policies you define to automate the cleanup of content through retention and disposition.

Once content ceases to provide value, then it is time to dispose of it; otherwise, it will accrue costs without providing any value. Content has value while it is usable to an individual or workgroup to support their job function, or while it provides information to processes, or while the organization depends on it to capture historical information. When your ECM system automates the disposition of content as it ceases to provide value, you save those costs.

What Is Enterprise Content Management?

Although the term *enterprise content management* has only been around since 2000, its concepts have been around as long as businesses have produced content and retained records. Before computers became so ubiquitous and digital files began to represent the bulk of content, physical files, folders, and filing cabinets made up the implementation details for enterprise content. The ECM processes at that time focused heavily on filing strategies, ergonomic cabinet layouts, and effective use of index cards to cross-reference content.

With the onset of computers and the ongoing exponential growth of digital content, organizations began looking for ways to manage the different repositories of content, to build an overall strategy for content. Motivated by things such as ensuring compliance, protecting intellectual property, or leveraging existing expertise, organizations have been evolving their enterprise content management from the world of physical content to digital content.

Before one can plan and design an enterprise content management solution, he or she first needs to understand the meaning of enterprise content management and what it represents in their organization. It is not a simple answer, and this is mostly because of the complexity of organizations and the range of information they process.

The Association for Information and Image Management (AIIM) International, the worldwide association for enterprise content management, defines ECM as the strategies, methods, and tools an organization uses to capture, manage, store, preserve, and deliver the organization's information assets over their life cycle and within the entire scope of an enterprise. This makes a nice overarching definition that I might sum up as *the means to manage information within an organization.* Let's break this concept down a little further and take a closer look at enterprise content management.

First, I need to define enterprise content. ECM is such a huge category, and you probably already have some familiarity with its vastness, hence why you might have reached for this book in the first place. There is so much content, for one, and it varies between departments with an array of different kinds. A piece of content can serve different purposes at different times or maybe even different purposes at the same time.

I created a model to visualize and make sense of enterprise content—the content life cycle model I will introduce and describe in detail in a later section of this chapter. This will help me describe content in the context of different phases or stages of an information life cycle within an organization. For now, I just want to point out the general idea of an organization and its different types of content existing in different stages, all culminating, forming the enterprise content.

I think of content as units of information—a slightly more abstract way than simply referring to *content*, but it also gives me a contained and countable unit, rather than the collective noun *content*. Focusing on a piece of content, or a contained and countable unit of information, eases the process of analyzing and designing an ECM solution, all from considering the actual items and generalizing or abstracting from there.

Units of information come in a variety of types in an organization, each with some degree of formality, some level of sensitivity, and some scope of impact on the organization. Managers may make budget and planning decisions based on the information; employees may make operational and career decisions based on the information; investors may base investment decisions on the information; and customers may make their decisions based on the information. Here's a list of some different types of enterprise content with different characteristics to consider:

- **A code of conduct policy manual:** This represents a formal document describing what is and is not acceptable behavior, typically forming a binding contract between the organization and its people. In some jurisdictions, this unit of information can protect an organization or hold it liable based on the policies it defines or omits, and whether it enforces the policies consistently.

- **An executive e-mail sent organization-wide announcing organizational change:** This represents a formal communication from one of the organization's leaders. Again, due to its formality and its reach, this unit of information usually has regulatory requirements because investors will base investment decisions on its content.

- **A product specification document:** This represents a formal document with intellectual property that an organization uses for a competitive advantage in the market. This unit of information usually has strict confidentiality requirements to secure and protect the organization's interests.

- **A document with the meeting minutes from a project team's status update meeting:** This represents a formal and historical account of the meeting, but its formality and impact on the organization depend on the scope of the project and its criticality to the organization. It may serve as a historical document for a limited audience, allowing project team members to track their progress on a minor internal project, or it may serve as a contractual document detailing delivery and sign-off for major milestones on a business-critical project.

- **A user's status update on the organization's microblogging site:** This represents a small piece of informal content, typically an opinion or reference-oriented unit of information, one created ad hoc for an internal audience and with limited structure. It usually does not drive formal or critical decisions in an organization, yet a disgruntled user may post an inappropriate or particularly offensive update, requiring an organization to capture its evidence to support disciplinary action

With such a range of content, content characteristics, and content requirements, you can see how complex the scope that enterprise content management represents. There are many variables and many things to consider at a very granular level, and they can vary by department or they can vary by stage in the content life cycle. By breaking down different parts and analyzing individual elements, you will be able to design and build up a complex enterprise content management solution, built from the ground up using each discrete class of information as building blocks. Figure 1-1 provides a partial view of the range of enterprise content in an organization.

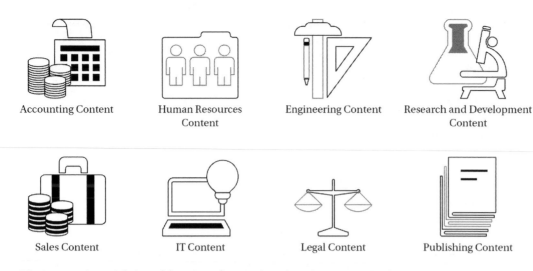

Figure 1-1. *A partial view of the range of enterprise content in an organization*

Users might need to analyze and describe each unit of information by applying policies and security to it, initiate workflows, and associate metadata to capture information about the content, such as how and why the organization uses it, its level of sensitivity, and other information to describe the piece of content. Figure 1-2 illustrates some of the different ECM components you can apply at the individual unit of information level. Not all of the information rolls up to a single universal rule you can apply to all content in an enterprise content management solution; instead, it entails a variety of cases and exceptions. You will have to analyze and work at this more granular level of content before you can build out and understand a comprehensive and global organizational view.

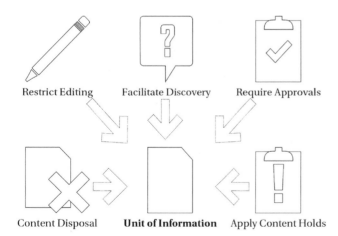

Figure 1-2. *The ECM components at the individual unit of information level*

This concept is akin to analyzing traffic in a city at rush hour. You cannot take a single aerial photograph and use this global snapshot to study traffic—although this view might play a part in revealing the heaviest congestion areas and highlighting where to analyze deeper. On its own, the global snapshot will not provide deep insights into what caused congestion, because if your city is anything like my city, *everywhere* will appear congested and busy with traffic. Instead, you need to look at relationships and the flow of traffic and traffic patterns, zooming in on individual streets and intersections, monitoring particular arteries and entry points, tracking a sample of cars to identify patterns, routes, and destinations. Similarly, with enterprise content, you will have to look at units of information, their relationships and patterns, and their flows and processes.

As you work through your enterprise content management solution, remember the key is to break down the concept of content to analyze its particulars and to look at units of information, studying their relationships and modeling their life cycle, and then you can combine your analysis to design and build your ECM solution. You can identify the characteristics of different types of enterprise content by the following content externalities:

- **Drivers:** Drivers answers questions about any motivating factors behind a type of content. What produces the content or causes it to come about? What conditions require the content? Who creates the content? How does he or she create it? Why do you even need a particular piece of content?

- **Constraints:** Constraints answers questions about how you have to treat a piece of content once it exists. Where do you need to store it? How long do you need to keep it? When do you need to dispose of it? Who can access it? Who has accessed it? What are its legal and regulatory requirements? What other enterprise content references it or bases its decisions on a particular unit of information?

I will look more closely at these questions and others in different sections throughout this book. Answering these questions and the other characteristics of content gets to the essence of enterprise content management. As I indicated earlier, enterprise content is a complex category that consists of many interrelated parts. Its parts can take many different forms and degrees of formality, and they all constitute how an organization produces, consumes, and manages its information.

Enterprise content is a term that summarizes all the content within an organization, the units of information at different stages, different uses, and different formalities. *Enterprise content management*, or as some people prefer, ECM, summarizes the concept of organizing and managing this diverse span of content with its diverse management requirements. The details for how you achieve this are the topic of discussion for the rest of this book.

Now that you have a good idea about what enterprise content and enterprise content management both entail, I want to build on this by defining core ECM concepts, establishing a shared understanding of the different technical terms I will use throughout this book. This will also help you understand the different aspects of an enterprise content management solution, laying the general foundation to design and build your information life cycle strategy on. In the next section, I cover and define different enterprise content management concepts that will help develop your familiarity with the topic.

Enterprise Content Management Concepts

Enterprise content management is a strategy for how to handle information within an organization. It implements a vision, encompassing how users interact with content and what the organization depends on with the content. It is not a closed system within the organization, because you cannot isolate and segregate it from how the organization functions.

It is not a packaged product nor is it a technology solution. However, technology can automate, control, and standardize certain aspects of your ECM implementation. You do not purchase an enterprise content management package, but you can purchase tools to implement your solution, a solution you design based on analysis of information within your organization and its related business processes—analysis this book will guide you through.

▓ **Caution**   Professional services consulting and product marketing language tends to focus on the technology aspect of enterprise content management, as if you can click through an installation wizard to solve your ECM challenges. Just remember, technology is only part of the solution and it represents the implementation details. There is no ECM easy button.

Your enterprise content management solution will consider your organization's content, from the formal to the ad hoc, from creation to disposition. The end state will certainly be a technology implementation, but there is a lot of analysis for you to do before you can design that implementation. You do not have to solve everything all at once; instead, you can tackle manageable chunks as you go. Figure 1-3 illustrates a phased approach to enterprise content management.

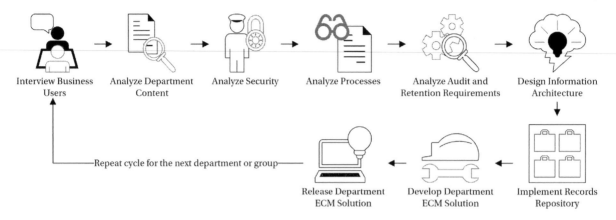

Figure 1-3. *A phased approach to enterprise content management*

This book will help you break down the challenge of ECM into those manageable chunks, first looking at an individual part, stepping through the analysis, and then guiding you on configuring the solution in SharePoint. Each of those parts may involve different technical terms or technical concepts, terms I will use throughout this book. As such, I think it is important to provide you with a description for some of the more popular terms, many of which you will already be familiar with, all to ensure we share a common ECM vocabulary.

The following sections list and describe popular ECM terms and concepts, grouped by document management, security management, business process management, and general information management. This is by no means an exhaustive list nor is it a conclusive glossary for this book; instead, it will help get you started with core terms I will use and later build on throughout the book.

Document Management Concepts

You implement document management using software to control and organize documents. This can range from a team's workspace or network file share to a sophisticated enterprise document repository. Within a document management system, users can interact with each other while creating and sharing documents. The system also hosts other related or complementary functionality, such as workflows and metadata. The following lists some common terms related to document management:

- **Content repositories:** Containers to store, manage, and organize content within the content management system, usually consisting of functionality to check-in and checkout documents, manage a version history of changes, and apply security settings.

- **Check-in and Check-out:** A feature within a document repository where a user can check out a document to lock it for exclusive editing, and then check in the document to make his or her changes available to other users.

- **Version history:** A set of previous versions of a document for each change, capturing snapshots of the state of the document at each point.

- **Collaboration:** A process that facilitates multiple users to author and work on the same content in a common environment.

- **Document imaging:** A process of transforming a physical document into an electronic document format and inputting it into the content repository.

▓ **Note**   Please see Chapter 5, where I discuss collaboration and document management in more depth.

Security Management Concepts

Security involves protecting an information asset to prevent disclosing its contents to unauthorized parties, to prevent unofficial content modifications, and to prevent unsanctioned usage. You apply security both to secure the storage and integrity of content, and to secure the transmission and use of content. The following lists some common terms related to security management:

- **Rights and permission levels:** Permission levels identify granular actions one could exercise against a piece of content, where rights identify actual permissions granted to a user, authorizing them to exercise the actions specified in each permission level.

- **Digital Rights Management (DRM):** An encryption technology to secure digital content delivered and circulated across a network, limiting it to an authorized distribution and use while preventing illegal access.

- **Digital signature:** An electronic signature using a cryptographic private key from a user's certificate, authenticating a user in message transmissions or approvers in business workflow processes.

- **Public Key Infrastructure (PKI):** A certificate-based encryption technology you use to secure transmission of content, where the sender encrypts content using a public cryptographic key that can only be decrypted using the receiver's private cryptographic key. For example, secure web sites (HTTPS) transmit web page data using PKI.

- **Audit trails:** A historical log of who performed what actions against a piece of content, such as who accessed or edited a piece of content, used to trace accountability

---

▓ **Note**   Please see Chapter 12, where I discuss security aspects in more depth.

Business Process Management Concepts

Workflows and business process management (BPM) standardize business processes according to a set of rules, automating some steps and system integration where possible to improve efficiencies or reduce redundancies in the process. A business process consists of a set of activities, tasks, and workflows that contribute to the organization's operations or administration in some way. The following lists some common terms related to business process management:

- **Workflow:** A system-managed process of step sequences and branching logic conditions to automate, track, and manage the state of a business process.

- **Electronic forms (e-forms):** Offers form capabilities for users to submit, process, and manage forms completely in a digital format.

- **Forms processing:** The process of transforming a paper-based form into a digital file by scanning and extracting data from the boxes and lines on the form.

- **System integration:** The capability for one system to utilize the data and processes provided by another system

▓ **Note**   Please see Chapter 8, where I discuss electronic forms and business processes in more depth.

General Information Management Concepts

Information management also includes concepts such as how you classify pieces of content, how users can search for content, and other types of repositories and policies you might include in your enterprise content management solution. I grouped these concepts in this section to quickly gloss over some other important terms without digressing too far into the details I discuss in more depth later in this book. The following lists some common terms related to general information management:

- **Categorization:** Organizes documents and other content into common groups based on the category applied to each piece of content, typically applied through metadata.

- **Metadata:** Terms users can associate with a piece of content to self-describe and categorize the content.

- **Content retrieval:** A system containing an index of content for users to query and find references to relevant content.

- **Archive repository:** A content repository where you store content for historical reference purposes, such as content your organization no longer actively uses.

- **Web content management (WCM):** A technology similar to document management, except users create and publish web pages, articles, and other web-based content on a portal.

- **Records management:** A system to capture and assign a specific life cycle to individual pieces of content that has evidentiary or essential value to the organization.

- **Content retention:** A policy where the system protects and retains a piece of content according to a set of predefined criteria and rules identifying the duration of time.

- **Content disposition:** A policy where the system deletes a piece of content according to a set of predefined criteria, such as disposing of the content after a certain duration of time or some other trigger.

▓ **Note**   Please see Chapter 15, where I discuss content retention and disposition in more depth.

Returning once again to one of the critical pieces of enterprise content management, the content itself, it is important to understand the difference between what content users are working on, and formal content that the organization uses to base its decisions and meet its compliance obligations. I separate these two views of content (or the content's formality) into two broad categories: transitory content and official records.

Transitory Content vs. Official Records

There is one major dividing line determining what content life cycle stage a piece of content is in, and this is the distinction between transitory content and an official record. These two major classification categories separate your focus for the content and its organizational purpose, such as the amount of rigor you want to apply to its policies and what regulations apply to a unit of information.

Transitory content represents the content an organization has not designated as an official record, although individual pieces may or may not become part of a permanent record or a historical archive. An organization can delete transitory content once its use turns dormant, because it has no retention requirements beyond the users' active and current need. Once transitory content reaches a stage with retention requirements, you designate a version as an official record.

Official records declare a unit of information as a permanent transaction or transcript resulting from an activity or decision, providing stable evidence the organization can base future decisions on. Typically, an organization must retain a record for a predetermined period, either to meet external requirements such as legal or regulatory compliance, or to capture internal historical archives.

One significant difference between transitory content and official records relates to how fixed or flexible a piece of content substance can be. With transitory content, a unit of information's subject matter and contents can change. In contrast, a record must remain immutable—once you declare a unit of information as a record, the entire unit must remain unchanged to protect the integrity of the record. Where a transitory piece of content may or may not retain a detailed history of any changes, a record is a snapshot of a unit of information at a specific point in time. Any other versions of a record are new snapshots at a different point in time, and thus they constitute a new and distinct record.

You can declare a record and move it or a copy of it to a records repository, or you can declare a record in-place. In-place records allow users to continue to find content in context based on its topics or usage, allowing the record to remain part of the SharePoint site. Records you move to a records repository will centralize the content into a file plan, routing the record to an appropriate classification container within the file plan.

■ **Note**   Please see Chapter 13, where I discuss file plans and how to design one with a content classification index for your organization.

A record often starts out as a piece of transitory content—a draft document a group of users collaborate on producing, an electronic form progressing through the early stages of an approval workflow, a spreadsheet with a manager's preliminary budget calculations—working its way through the transitory phase as its creators finalize the contents. Figure 1-4 illustrates transitory content progressing into an official record. A record can also skip any transitory phase, at least from the organization's perspective, such as vendor invoices that users receive by e-mail and directly upload and declare as a record in the repository.

| Authoring Document | New Document Created | Team Collaboration On Document | Document Editing and Review | Final Version Approved | Document Signoff | Document Submitted to Records Repository |

Figure 1-4. *Transitory content progressing to an official record*

You will capture different types of records and you can treat them each in their own way, accomplished by applying the implementation details to an area in the file plan or to the content itself through SharePoint workflows and policies. For example, you might want to offer an archive repository to store project information for a period for reference purposes. The requirements for this particular scenario can vary greatly, depending on the archival and retention requirements.

Your requirements for content archival and retention can range from informal to formal, from internal historical interests to external compliance stipulations. For some records, your requirements might be to retain nonbusiness critical, nice-to-have historical information, all to make available just in case a user wants to reference it in the future. For other records, your requirements might be to retain legally binding information with a detailed audit trail, records that external agencies require you to maintain with some rigor.

To return to the example I just mentioned (the project team archiving their project information), this can range from informal to formal, depending on things such as the scale and scope of the project, the nature of the project information, and the ongoing business impact of the project. On the informal end of the range, you might imagine an IT project team deploying a simple intranet homepage for a department to describe the services the department offers. The documentation work products from this project might include things such as a design document and a project schedule. Neither of these documents provides any ongoing business contribution nor do they have any future business impact. However, the project team wants to archive them to allow another team to copy and reuse sections from the documents on another project.

In contrast, imagine a real estate development project team purchasing land and developing a property there on behalf of investors. The documentation work products from this project might include things such as building blueprints and financial reports. They may need to capture the blueprints for historical purposes; and since buildings last a long time, they have to archive them for at least 50 years. They also have to meet financial regulations to retain any financial reports and transaction content. The organization may need to produce either of these documents in the future to comply with an external agency's review, such as a building inspector or tax auditor.

■ **Note**   For more on planning and implementing records management, please see the chapters in Part IV.

Your transitory content is even more diverse because it includes a huge category of content—everything from a user's status update on a microblog site to detailed documentation a team is collaborating on and producing, or from an e-mail thread between colleagues to article pages posted to a portal. Up until someone designates a piece of content as a record, it is transitory. This represents a massive corpus of content and a major component of any enterprise content management solution. As such, I dedicated a deserving potion of this book to help you plan and design this aspect of your information life cycle strategy.

■ **Note**   For more on planning and designing solutions for transitory content, please see the chapters in Part II.

Just because it is transitory does not mean that the content is not included in any compliance, regulatory, or legal implications. If a case comes up, your organization has to identify all content relating to the case, whether or not a piece of content is officially a record yet. To an outside agency or legal counsel, any related content is relevant content. SharePoint eDiscovery manages this by enabling a case manager to discover content across any repository the search engine indexes, allowing him or her to capture and place any content on hold to preserve its integrity for the case.

■ **Note**   Please see Chapter 11, where I discuss managing eDiscovery and discovery cases in more depth.

I spent some time in this section defining transitory content and official records, taking a closer look at the difference between the two, and discussing how each divides the mass corpus of enterprise content into one of these two categories. For me, this is a helpful division to keep in mind when I analyze content life cycle details and I design an enterprise content management solution for an organization. I find that this is the first step to break down the complexity and sheer size of enterprise content management.

Transitory content and records also make up two major states of a more detailed information life cycle. As I continue to break down enterprise content management into its more granular parts, I look at details and stages within the information life cycle. I designed a generic model, one I called the *content life cycle model*, to apply and make sense of the enterprise content management problem I am addressing, a concept and process I describe next.

Understanding the Content Life Cycle Model

A model serves as a representation of a more complex system or process, providing a framework or pattern one can use to make sense of the complexity and to understand how to manage it. In this way, I designed my content life cycle model to represent the more complex concept of enterprise content management, providing a framework you can use to analyze the different aspects of your content, all by tracing the life cycle of different units of information. From there, you can design and implement an elegant enterprise content management solution in SharePoint 2013.

My content life cycle model is not the first model for enterprise content management, nor does it replace any other model you might have familiarity with. In fact, there is the Association for Information and Image Management (AIIM) International, a nonprofit organization conducting and documenting information-related research. They provide a popular information life cycle model, one often referred to by some as the "ECM 101 poster." AIIM separates the information life cycle into these five phases:

- **Capture:** The process to move content into your content repository through human-created or application-created business processes.

- **Manage:** The tools and techniques for controlling content within an organization.

- **Store:** The repository for the content, including library services and any other storage technologies.

- **Deliver:** The means to provide relevant content for an interested audience on their preferred device through data transformation, security, and content distribution.

- **Preserve:** The long-term archival and storage solution for content continuing to provide organizational value or meeting an organizational obligation.

I find this model useful in considering the different aspects of an enterprise content management solution from a high level, but for my purposes in this book, I find the phases on their own overly abstract and generic, making them difficult to apply and difficult to analyze a specific piece of content within an organization. For me, the AIIM information life cycle model works well for theorizing the life cycle of information in general, but I created my own content life cycle model for looking at actual content within an organization's SharePoint environment. In this book, I use my model to analyze how users interact with the content.

▒ **Note**   To learn more about AIIM, and to access its white papers or join its community of information professionals, please see their web site at www.aiim.org.

Information goes through a life cycle within an organization, not always starting from the same place nor always ending up in the same place, nor even following the same path in between. Yet the general outline or pattern of this life cycle stays reasonably consistent, at least enough for me to model a basic framework. I will build up my content life cycle model slowly for you, stepping through each part to make it clear. To start, content comes into being either from a user creating it or from a user receiving it, such as with an e-mail attachment that a user receives and then uploads to a SharePoint site. Figure 1-5 illustrates this early portion of the content life cycle where content comes into SharePoint.

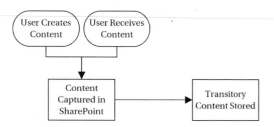

Figure 1-5. *Content coming into SharePoint*

Once content is in SharePoint, SharePoint begins to manage it through the product's different features and capabilities. SharePoint manages content through specific sites using features such as policies and workflows. Figure 1-6 illustrates where in-the model SharePoint manages content in the process, and in the context of disposing of transitory content using policies and workflows.

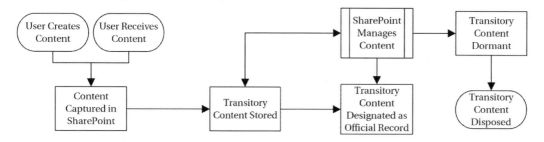

Figure 1-6. *SharePoint manages the content with its features and core capabilities*

▧ **Note** Please see Chapter 2 for more details on the features and core capabilities in SharePoint.

With content stored and managed within SharePoint, users will want to interact with it to base decisions on and to support their job functions. Users first need to discover content in order to interact with it, which from the system's perspective, entails a user noticing relevant content on his or her newsfeed, or a user explicitly searching for content, such as by using the SharePoint search engine or by clicking through directories. Figure 1-7 illustrates where users discover and then interact with content in the life cycle model.

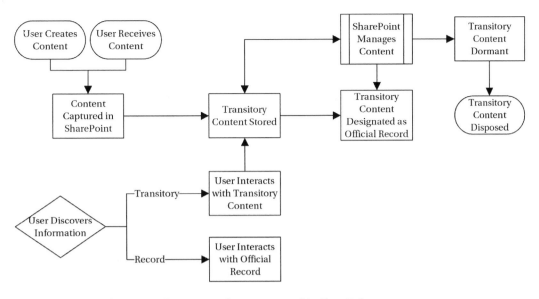

Figure 1-7. *Users discover and interact with content stored in SharePoint*

Finally, an organization needs to retain certain content for regulatory compliance reasons, evidentiary reasons, or historical reasons. SharePoint preserves content by designating it as a record. Figure 1-8 illustrates where in the model SharePoint preserves content as a record until a retention policy disposes of it.

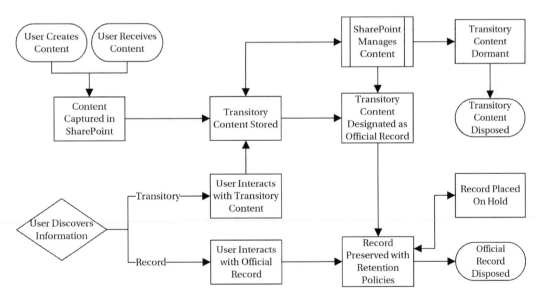

Figure 1-8. *Content preserved as an official record*

If you compare my content life cycle model with the AIIM information life cycle model, you will notice some similarities and consistency between them. Indeed, my model follows the pattern of the life cycle that a unit of information might go through. I added some extra detail and phases to the model and I increased the verbosity to phase labels, making the models similar but not the same, increasing the details and zooming in on parts to increase its application for a SharePoint ECM solution. Figure 1-9 overlays my content life cycle model with phases in the AIIM information life cycle model to illustrate how the two models relate.

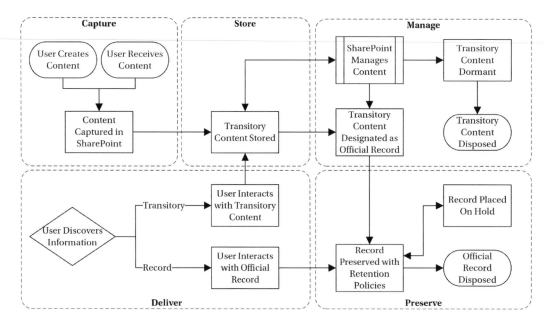

Figure 1-9. *The content life cycle model*

■ **Note**   To learn how to apply the content life cycle model to your organization, please see Chapter 3.

As you consider the content life cycle model, one of your critical tasks is to identify every process within the model that you can automate—from creation to disposition, and everything in between. The more you can automate in the content life cycle, the more standardized and mature you will make your enterprise content management solution.

ENTERPRISE CONTENT MANAGEMENT AND COMPLIANCE

Compliance involves an organization fulfilling its legal and regulatory obligations through identifying and preserving records, as well as capturing the audit trail of a record's history, including evidence of executive signoff where required. The evidence of the record and its history comprise the essence of many compliance requirements, all of which SharePoint supports, from basic to sophisticated implementations, depending on what you need.

Many compliance requirements come with penalties if an agency catches an organization out of compliance, such as significant fines or even jail time for executives. The risk of these penalties serves as an impactful motivator for many organizations to mature and formalize their enterprise content management solution with sophisticated policies and processes.

The following lists some popular compliance-related acts, standards, or commissions from different regions:

- The Sarbanes-Oxley Act (SOX): A United States law that sets standards and regulations for all US public company boards, executive management, and public accounting firms.

- The Health Insurance Portability and Accountability Act (HIPAA): A United States law that sets standards for electronic health care transactions and identifiers.

- The Payment Card Industry Data Security Standard (PCI DSS): A set of payment processing standards.

- The Australian Securities and Investments Commission (ASIC): An Australian commonwealth government agency that enforces and regulates company and financial services laws.

This illustrates the range of information types that relate to compliance requirements. Depending on your region and your industry, you may face financial, health, privacy, environment, or a host of other types of compliance requirements. In a large and complex organization, this can be difficult to track and enforce without a system to automate it.

It is important for an organization to comply with any regulations that apply, but it is also important to plan for a level of information usability—usable internally within your organization and usable for your legal or records team with the external governing body. In addition, if you have internal corporate or legislative standards to meet, you can treat those in the same way as any external compliance requirements.

Comparing ECM Costs and Value

Aside from the smallest and simplest organizations, an enterprise content management solution is going to be costly—the deep and thorough analysis you require to design an effective solution will require a significant investment in terms of both expense and effort. Its magnitude is just too colossal and complex, particularly leading up to and including its implementation.

If you think of ECM as an all-encompassing program rather than simply an implementation project, you can calculate and weigh its costs against its value to form a clearer picture of your long-term investment and your expected return. You frontload the bulk of your investment into an ECM program as you analyze, design, and implement an ECM solution. After you have a solution implemented, your ECM program can begin to deliver value to offset its costs. As Figure 1-10 illustrates, once you spread the program costs over the life of an ECM program, the magnitude of the costs begin to diminish, while the magnitude of value climbs.

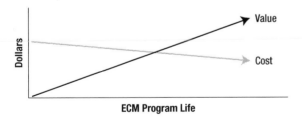

Figure 1-10. *The relation between cost and value in an ECM program*

Other costs related to an enterprise content management solution and the value derived from it are harder to quantify. For example, as I noted in the sidebar, compliance is a major component to an enterprise content management solution, and those costs associated with any risks from being out of compliance are difficult to calculate. Will a judge consider the organization in contempt of court and issue a fine if content related to a case is not forthcoming in accordance with a court order? What is the cost if an organization is unable to find a contract to exonerate their liability in the case of a lawsuit? What is the value of being able to audit and systematically prove that an organization complies with any regulatory or legislative obligation?

Some of your investment costs and the value they return are easy to calculate and quantify. Others are less explicit or only probable. Still others are more indirect and less monetary-related, such as reducing lags or wait times with automation, and facilitating group collaboration with shared workspaces. As you factor your cost-benefit analysis of an enterprise content management program, remember to consider the long-term value that a mature and sophisticated ECM implementation will return for the organization, not just its upfront implementation costs.

▓ **Tip** You should consider breaking down your enterprise content management program into phases, implementing a series of phases with a smaller scope that work toward an ECM solution, rather than attempting a massive ECM undertaking.

Approaching an ECM Program

Where do you start? These enterprise content management concepts and theories all sound great, I bet; but you might be wondering how you get started with your own ECM program. After all, enterprise content management is a massive topic and it encompasses every aspect of content within your organization, which is no small matter. The idea of attempting to take this all on at once can seem daunting, at least for me.

I am a firm believer in breaking down complex problems into smaller, more manageable units. I look to do this on almost every project that I am on, and enterprise content management is no different. If you are familiar with how I like to approach anything in SharePoint, then this will not come as a surprise to you. Essentially, my formula for SharePoint project success, whatever the project or project scope, follows a consistent cycle of phases. I always try to start with a pilot deployment of basic SharePoint functionality, something that provides a baseline to reference and expose to stakeholders, and then I build on that base with a series of project phase iterations.

I prefer frequent and focused iterations that include the following stages, achieving a tiny bit at a time within each iteration cycle, building on the previous iteration and delivering incremental value:

- Select a small piece of the larger problem

- Analyze the different aspects of the narrower scope

- Envision a solution concept and design the solution details

- Build the solution

- Test and stabilize the solution

- Release the solution

I continue repeating this cycle until I solve the larger problem or deliver enough value that my client or stakeholders are satisfied. If there are any unknown variables or unclear requirements, or if there is a high degree of complexity with an aspect, then I focus on a proof of concept deployment to mitigate any risks and refine the solution by proving out any solution concepts and assumptions before over committing the project direction on risky aspects in the solution design.

Once I am successful with releasing one focused and limited aspect of the solution, I repeat the cycle on another piece of the overall business problem that the project is working toward solving. You might notice that these phases and iterations closely resemble the Microsoft Solutions Framework (MSF), and this is because I generally adopt and apply the framework to my projects. The phases of MSF are envisioning, planning, building, stabilizing, and deploying, as illustrated in Figure 1-11.

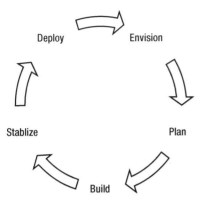

Figure 1-11. *The MSF phases within an iteration cycle*

For me, these phases provide a natural and productive progression through project iterations, frequently delivering smaller iterations, ultimately reducing the overall project risk while the process propels a project forward. Trying to take on too much at once will take excessive amounts of time to deliver anything, and it could even lead to a paralysis of the team's momentum as the ominous task of solving the enterprise content management problem stares down at you. Yet when you scale the problem down into manageable chunks, it does not seem as intimidating.

This type of phased approach seems like a good fit for more straightforward aspects of a SharePoint deployment, such as basic collaboration sites or departmental portal sites, but the approach also works for something as large and complex as enterprise content management. In fact, you may find, as I have found, that overly large and complex projects are the most successful when you simplify them by taking an iterative approach. Do not fall into the trap of trying to tackle everything all at once; instead, break it down into simpler pieces, and then select one to start with the first iteration.

That leads into the next set of questions: How do you decide where to divide the scope of the iterations, and which one do you start with? This can present a bit of a dilemma, because you should start with a small focused piece of the your overall enterprise content scope, but you do not want to have one area within your organization dictate how every area will categorize and manage content, simply because that area went first in your project delivery. For example, if you start with the IT department, you might find they have a detailed and heavily engineered process for categorizing and managing content, simply because the department is technical by nature and people in it tend to take a system-oriented view of things. In contrast, if you started with the sales department, you might find they take an opportunity or a campaign-oriented view of things, focusing on how different aspects relate to their sales pipeline and the percentage a lead is progressing through the sales process—a much less systematic and system-driven process, resembling a more intuition and relationship-driven process.

If you focus too heavily and exclusively on a single department, you risk that department influencing, and possibly distorting, the organization-wide requirements. Conversely, if you try to implement an enterprise content management solution for every department, you will probably struggle with trying to scale to balance and manage the volume and intricacy of information across the organization.

I prefer to divide my ECM implementations into phases separated by departments, because they already form a discrete unit within the organization with an existing reporting structure of stakeholders and processes that I can use to build a project plan. However, I first like to take an enterprise-wide view of the content and common ways to categorize and manage it. For this first phase, I do not perform deep analysis, and instead I make a quick pass over the main kinds of content for each department, only doing some preliminary analysis to identify commonalities and standards that I can consider when doing a closer and more detailed analysis for each department.

From there, I divide an ECM program into departments or groups within departments, where I analyze, design, and implement an enterprise content management solution based on their requirements. For the most part, I find success through this approach of taking a quick pass for an enterprise-wide view followed by project iterations that focus on smaller groups within the organization. I may have to revisit an earlier department's design and implementation based on new knowledge uncovered in a subsequent phase with another department, but this is not terrible and the idea of minor rework should not scare you away from taking this phased approach. Besides, you can usually automate most changes and rework through a PowerShell script.

To organize your plans, I recommend building a project plan, using either a SharePoint project task list or a Microsoft Project plan, or both. I like to build out a work breakdown structure (WBS), starting with the main project phases that I will use to divide the project into defined iterations, and then I begin to fill in the details of the summary tasks within each phase before moving down to the individual work item details. This project plan will help you plan your resources and coordinate activities with different departments and groups your project team will need to work with. Microsoft Project is usually my tool for this planning, but I also like to synchronize the project plan with a SharePoint list to communicate it with the rest of the project team and any stakeholders.

■ **Note**   For more information on how to synchronize your Microsoft Project plan with a SharePoint project task list, please see my blog post on this topic at http://stevegoodyear.wordpress.com/2012/08/27.

One technique I like to use is diagramming a visual representation as I plan a project approach and the major work items in a project. Figure 1-12 illustrates an example of how I might use a workflow diagram to provide a visual summary of major project tasks or phases. I use this technique both to organize my thoughts during my project planning process and then to communicate a high-level overview of the project. During the project delivery, I include copies of this visual summary to provide status updates by color-coding or adding check marks to highlight progress through each iteration cycle.

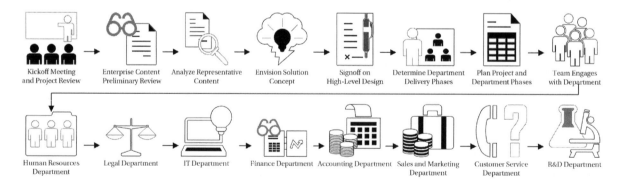

Figure 1-12. *A visual workflow representation of a project plan*

With a project plan detailing your phased approach, all you have to do now is execute on your project plan. Project plans change, timelines shift, and new work items come up all the time, but for the most part, they give you direction and they organize everyone's efforts. I find that I revisit my project plan after each iteration phase, where I prepare for the next phase by building out a detailed list of tasks for that phase, and then I adjust any timelines or dependencies for the subsequent phases. One of my favorite benefits derived from a phased approach is that it provides a regular checkpoint where I can assess the project team's overall progress and I can check for any problem areas that might affect the ECM program.

Wrapping Up

Enterprise content management is a complex topic—complex enough to warrant this book and many others, dedicated entirely to the subject. In its essence, it is how you manage content through its life cycle, from facilitating users who are creating or capturing content, to surfacing relevant content to users through search or social feeds, to retaining evidentiary content that the organization depends on in the future, to disposing of content once it is no longer of value. In this chapter, I provided an overview of enterprise content management and some of its core concepts, which I will build on throughout this book. From there, I explored the difference between transitory content and official records, with transitory content representing any content not designated as an official record, and official records representing evidence that an organization can base future decisions on. Finally, I described the content life cycle model and I considered the costs and value associated with an ECM solution.

Understanding enterprise content management in general is vital for designing and implementing an ECM solution in SharePoint, because the industry ECM concepts remain consistent, whereas only the implementation and configuration details are specific to SharePoint. With an understanding of SharePoint and its capabilities, you can begin to translate these general ECM concepts into the aspects of a SharePoint deployment that you will need to enable. In the next chapter, I shift to provide you with an overview of the ECM features built into SharePoint 2013 and how these features and the different SharePoint capability areas build on and complement each other as part of a comprehensive enterprise content management platform.

CHAPTER 2

■ ■ ■

SharePoint 2013 Enterprise Content Management Features

The beginning of wisdom is to call things by their proper name.

—Confucius

How does SharePoint implement and support enterprise content management (ECM)? In this chapter, I provide an overview of SharePoint 2013 and its ECM-related features. I also discuss how each of the main capability areas within SharePoint relate to or complement each other, particularly as they relate to the information life cycle within your organization.

After reading this chapter, you will know how to

- Describe SharePoint 2013 and its purpose.

- Describe how SharePoint capability areas relate to and complement each other.

- Explain the SharePoint site and content container architecture.

- List SharePoint list and library types and their uses.

- List SharePoint site types and describe their uses.

- List and describe the SharePoint 2013 ECM features.

Overview of SharePoint 2013

SharePoint, at its simplest core, is a platform that an organization uses to manage and work with information—knowledge that an organization produces or acquires, and then uses as part of its operations. This is a very abstract description, but SharePoint has grown into its current version as a vast array of different features and functions that make up a set of diverse yet interrelated capability areas. Still, at its core, it provides a way for knowledge workers to interact with information, the enterprise content.

Enterprise content within SharePoint ranges from documents and web pages to electronic forms and social feeds. The platform provides containers to capture, manage, and interact with these different types of content at granular degrees and across the network. In its first version, SharePoint 2001, it began as a document management and collaboration system, providing users with a centralized document repository and richer document management features than a simple network file share.

As SharePoint matured over the years, Microsoft continued to invest in the collaboration experience for users in an organization. The product team built out SharePoint to serve as a platform to host and collaborate on different types of information in an enterprise, and they refined the user experience to encompass more of the information life cycle—from content creation to content discovery to content retention and disposition.

With the product evolving its capabilities to manage more of the content and life cycle, it has also grown in size and complexity. Now, rather than just providing document repositories and enabling collaboration, SharePoint 2013 offers a range of other features for information workers to capture knowledge and work with information. I like to group these other features into what I refer to its seven core capability areas, which are:

- Collaboration
- Social computing
- Portals
- Search
- Records management
- Business intelligence
- Composite applications

Within the collaboration capability, I bundle the different aspects of creating and collaborating on content, as in team or project workspaces. In this book, I refer to the type of content within the collaboration capability as *transitory content*. Knowledge workers collaborate by creating drafts and working with different pieces of content within a workspace container such as a SharePoint site. This interaction may involve content such as Word documents or wiki web pages, but collaboration is less characteristic of the type of content and more with the nature of how people create and share information collaboratively.

▨ **Note**   I discuss transitory content in more detail in Part II and I devote Chapter 5 specifically to look closer at collaboration-related content.

Social computing relates to collaboration, and the two have some overlap—particularly with functional aspects such as wiki pages or blogs. For my purposes in this book, I classify social computing as those features that enable people to discover information and their peers through other people. Whether a knowledge worker creates a collaborative piece of content as a Word document or as a wiki page, the social aspect includes things such as his or her tagging the content with metadata so other users interested in that tag will discover the content. For example, in Figure 2-1 a user can discover the new document based on the #Marketing tag he or she follows.

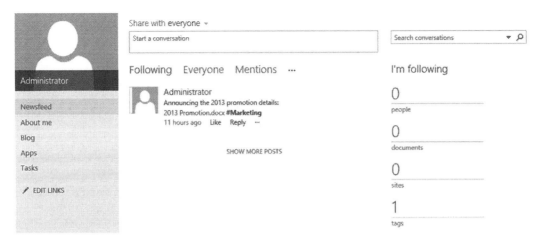

Figure 2-1. *Social tags to discover content from a SharePoint My Site*

■ **Note**   Please see Chapter 10, where I discuss newsfeeds and social tagging in more detail.

Portals also overlap and relate with the other capabilities, such as a user's personal portal or their My Site. At their essence, portals provide a means to communicate information to a particular audience and provide a gateway to access other web properties and processes on the network, such as other more specific portals and workflow applications. A portal's audience can be internal users, as with an intranet, or it can target external users, as with an organization's public web site.

■ **Note**   Please see Chapter 7, where I discuss portals in more detail.

Search relates and complements the other SharePoint capabilities by providing the functionality for a knowledge worker to search and find information of interest. Users can use keywords or more advanced query criteria and find relevant documents or web pages within SharePoint or any other content source you have configured for the SharePoint search service to index. Users can also search for and discover other people based on metadata associated with user profiles. This enterprise search capability provides users with a means to discover content based on its relevance to the search terms, and it offers an entry point to the other capability areas.

■ **Note**   I discuss content discovery in more detail in Part III and I devote Chapter 9 for a closer look at SharePoint search specifically.

Records management extends the information life cycle to manage content retention and disposition once content progresses beyond the transitory phase. This capability provides a repository and the functionality associated with capturing an official unit of information that the organization can or has used to base decisions on. The content captured provides a historical record of decisions or information at a particular point in time, which can serve to meet legal or regulatory requirements in the future.

■ **Note** Please see the chapters in Part IV, where I discuss topics related to records management in more detail.

Business intelligence includes features that aggregate and report on data, such as Key Performance Indicators (KPI), scorecards, dashboards, and other types of analytical reports. This capability provides a means to analyze data, and then report on statuses, relationships, and trends. A knowledge worker or organizational leader can use this information to base their decisions.

■ **Note** Although you can make official business decisions based on business intelligence dashboards and the like, I have chosen not to treat this capability distinctly as an official record. Instead, I grouped it with other transitory content—for example, you can capture a snapshot of a report or dashboard if you require capturing an official record at a point in time.

Composite applications cover a range of features. It is the capability that I group those aspects where you extend and customize SharePoint. Here, I include custom applications built on SharePoint as well integration with other enterprise systems. Specifically as it relates to enterprise content management, this is where I include electronic forms such as InfoPath forms to capture business process information. This is also the capability where I include workflows to manage and automate business processes ranging from approval workflows to automated content retention and disposition workflows.

■ **Note** Please see Chapter 8, where I discuss electronic forms and workflow processes in more detail.

I already alluded to how each of these capability areas relate to each other, but in the next section, I look more closely at the different ways that these capability areas complement and build on each other by sharing functionality and services.

Relating SharePoint Capability Areas to Each Other

I often describe the relationship between different capability areas as one similar to puzzle pieces fitting together—each complements each other as they add on and build out a larger overall picture, as I illustrate in Figure 2-2. Microsoft designed the product in a modular and service-oriented fashion so that you can reuse common functionality across different capabilities. Ultimately, at the component level, this leads to a more efficient system; but at the capability level, this allows you to continuously add on and grow your SharePoint environment as you need to and as you are ready for new capabilities, all without requiring you to over-architect a complicated deployment up front.

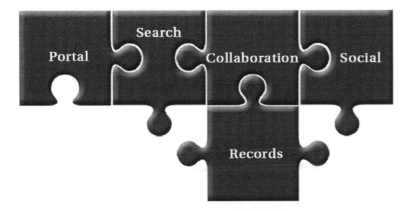

Figure 2-2. *Conceptual SharePoint capability puzzle pieces fitting together*

For me, each of the SharePoint capabilities build on or complements the others, offering specialized individual functionality while also leveraging or enhancing features in the other capabilities. In a general sense, you can extend your SharePoint service by adding additional capabilities, and this will add new features and functionality for your end users. This could be a drastically new capability area, such as adding business intelligence dashboards to an intranet portal, or it could be a related capability area, such as adding an enterprise search portal to an intranet portal.

Whatever the extension, the capabilities will still loosely relate to each other, and Microsoft designed the SharePoint platform such that the different capabilities will all work together to create a better or more feature-rich end-user experience. This design allows you to take and enable the capabilities you need, and leave the rest disabled. From an architectural perspective, the product team implemented a module pattern to design the infrastructure for capabilities, features, and any general product add-ons. Essentially, a module component provides loose coupling with high cohesion; it is an independent and self-contained component that you can include or not, and if included, it will work well with the other components.

The ability for capabilities to work together in a well-coordinated fashion is especially important for planning and designing enterprise content solutions, precisely because of the information life cycle I discussed in the previous chapter. Information in an organization is fluid and in flux as it flows through an organization and as it progresses through its life cycle. Whatever system you use to capture and manage information within your organization will resemble a kaleidoscopic of enterprise content that users interact with for different purposes and at different points in the cycle.

Such a complex relationship among enterprise content within an organization requires a flexible enterprise content management system, and this is particularly true as the complexity and the types of information will vary from organization to organization. For example, a legal firm may track contracts with precise security and retention requirements, while an advertisement firm may collaborate on copy and visuals for an advertisement campaign. Their needs are similar, as the information life cycle is similar for each; however, they expand or contract at different stages with different levels of formality. With the module design in SharePoint, they can each enable the capabilities they need and configure them to serve their distinct purposes.

Enterprise content management is a concept that spans all of the SharePoint capabilities that you have deployed. And as I just mentioned, the mix of capabilities you enable will vary depending on your organization's needs and the type of information it creates and consumes. Nevertheless, each of the SharePoint capabilities you have deployed will play a part in your information life cycle strategy, and you can continue to build on and evolve your strategy over time as you enable additional capabilities and as your enterprise content management requirements mature or change.

From a general enterprise content management perspective, the capabilities relate together as information progresses through different uses and through different stages in its life cycle. As your users generate and create content in a collaboration environment, other users might want to discover it using search or social capabilities, or a content manager might include a link on a portal page. Meanwhile, your records managers might want to use workflows to capture the content and apply policies, and they can report on compliance using a business intelligence dashboard.

In a simplified and quick synopsis of enterprise content management, you can see how all the main SharePoint capabilities can come together at different points in the information life cycle. This example presents a user story of how the different capabilities relate to each other from the perspective of the business value and usage. The relationship between capabilities also runs deeper than the flow of information participating in the information life cycle. Capabilities can also provide services to other capabilities, which enables a SharePoint capability to leverage the features in a component hosted in another capability while providing its own functionality.

Capabilities such as search include underlying components that other capabilities can leverage. For example, a portal can provide a dynamic navigation by using search refiners, a social computing site can provide recommendations based on similar content search crawled, a portal site can provide usage analytic reports based on crawling data from search, and an eDiscovery case manager can discover content by querying the search index.

As a result, some capabilities will depend on other capabilities to provide their features and functionality. They also may share the same underlying service application in SharePoint—an application that exposes its features through a Windows Communication Foundation (WCF) web service hosted in Internet Information Services (IIS). A service application extends SharePoint with additional functionality by providing sets of features that can make up an entire application, and it can include its own data sources or external system integration points.

You associate a service application with one or more web applications, and then the sites within these web applications can consume and interact with the services that the service application provides. You can share the same service application instance across many web applications, which centralizes and reuses its services, or you can create several instances of a service application and isolate each from other instances, either providing each web application with a dedicated and isolated service application or providing multiple service application instances to a single web application. Figure 2-3 provides a conceptual example of SharePoint farms that share some service applications but not others.

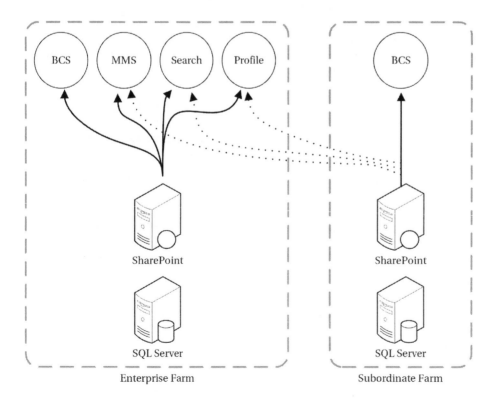

Figure 2-3. *Service applications associated with multiple SharePoint farms*

A service application can also provide services to one or more of SharePoint's capabilities. For example, the Managed Metadata Service provides metadata and taxonomy services to tag content in every capability. The User Profile Service, which provides core social computing features, depends on the Managed Metadata Service to provide profiles and to link relevant content in a user's newsfeed. The Search Service also depends on the Managed Metadata Service to store the dictionaries of custom spellings, synonyms, or terms to ignore.

I use the concept of SharePoint capabilities as a logical way to group core functional areas to simplify and abstract the vastness of SharePoint; in contrast, service applications are more granular and their actual implementation details map specific feature sets to one or more capability area. I loosely relate SharePoint capabilities to underlying features and service applications in the product, but this is only one logical way to divide the product and plan its different aspects. This division and simplification of the product is what I found works well for me when I plan and design a SharePoint solution, but you are welcome to adapt it to whatever model works best for you.

This section is simply a long way to say that SharePoint offers an array of features and capabilities, and the product team designed the core architecture so that you can enable the functionality you need and leave the rest disabled, all in a coordinated and complementary fashion. As a result, SharePoint is flexible enough to adapt to a variety of situations, allowing you to tailor it to suit your enterprise content management needs, whether they are complex and rigid or they are straightforward and open.

As I discuss different phases of the information life cycle in different chapters of this book, I provide you with guidance on planning and implementing the different SharePoint capabilities and their underlying features. For now, I just wanted to point out how they all work together and build on each other. You can build out and mature your SharePoint service by enabling additional capabilities like fitting puzzle pieces together to form a richer and fuller picture of your information life cycle strategy.

With service applications and major feature sets making up the conceptual capabilities at the product level, your SharePoint service exposes these capabilities at the site level. A SharePoint site provides a granular container that contains functionality and content for users to interact with their content. As SharePoint sites provide the most significant container for interaction and information in any SharePoint deployment, I discuss them in depth in the following sections, starting with a look at the site architecture.

Understanding the SharePoint Site Architecture

Every architecture decision in a SharePoint deployment either directly or indirectly revolves around SharePoint sites. This is because SharePoint sites are at the essence of SharePoint and its capabilities. You can choose not to deploy certain aspects of SharePoint, but if you omit deploying any sites, then your SharePoint deployment will not be useful to users. However, even though you might deploy a SharePoint farm strictly to host services such as search, somewhere along the way you will need to create a SharePoint site to provide a user interface for this service, whether in that particular SharePoint farm or in another.

SharePoint sites are the entry point for users to create and interact with enterprise content. They are an essential piece of your SharePoint deployment and your information life cycle strategy. They intertwine so deeply with the product that you will find them throughout your SharePoint service, even if you have not previously given them any conscious thought. So, what makes a SharePoint site so essential and paramount in a SharePoint deployment and with enterprise content management? The answer lies in the site architecture and the hierarchy of containers in SharePoint.

The following lists the main containers in the SharePoint hierarchy, which I also illustrate in Figure 2-4:

- SharePoint farm
- Web application
- Site collection
- Site
- Lists and libraries
- List items

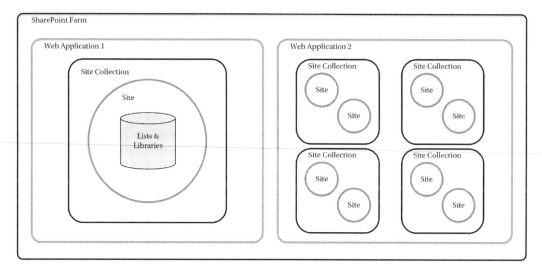

Figure 2-4. *The hierarchy of SharePoint containers*

At its most macro level, a *SharePoint farm* is the highest container—or at least it is the most encompassing container for the farm itself for my purposes to simplify this discussion, even though an organization can deploy multiple farms and spread services and content across these farms. Service applications branch off and provide another container for the functionality and data the service provides, and depending on the service application, it can share its services across web applications and even farms in some cases.

The next major container in a SharePoint farm is the web application. *Web applications* consume service applications and they manage settings such as security providers and other policies. A web application will have one or more content databases that associate with it and that provide the storage for sites within the web application. A site collection can only belong to a single content database within a web application, but different site collections can belong to different content databases or the same one, depending on how you want to segregate and spread the data out within a web application.

Site collections make up the next container in the SharePoint container hierarchy. A *site collection* is what its name implies: a collection of one or more sites. In addition to its storage boundaries, it also serves as a security boundary where a site collection administrator can manage security groups and permissions for all of the sites within the collection. It is a self-contained unit that you can delegate its ownership and management to regular users.

A site collection will contain one or more *sites*—a root site with optional child sites. A site can optionally contain other child sites or other types of content containers, such as document libraries or lists. A site serves as the main unit in SharePoint that users interact with because it hosts the user interface and any content containers.

Content containers within SharePoint provide places for users to store and collaborate on content. They consist of a specialized type of list or library to store content items, depending on the type of content you are working with. For example, to capture and work with announcements, you would use an announcement list; for PowerPoint slides, you would use a slide library; and for web pages, you would use a pages library.

Each specialized type of list or library manages the settings for the content stored within its container, except when you are using content types. *Content types* provide a means to identify a type of content, and then associate policies with it. For example, you can create a Press Release content type and associate a default Word template with it, as well as approval and retention workflows, and any relevant metadata fields you want to capture with this type of content. If you do not wish to manage this policy, workflow, and metadata information through content types, then you can manage it directly in the list or library.

Optionally, a library can contain folders to organize files within the library, further nesting the container hierarchy. A library can also contain document sets, which are a special type of library item that can contain a group of other items and treat them all as a single unit. You would use a document set when you need to group items together to apply the same retention policy and workflows to them all. For example, in a procurement process, you might want to capture supporting information such as the original quote, your purchase order, the vendor's invoice, and any other related documents to the purchase. You could capture those together in a document set to enforce the same information life cycle to the document set package.

At the lowest level in the hierarchy are the individual items within a list or library. These can be the announcements within the announcement list or the PowerPoint slides within the slide library. They could be pages within a page library or documents within a regular document library. Their essence is the same: they are a list item contained within a list or library. They may or may not have multiple versions and extra columns of metadata associated with them, along with other potential settings available. But at their core, they are a unit of information contained within SharePoint.

These units of information within lists and libraries are going to be my focus throughout this book. There are other places for units of information, both inside SharePoint and not, and I will discuss some of those as they come up. However, my primary focus is on those units of information you create and work with in a SharePoint list or library, because those items usually make up the majority of the content in one's information life cycle, at least from the perspective of a SharePoint environment. As such, they are a crucial piece of your information life cycle strategy and they are the key pieces around which to build your enterprise content management solution.

Think of the information hierarchy like words in a book: you have different containers, such as the book itself, chapters, and sections within chapters. Then you have the sentences, the units of information. Within a sentence, you have words, which make up the contents, but that individually do not contain information on their own. The sentences form a unit of information because they contain one or more propositions. There is a structure that then all comes together (hopefully) into a cohesive whole. Likewise, your enterprise content also consists of a structure, managing which is the heart of enterprise content management.

Now, you will not get far or you will quickly become over-consumed if you try to manage each individual unit of information yourself. Most organizations generate too much information for one person to track and manage at each individual item level. Quite simply, you will not scale by focusing on each individual item, even though those units of information are the critical component around which to build your enterprise content management solution. This is why understanding the content hierarchy in SharePoint is crucial, because unlike sentences in a book, you can automate a lot of the management of items by managing aspects at one of the container levels.

Containers in the hierarchy contain and manage other containers or the actual units of information. The site collection provides the main security and content boundary to isolate content and processes from other sites. As a container, they are largely generic and standard—a site collection is a site collection and does not vary much as a container beyond its configuration settings. Similarly, a web application is a standard container that does not vary from its default a great deal. You can set policies and settings at these container levels and they will apply to the items that they contain.

Once you move down the hierarchy to one of the lower containers, the site or list and library containers, you can specify a specific type of container. Types that are more specialized include predefined settings and functionality to specifically manage and interact with the particular type of information stored in the container. Using specific types of containers can help ease your enterprise content management implementation details.

In the next section, I look at some of the different types of sites you can choose from—more commonly referred to as the different site templates. I also share some considerations for deciding between different site types and their appropriate purposes. Following my discussion on the site types, I shift to look at some of the different lists and library types available in a default SharePoint deployment.

SharePoint Site Types

As I mentioned previously, a site collection will have one or more sites, beginning with a single site at the root of the site collection. Sites can then contain one or more child sites, and those sites can contain other sites, and so on. You can choose the site type for each of those sites independently from each other—meaning you are free to choose whichever site template is available when creating a new site, regardless of what any containing or peer site template you previously choose. (Although not every template will always be available, as some may only be available for root sites and some parent sites may suppress certain site templates).

You can create a new site collection from SharePoint Central Administration by clicking the Create Site Collections link found under the Application Management section. On the Create Site Collection page, you will also see a Template Selection section, as shown in Figure 2-5, where you can select a site template for the initial site in the site collection—the site collection's root site.

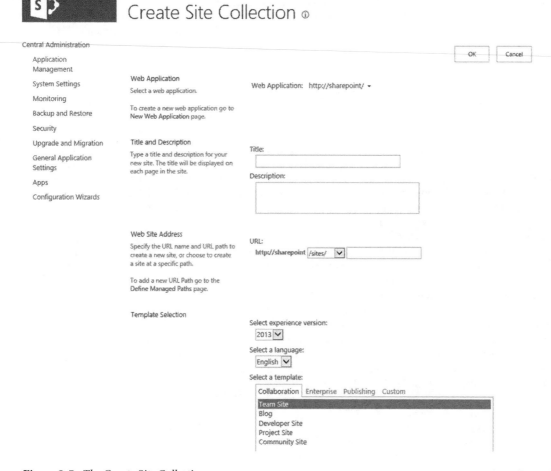

Figure 2-5. *The Create Site Collection page*

The following lists and describes the main site templates on the Create Site page you can use to base a new site on:

- **Team Site:** This template creates a basic SharePoint site with only a document library provisioned within it. It provides the fundamentals that all other site templates include and build upon. Users can activate additional features or provision additional SharePoint apps to tailor the site to their needs. You can use team sites to host and facilitate team collaboration on content such as documentation and reports. Figure 2-6 shows the default homepage for a team site.

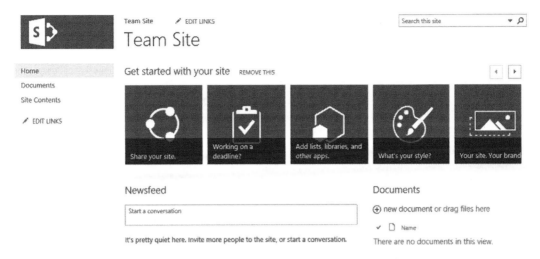

Figure 2-6. *The default Team Site homepage*

- **Blog:** This template creates a site designed around blog posts where one or more users can create blog posts, tag and categorize their posts, and even schedule their posts. It also provides functionality for users to comment and rate different posts. You can use blog sites to host and publish blogs, either for individuals or for groups of individuals, such as in a personal My Site or a shared group blog site.

- **Wiki:** This template creates a site that uses wiki pages for its welcome page and any subsequent pages. It facilitates creating additional wiki pages in a wiki fashion: by adding a link to a new page, and then clicking the link to generate the new page. You can use wiki sites to capture and collaborate on information such as documentation that you generate across pages in the wiki. Figure 2-7 shows the default wiki site welcome page.

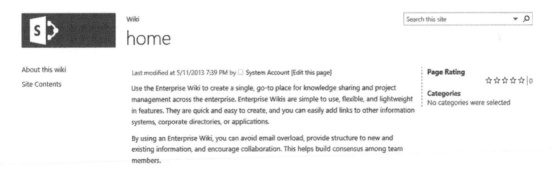

Figure 2-7. *The default enterprise wiki site welcome page*

- **Publishing Portal:** This template creates a site with the publishing features activated and organized with a portal welcome page. It also facilitates publishing portal content such as different types of articles or product catalogues. You can use the publishing portal sites to create a public web site or an internal intranet portal.

- **Search Portal:** This template creates a site with a default search landing page and an advanced search page. It also includes a search results page with preconfigured search refiners. You can use a search site for search-related requirements, such as for your enterprise search portal or for a departmental search application.

- **My Site Host:** This template creates a site to host the shared My Site pages and features, such as the newsfeed, sites listing page, and the main people profile page. It also provides the functionality for users to update their profile, add a profile picture, and manage their newsfeed and social tags. You can use a My Site host site as a starting point for your My Site and User Profile Service implementation.

- **Community Site:** This template creates a site for a community of practice to ask questions and discuss topics on a forum within the site. It also keeps track of the reputation for community members and contributors, scoring ratings based on the number and community-voted value of contributions. You can use a community site for a knowledge management portal, a frequently asked questions site, or a community of practice site. Figure 2-8 shows the default welcome page for a community site.

Figure 2-8. *The default community site welcome page*

You can find the different site templates available by clicking the different tabs in the Site Template section. This is not a fixed list, because Microsoft or other vendors can add additional site templates along with their custom applications or SharePoint extensions. Your developers can also add to the list of site templates with any templates they create in a SharePoint feature, and then deploy in a SharePoint solution package. Finally, site collection administrators can add custom site templates by saving a site as a template or by uploading a site template package to the site template library in a site collection.

Each site template has a specific purpose and provides a specific user experience. Which one you choose will depend on the aspect it will fill for your enterprise content management implementation. You do not have to create a site for each, but you may, depending on your requirements.

For some site types, you might only create a single site based on the template. For example, you might only create a single enterprise search portal based on the search template. For other site types, you might create many instances of sites based on those templates. For example, you might create many collaboration sites based on the Team Site template. The choice of site type and site structure makes up your information architecture. Figure 2-9 provides a sample of a simple information architecture consisting of different site types.

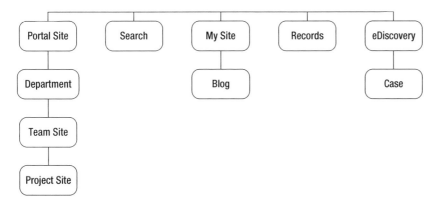

Figure 2-9. *A sample information architecture of different site types*

▓ **Note** For more on how to plan and design your site information architecture, please see Chapter 4.

Some of these sites in the sample information architecture exist in separate site collections. For simplicity sake, I used a single web application, but you can also spread these sites across different web applications as well. SharePoint has an important concept for how and where you create sites, referred to as a managed path. A *managed path* is what SharePoint uses to organize the URL for where you can create a site collection in a web application, and it comes in two flavors:

- **Explicit managed path:** Specifies an explicit URL path where you can create a single site collection. For example, if you create a `search` explicit managed path on the `www.contoso.com` web application, you can then create a single site collection at `www.contoso.com/search` to host the search portal.

- **Wildcard managed path:** Specifies a path under which you can create multiple site collections. For example, if you create a `sites` wildcard managed path on the `www.contoso.com` web application, you can then create multiple site collections under that path, such as `www.contoso.com/sites/hr` to host an HR team site and `www.contoso.com/sites/it` to host an IT team site.

▓ **Note** In addition to path-named site collections under a managed path, you can also create host-named site collections, where each site collection uses its own URL. For more on host-named site collections, please see the MSDN article at `http://technet.microsoft.com/cc424952`.

Once you create your site, the template you used ceases to remain relevant. At its essence, a site is just a site, and as I mentioned, the team site provides the fundamentals of any site. Anything beyond the team site simply consists of activating different features, adding different SharePoint apps, or provisioning different types of content. In most cases, you can activate these features or add these apps when you need them, evolving the site beyond its original site template to adapt it to new site needs.

A site can and probably will evolve over time, transforming into other purposes or expanding to meet new requirements. The site template simply defines a site's initial functionality and layout, and then the template ceases to contribute anything to the site. You also cannot make changes to the original template to cascade changes down to sites. Site templates are limiting from a maintenance perspective, and they do not offer a lot of value beyond automating the initial site configuration and providing a friendly name for this automation on the Create Site page. For this reason, I try to minimize any extra templates and avoid what I call *template bloating*, as I describe in the sidebar.

AVOID TEMPLATE BLOATING

I noticed that it can be tempting to create a lot of site templates for specific purposes, and I want to caution you here. Creating excessive amounts of templates just for subtle changes in the site purpose only leads to template bloating and a maintenance headache down the road.

There are valid reasons to create new templates, and this is why Microsoft made the option available. However, I have seen people go too far with this, usually with the best intentions to help their users. It usually relates to attempting to be helpful by specifying the initial setup and layout, which has the site provision and configure things for a particular group's use case. I recommend against creating new templates simply to ease the initial setup—instead, use another technique such as feature stapling and an event receiver or a SharePoint app to arrange the initial setup because, as the users' processes change, those are easier to change and adapt than templates.

When considering new templates, base them on custom applications you want to provide, not layouts or initial setups. For the most part, I think of site templates as a means to hook a group of custom SharePoint features for a specific application I want to provide. What I never consider is using a template simply for an initial folder structure to populate in a site, for example.

Where possible, I try to stick with the default site templates, activating features and hooking into events to provision or configure aspects of the site, resulting in a customized site experience based on a default site template. I do this to ease the future upgrade supportability, because Microsoft usually provides a seamless upgrade experience for those sites based on the default site templates.

SharePoint List and Library Types

In much the same way that you can use templates to create different types of sites, you can do the same to create different types of lists and libraries. Unlike a site, however, lists and libraries are specialized with particular functionality to work with certain types of content, remaining specialized throughout their continuation.

You cannot, for example, easily transform or evolve a document library into a picture library with all its picture-related functionality, although you can add pictures and other content types to a document library. Lists and libraries are specialized by design to manage specific types of content through the information life cycle.

Lists and libraries provide the primary and most significant container for enterprise content in your SharePoint environment, establishing and sorting the variety of content in different containers. The lists and libraries also provide a container for other aspects to manage your information life cycle, such as associating metadata with content, hosting workflows to process and manage the content, and applying retention and disposition policies to the content.

I am stressing the importance of SharePoint lists and libraries because they are a critical component to any enterprise content management design and implementation. Indeed, this is where the majority of your configuration and policy settings will apply, allowing those details to cascade down to the individual units of information stored within the container, thus enabling you to scale. Instances of the policies and workflows apply to individual units of information, but you define and apply them at the content's container, either directly implementing them through lists and libraries, or through a content type.

▪ **Note** For more information on how to plan and configure settings for the list and library content containers in your information life cycle strategy, please see the chapters in Part II, where I go into those topics in more depth.

You can add new lists and libraries to your site by adding new SharePoint apps, the site component through which SharePoint adds new functionality and containers to a site. Apps can be a little confusing at first because they include a variety of options to add to and enhance a site. For example, you can add an app to provision a new document library in your site for storing content, and you can add another app to add a web part with functionality for user interaction rather than content storage.

Apps also come from a few different sources, adding to the potential confusion when one initially tries to understand their purpose and what they do. SharePoint organizes apps in different catalogs, which are simply different sources of finding apps, some built into SharePoint itself, others developed by your internal developers, and still others licensed through third-party vendors. The following lists and describes the different app catalogs:

- **Site Catalog:** This catalog exposes all of the apps built in or installed directly on the SharePoint farm. It includes apps such as the core lists and libraries as well as the product's core web parts.

- **Organization Catalog:** This catalog exposes your organization's internal apps, built either by your internal development teams or outside consulting service firms. You use this catalog to host your custom developed apps, providing a well-known and centralized location for users to discover relevant apps for their sites. This catalog also manages your organization's app licenses and user requests for apps from the SharePoint Store.

- **SharePoint Store:** This catalog exposes Microsoft's marketplace where Microsoft and third-party vendors list their apps—some for sale, some for free. You can use this catalog to acquire new apps rather than develop them yourself. This provides a centralized and trusted location to add new functionality, leveraging the global community for site-specific extensions while standardizing the procurement process.

At their most basic sense, SharePoint apps package instructions to configure or add functionality to a site, including adding a list or library definition, creating an instance of a content container to capture and manage units of information, as well as adding other site aspects such as web parts. SharePoint contains apps within a site collection, isolating them from other sites and the system itself. It also prevents any custom code from executing on the servers in the SharePoint farm, instead requiring the app to execute any custom code directly on the client, typically using JavaScript, or on a vendor-hosted server using a web service.

You can add a new SharePoint app to you site from the Site Content page, easily accessed by clicking the Site Content link in the quick launch navigation menu, usually located in the left area of a site page. Alternatively, you can use the site Settings menu found in the top-right area on a site page and represented by a gear icon. On the Site Content page, click the Add An App link to open the Add An App page, similar to the one in Figure 2-10. You can select a desired SharePoint app from one of the categories by clicking it.

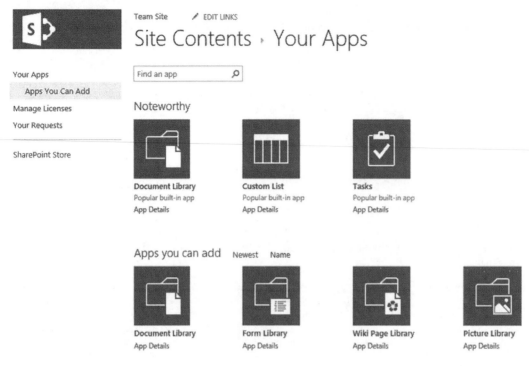

Figure 2-10. *The Add An App page*

For my purposes in this book, I primarily focus on the apps for content containers, and for simplicity sake, I refer to those containers directly as the lists and libraries in general, or the specific type of list or library. The other apps are valuable and I encourage you to explore them and experiment with what they can offer to your site, but except where they relate directly to designing your enterprise content management strategy, I do not discuss them further in this book.

As I mentioned, content containers divide between two main flavors: lists and libraries. The following lists and describes the main libraries available in SharePoint 2013, accessed through the Add An App function and by selecting the library filter:

- **Document library:** This library is the core content container and one of the most popular libraries your SharePoint deployment will probably use. Users can upload any type of file, not just Microsoft Office files, as long as its extension is not on the exclusion list for file extensions.

- **Pages library:** This library stores and manages SharePoint pages—ASP.NET pages as well as basic HTML web pages. When combined with the publishing features in a SharePoint site, it can merge page content with layouts pages, rendering consistent and efficient content pages for site visitors. Wikis also use a page library to store wiki pages.

- **Picture library:** This library is a specialized library for storing and managing pictures and their associated metadata. It also provides functionality to preview pictures at different sizes or view a slideshow of selected pictures. You can use this library to share pictures and host picture galleries with the site visitors.

- **Form library:** This library stores and manages InfoPath forms. It also provides the ability to link a column in the library with a field in the InfoPath form. You can use this library to capture electronic forms, execute their related workflow processes, and track or audit their history.

- **Asset library:** This library stores and manages different types of media assets, including video, audio, and pictures, as well as their associated metadata. It also provides functionality to preview media assets. You can use this library to organize your rich media content.

- **Slide library:** This library is a specialized library for storing and managing PowerPoint slides. User can upload PowerPoint files and then interact with individual slides from those presentations. You can use this library to share presentations with teammates, allowing them to mix and match slides when they need to make a presentation of their own.

▓ **Tip**   When I worked for Microsoft, there was an unwritten rule where we were supposed to share our PowerPoint slides for any presentation we gave, allowing my colleagues to leverage any of my slides and me to leverage any of theirs. At the time, this was a network file share named "showsrus" with a hierarchy of folders organized by conference. You can copy this idea for your organization, making it even more efficient with a SharePoint slide library, enabling your users to leverage and reuse each other's presentation slides.

Where libraries mostly entail files, lists mostly involve strings of text directly as the unit of information. (Both lists and libraries further include metadata as part of the unit information, self-describing an item along with the item's content). The following lists and describes the main lists available in SharePoint 2013, accessed through the Add An App function and by selecting one of the list filters:

- **Announcements:** This list allows you to post and schedule announcements for site visitors and teammates, keeping everyone updated and aware of developments. It also exposes enhanced formatting capabilities to embed images and hyperlinks with rich formatted text. You can add a web part to a site page to display recent announcements.

- **Calendar:** This list essentially serves as a shared calendar, allowing site members to post event details and schedules. It also exposes functionality for users to open the calendar in Outlook, optionally layering it over their personal calendar, providing a global view of their commitments and availability.

- **Tasks:** This list provides task management capabilities, including task details and task assignments. SharePoint can aggregate tasks from tasks lists on different sites, as well as other task repositories such as Project sites or Exchange mailboxes, displaying an aggregated list of tasks on each user's My Site.

- **Project Tasks:** This list captures task information in a similar fashion to the task list, extending that list to provide a visual or Gantt view with progress bars consistent with common project management formats. It also exposes functionality to open and interact with a project task list in Microsoft Project 2013. You can use this list for more consistency with traditional task tracking in project management.

- **Issues:** This list captures issue details and manages open issues, tracking their progress and status. It also exposes functionality to assign issues to site members, categorize issues, and relate issue items to other issues. You can use this list to track bugs, risks, or other types of issues you want to capture and monitor through until the issue's resolution.

- **Contacts:** This list stores contact information such as names, phone numbers, e-mail addresses, and postal addresses for individual contacts. You can use this list for different types of contacts, depending on the site's purpose, including customers for a service or stakeholders on a project.

- **Discussions:** This list stores discussion topics and their replies in a similar format to forums or newsgroups. It also exposes functionality to receive threaded e-mail discussions, set by configuring the list to receive and post inbound e-mail messages. You can use this list to brainstorm ideas or capture discussion topics for future reference.

- **Links:** This list stores link information such as a URL and title for a web link. You can use this list to display links to relevant web resources for site members and site visitors to reference.

- **Surveys:** This list allows you to define survey questions and capture survey responses. It also provides reports on survey results, both aggregating and reporting on individual responses. You can use surveys to gather information from users based on a series of questions.

As you can see, there are many different containers to capture and manage enterprise content in. They provide the entry point to capture knowledge and information, then transforming themselves into a storage role to provide ongoing access, consumption, and management of a unit of information. Some are specialized to manage particular kinds of content, whereas other containers are more generic. They all combine in your enterprise content management implementation, working together to provide the storage and item handling.

All of these content containers share some underlying core functionality and settings, such as access control, retention policies, and workflows, among others—all vital features to facilitate a productive and automated content life cycle. These content containers establish the foundation for an ECM solution, capturing and managing the individual content items, providing a means for enterprise-wide ECM features to interact with and manage your content. In the next section, I summarize the different ECM features in SharePoint, looking at how they provide tools to manage the content life cycle across all lists and libraries, among other content repositories.

SharePoint 2013 ECM-Specific Features

SharePoint offers a compelling range of enterprise content management features for your deployment, establishing a platform with rich feature sets for each stage of the information life cycle, allowing you to deploy a single platform, growing and adapting it over time as your enterprise content management matures. You do not have to stick with a single platform, as SharePoint can integrate and coordinate with other platforms. But for now, let's just focus on SharePoint as your ECM platform.

I already noted some low-level, particularly crucial components for managing your enterprise content: the SharePoint lists and libraries. These are where your ECM solution design begins, because this is where the content lives. I like to build out from there. I touched on another useful, and somewhat related, aspect at the list or library level when I mentioned content types—every item in a list or library belongs to a content type, whether a more generic content type or a specialized one for certain kinds of content.

Where SharePoint lists and libraries handle the capture and storage of content, content types offer a granular method to apply policies to a specific type of content wherever it resides, rather than applying policies to everything in a content container. It also offers a means to define the metadata. Defining the content and its policies through a content type empowers you to organize the content by what makes sense for the information and how users want to work with it, instead of having to organize it by how you want the system to manage the content.

At its essence, a content type is really just another piece of metadata that categorizes content as a specific type. SharePoint uses this metadata category to group and marry other content-related aspects to the unit of information, such as retention policies, workflows, and other metadata columns, as illustrated in Figure 2-11. The product simplifies these underlying details and exposes the implementation details relating to a unit of information as a content type.

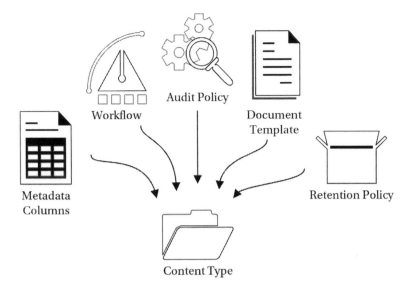

Figure 2-11. *Conceptual overview of content types*

Content types enable you to manage different kinds of content in the same list or library, but that is just the start of their value. You can reuse content type definitions across different content containers, facilitating consistency and standardization for your units of information, no matter where users create particular kinds of content and no matter where users move the content items. Indeed, one other feature of content types is that you can standardize and share them across your enterprise, a feature known as the *content type hub*.

When you create a content type hub, you specify a site collection to host content types that SharePoint will then replicate to the other site collections across your organization (or at least replicating to those site collections in a web application that consumes the same Managed Metadata Service managing the content type hub). This manages units of information as users move them to new locations, progressing through stages of the content's life cycle.

For example, a user can create a document in his or her My Site, associating it with a particular content type, and then later he or she can move it to a shared team site for group collaboration, before finally moving it once again to a records repository to designate it as an official record. In each location, the SharePoint site is aware of the content type and any policies or metadata associated with it, regardless of the site or document library. Furthermore, as I discuss in Part IV on records management, a records repository can automatically route and apply the applicable retention policies for content based on its content type.

▓ **Note**   Please see Chapter 6, where I step through how to plan, design, and implement content types and their related metadata, policies, and workflows.

So far, I have discussed granular aspects relating to enterprise content management in SharePoint. Lists and libraries, along with content types, set the basic building blocks for everything else in your information life cycle to interact with, extend, and depend on. Working out from here, the different kinds of SharePoint sites are the next major aspect for managing units of information, depending on the type of site, as I discussed previously.

A major component of a content type includes the metadata to tag and classify content. Metadata itself plays an integral part of any enterprise content management solution, because this organizes content and it establishes the criteria for most of your policy rules to apply to the content. SharePoint implements metadata through its Managed Metadata Service (MMS)—a service application that hosts your enterprise taxonomies and other term-based structures and lists.

■ **Note**   Please see Chapter 4, where I discuss designing your enterprise taxonomy and implementing it in the Managed Metadata Service.

Workflows establish another major ECM feature exposed in SharePoint. The Windows Workflow Foundation in the .NET framework provides the underlying workflow engine and framework for SharePoint, enabling sophisticated workflows to manage and orchestrate activities and automate processes. SharePoint leverages these workflow capabilities in the .NET framework, extending them with its own workflow implementation, hosting workflow instances, managing workflow state, and providing an integrated workflow user experience consistent with the rest of the SharePoint user experience.

You can apply and associate workflows at any stage of your information life cycle. For example, you can create an approval workflow for documents or portal pages as a team collaborates on them, defining a system-managed process for documents or portal pages to move from a draft status into a published state, as illustrated in Figure 2-12. This both formalizes and enforces the process to progress from draft to published content.

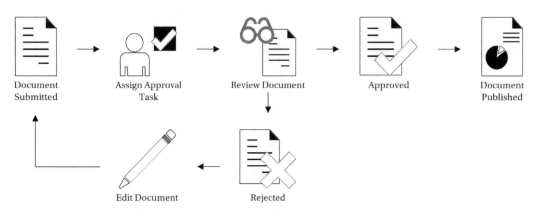

Figure 2-12. *An example of steps in an approval workflow*

With users constantly producing new units of information, your corpus of enterprise content continuously grows, some portions valuable, others not at all or only temporarily. This presents the need to retain some content and dispose of other content when it no longer provides value and is no longer required for historical purposes. SharePoint solves this scenario through retention policies, and these are especially effective when you combine them with custom workflows and associate them with content types, enabling you to manage major categories of content in an efficient and effective manner.

■ **Note**   Please see Chapter 15, where I discuss managing content retention and disposition in more detail.

Electronic discovery (also referred to as eDiscovery in SharePoint 2013) provides a means to discover relevant content based on a range of query parameters. This allows an organization to respond to compliance, regulatory, and legal cases by discovering any relevant units of information within the corpus of enterprise content. An eDiscovery manager can create and manage a discovery case, discover content related to the case, and place a snapshot of the content items on hold to preserve and protect their integrity for the case. You can use eDiscovery in response to an incident or external obligations, or for a proactive internal content audit.

▓ **Note**   Please see Chapter 11, where I discuss eDiscovery and managing discovery cases in more depth.

Managing the process to capture, store, and control units of information make up the majority of an enterprise content management solution, but you also need to manage how users can find and discover information, whether managing eDiscovery cases or generally searching for relevant content. The SharePoint search service is the underlying component and the essential functionality to query for content, from users executing a search query to aggregated rollups displaying related content suggestions.

I discuss these features and others in more depth throughout the rest of this book. For now, I just wanted to give you an overview of some key functionality, a taste of what SharePoint brings to the table, to whet your appetite for the rest of the book, where I lead you through how to plan and design solutions around these functions, and then how to implement them in your SharePoint environment.

Although this is not a deployment book on how to set up and configure SharePoint itself, as my limited space for topics constrains me from including detailed SharePoint deployment guidance, I think it is important to ensure a general understanding of what a SharePoint farm entails. As such, I shift now to give you a succinct overview of the infrastructure that makes up a SharePoint farm.

Overview of the SharePoint Infrastructure

Any SharePoint farm will consist of at least a SharePoint server and a SQL Server database server—these may coexist on the same Windows server instance, but in all but the smallest and most basic deployments, you will generally install them on separate servers. As I indicated, you install the SharePoint and SQL Server application software on a Windows Server (either 2008 R2 or 2012), building your servers on virtual or physical servers, depending on your preference.

These servers make up the essence of a SharePoint farm, ranging from small farms with just those two servers, to larger farms consisting of multiple servers to process a greater load in parallel. The number of servers your SharePoint farm requires depends on the number of users you support, their usage characteristics, and how powerful the servers are.

▓ **Note**   For more information on how to install and set up a SharePoint farm, please see my SharePoint 2013 Build and Installation Guide at `http://stevegoodyear.wordpress.com/sharepoint-2013-build-guide`.

One of the great things about SharePoint is its flexibility to change over time. Indeed, Microsoft designed SharePoint to maximize its adaptability to future requirements and the inevitable changes as the future reveals itself. As your users grow in numbers or their usage characteristics change, you can join additional servers to the farm to handle the increasing load. This is as simple as the following steps:

- Install the SharePoint software and any applicable language packs.

- Apply the latest service pack, security updates, and patches.

- Run the SharePoint configuration wizard.

A SharePoint server is a server on which you install the SharePoint software. SharePoint servers run services, and each of those services process some aspect of the farm's workload. You can allocate a server to different conceptual roles in a SharePoint farm by starting the relevant services on that server and stopping other services. For example, you can designate a web server by starting the Microsoft SharePoint Foundation Web Application service; or you can designate different application roles by starting the application's respective services on the server. A server can run all or some services, and multiple servers run the same service, in which case SharePoint will manage the load balancing for the service.

Basically, I want to show you that your SharePoint farm is not fixed or limiting, and this is because you can adapt the number of servers and the distribution of services on the servers with ease. I like to highlight this because it is important: you do not have to worry about thinking of every possible future scenario ahead of time, alleviating the need to over-architect an implementation up front. You can grow and adapt your farm as the load warrants, and you can discover your farm loads by monitoring the performance levels of servers in the farm.

■ **Note**   For more on performance monitoring in a SharePoint 2013 farm, please see the MSDN article at http://technet.microsoft.com/ff758658.

Now you know the main infrastructure components involved in a SharePoint farm; but SharePoint farms rarely operate in isolation. In fact, I like to think of SharePoint as the application that integrates or interacts with almost every other enterprise application, and this can quickly add to the complexity with understanding the infrastructure that surrounds a SharePoint farm.

Some of these enterprise systems are natural and almost seamless for SharePoint to integrate with and consume data or services. For example, a SharePoint farm probably uses an identity management system such as Active Directory to authenticate its users. A SharePoint farm may send e-mail alerts and even receive inbound messages to discussion boards or document libraries, interacting with an e-mail system such as Exchange. SharePoint can interact with other enterprise systems through custom integration points as well, such as through Business Connectivity Services (a service application that provides external data connectivity and integration services to the SharePoint farm).

Figure 2-13 illustrates the different servers making up a sample SharePoint farm, as well as servers from other enterprise systems that the SharePoint farm integrates with.

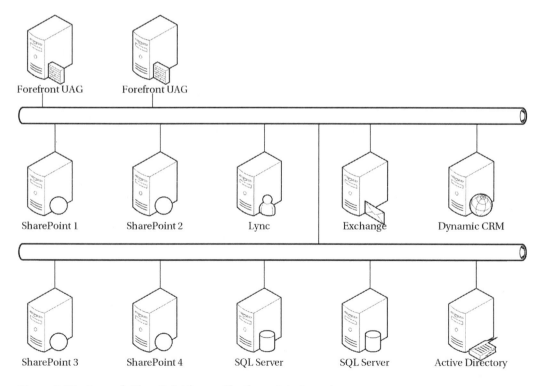

Figure 2-13. *A sample SharePoint farm with other enterprise systems*

As you can see, a SharePoint farm can interact with some critical enterprise systems, and in some cases, these are some of the most critical enterprise systems in an organization—take Active Directory or Exchange, for example, since these are among the most critical systems for many organizations. But even more than simply interacting with critical enterprise systems, I find that SharePoint is itself frequently a critical enterprise system as well.

With SharePoint reaching the status of a critical enterprise system, you can take comfort in how capable the product is to hold this status. For one, it is generally stable and built well. However, for my money, I think its service-oriented design and overall scalability are what make it particularly capable for you to treat it as enterprise critical.

SCALING UP AND AMDAHL'S LAW

Amdahl's law, named after Gene Amdahl, provides an algorithm to identify the maximum expected improvement in a system when you only improve part of the system. The following is the formula for Amdahl's law:

$$1 / (\alpha + \frac{1-\alpha}{\rho})$$

You can apply this formula to your SharePoint 2013 farm to give you an indication of the expected performance improvement in the farm if you change one part. For example, if you have a single SharePoint 2013 server instance and its four processors are running at 80% utilization, you can use the formula to calculate the improvements by scaling up to eight processors. First, you plug in the numbers to the first formula—0.2 (or the 20% in available processing power) and 4 (for the four existing processors), as follows:

$$1 / (0.2 + \frac{1-0.2}{4}) = 2.50$$

Next, you calculate the performance improvement you can expect from doubling the amount of processing power by plugging in the numbers 0.2 (or the 20% available processing power) and 8 (for the eight processors) to the second formula, as follows:

$$1 / (0.2 + \frac{1-0.2}{8}) = 3.33$$

Using this formula, you can see that by doubling the processing power, you can expect to increase performance by about one third or 33%—(3.33-2.50)/2.50. This can help you to determine whether scaling up by improving a part of the system will be the optimum solution to your performance needs. When you scale out, you can duplicate the entire system, and as such, you will have a more linear relationship between scaling out and the increase in performance. The optimum scaling solution will relate to your performance needs and consider the expected performance gains against the scaling costs involved with each approach.

Wrapping Up

SharePoint offers a range of ECM features to implement and support your ECM solution, from collaboration sites and content types to eDiscovery and content retention workflows. In this chapter, I provided an overview of SharePoint 2013 and its core capability areas—namely, collaboration, social computing, portals, search, records management, business intelligence, and composite applications. From there, I described the site architecture in SharePoint, paying particular attention to the hierarchy of content containers as well as the types of sites, lists, and libraries. I stressed understanding how SharePoint captures and manages content will help you with your information life cycle strategy, and then I highlighted some of the main enterprise content management features in SharePoint.

Knowing how SharePoint manages content is critical for implementing your enterprise content management solution, but before you get to that stage, you have to design a solution that fits your organization's needs. The first major step in designing your enterprise content management solution is to analyze and understand your information life cycle. In the next chapter, I return to the content life cycle model I introduced in Chapter 1, and I show you how to apply it to your organization and how to use this to analyze its information life cycle.

CHAPTER 3

■ ■ ■

Analyzing Your Information Life Cycle

"Think simple" as my old master used to say—meaning reduce the whole of its parts into the simplest terms.

—Frank Lloyd Wright

Understanding how information flows and progresses within your organization will reveal and steer you toward an elegant enterprise content management solution. In this chapter, I provide guidance on how to analyze information life cycles within an organization by applying the content life cycle model I introduced in Chapter 1. I also share techniques for how you can build an inventory of your organization's content and how you can analyze business processes relating to your content. Finally, I discuss how you can identify your content's security requirements.

After reading this chapter, you will know how to

- Apply the content life cycle model to your content.

- Build an inventory of your organization's content.

- Analyze and diagram your content-related business processes.

- Identify your information security needs.

- Document your content life cycle requirements.

Applying the Content Life Cycle Model

Models make complex information easier to understand and easier to communicate. They reveal patterns and dependencies that otherwise might not be noticeable, helping to elaborate or clarify requirements, highlighting any exceptions or outliers to consider, all to help analyze a problem and to support designing a solution. Applying the content life cycle model to your organization's content will guide your analysis by helping to reduce the complexity and scale of enterprise content into a comprehensible model.

You might recall the content life cycle model I introduced in Chapter 1. As I mentioned then, I expanded the details for my content life cycle model from the AIIM information life cycle model, a model focusing on five life cycle phases: capture, store, manage, deliver, and preserve. I did this to make the model more concrete for analyzing content and its life cycle within a SharePoint environment. With a few extra details, I maintained most of the simplicity of the model so that it is easy to follow and can fit a variety of scenarios, but I added some hooks or anchor points where you can apply it to an actual content instance.

Figure 3-1 illustrates the content life cycle model, included again here for your convenience. This model provides several entry points into the life cycle, including the beginning with a user creating or receiving a piece of content and capturing it in SharePoint. The model also includes a convenient entry point where SharePoint manages the content, if you would rather take a more system-oriented functional view. Alternatively, you can start with how users discover content and then interact with it, if you prefer to analyze your existing content. Wherever you start, eventually you will apply and work your way through the entire content life cycle.

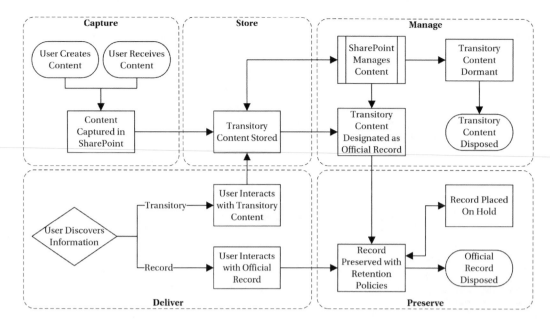

Figure 3-1. *The content life cycle model*

Before I jump into applying the model to your content, I want to offer a word of caution if you choose to start with analyzing how SharePoint manages the content, that is, the functional view. This can be a tempting entry point, because the functionality in SharePoint is already architected and documented, leaving you to make configuration decisions for each aspect. Its functions gives you a known list of things to configure and decisions to make, which can feel comforting at first; however, without the information about the actual content and its uses, those configuration decisions will not be as obvious or as comfortable as they might first seem.

I find this comes up when well-intentioned business analysts want to make progress and work with the information they have, which initially is product guides and other materials documenting SharePoint features. It could stem from some of the marketing language around the product and its capabilities, but an effective ECM program goes beyond working one's way through a list of product features, deciding what to enable and how to configure it. This always seems to constrain a design where a team ends up trying to pigeonhole a use case into some functional constraint the team decided on too early in the process. Forcing something to fit with a contrived constraint only builds up complexity and complications through your ECM solution design and implementation, and ultimately it has a negative effect on user adoption.

Another danger I see occurs with project teams that are replacing one system with SharePoint as part of the project delivery, and in their approach, they heavily document the existing system and all of its features, a document that then serves as a requirements list for the SharePoint implementation. As far as I can tell, this seems to stem from a desire to avoid upsetting users with the system change, and so someone announces that the change will not lose any functionality—in essence making a promise to users that anything they can do in the old system, they will also be able to do in the new system. I see this run into trouble when the project team takes that promise too literally as they document every function in the old legacy system, only looking at the new system from the perspective of how it can replicate the old system.

■ **Tip**　There is generally no point to replace old systems, only to reproduce the old system on a new platform.

Instead, I recommend you start with one of the other entry points and follow the content, from either creation or discovery, tracing it through the life cycle, using the content to drive design decisions. When you understand the content and its use cases throughout the life cycle, you are then in a good position to make solution design decisions by looking at how SharePoint can implement and manage the content while supporting its use cases. You might even find that SharePoint alone cannot support one of your use cases, indicating that you might need to integrate with another system, procure a third-party extension for SharePoint, or include custom development as part of your ECM solution.

■ **Important**   Start with the content and let the content and its use cases drive your enterprise content management design.

Following my advice, let's start with where the content starts: when a user or automated process captures content into the system. For my purposes here, I will refer to the system as SharePoint, since this is a book about ECM in SharePoint. Often during the analysis phase, I prefer to remain more abstract and general in documenting the process to avoid having technology drive a solution, such as capturing content into the system. Although in this case, I know the system is SharePoint, but I still avoid getting too specific on the functionality or the technical details at this point. I do not say, for example, capture the content in a team site's document library, because at this point, I want a higher-level view of the life cycle.

If you pick a piece of content and look at its capture process into SharePoint, you might notice that you can move backward from the capture point to identify stages in the content creation not captured in the content life cycle model. This can include a stage where a user creates and interacts with the content outside SharePoint. For example, a user might create a funding proposal document on their desktop and work with it for a period, even e-mailing it around to different users who provide input on the document, before eventually uploading it to a SharePoint site. Figure 3-2 illustrates the activities in the creation process for a document prior to its capture in SharePoint.

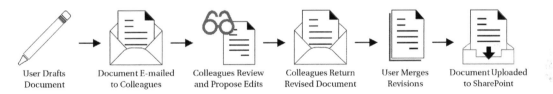

User Drafts   Document E-mailed   Colleagues Review   Colleagues Return   User Merges   Document Uploaded
Document   to Colleagues   and Propose Edits   Revised Document   Revisions   to SharePoint

Figure 3-2. *A content creation process for a document prior to its capture in SharePoint*

This proposal document is a perfect example for how you can refine requirements and solution designs by applying the content life cycle model to your organization's content. The most notable thing the model does is highlight an exception to the model: the content goes through a fragment of a life cycle before it enters the SharePoint ECM model. This may or may not be how you want the process to flow in the future, but for now, the model helps you to uncover where the exceptions exist. Perhaps this exception is one you can resolve by guiding the users to collaborate on the content entirely within SharePoint, either in a team site or a My Site library.

You might find a similar exception for a piece of content that a user receives and eventually captures in SharePoint. For example, a vendor might e-mail an invoice to a user in the organization, and then it sits in the user's inbox for a time before he or she forwards it to someone else, who then captures it in SharePoint. Again, there is a fragment of life cycle not captured prior to the content life cycle model for SharePoint. Figure 3-3 illustrates the phases in this receiving process for an e-mailed invoice.

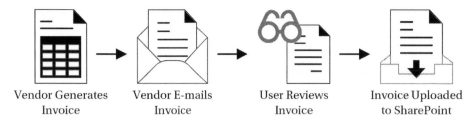

Figure 3-3. *A content receiving process for an external user's report*

This e-mailed invoice process reveals another exception to the content life cycle model: the content lives in the organization for a time outside the boundaries of the model. Now, this is not to say the exception is bad and that you should alter the process; it merely highlights that an exception exists, allowing you to analyze it further to make those types of process design decisions. If you did want to resolve this exception, you could alter the process by e-mail-enabling a document library or discussion board to capture the content directly into SharePoint and into the model.

How users discover content provides another area for you to analyze and uncover exceptions. In the content life cycle model, I included discovery from the system's point of view—meaning that the model begins with users discovering content from within the system. You might come across exceptions to this discovery entry-point, with the most popular being a process similar to e-mailing a colleague and asking if they can recommend any content. This would be a fragment of life cycle not captured in the discovery process, because the user is going outside SharePoint to discover relevant content. Figure 3-4 illustrates this process where a user discovers content by using the SharePoint search portal.

Figure 3-4. *A content discovery process involving direct user interaction*

Bypassing the search portal and directly asking colleagues for references to content may not be a negative process, particularly if you want to encourage users to interact with each other to leverage one another's expertise and to cultivate teamwork. However, it does highlight an exception to the model where users rely on other users rather than on the system to discover certain kinds of content. With any exception, this gives you an opportunity to investigate and analyze deeper, where a closer look might reveal that the search engine does not provide results with enough relevance to locate this content efficiently, or it might reveal that the content's metadata does not align with the recommendations on a user's My Site. Whatever the underlying drivers behind an exception, the model will help you identify and analyze them, and through this process, you have the opportunity to optimize processes where appropriate.

■ **Note**   This exception of users asking for content rather than searching for it themselves reminds me of a web site (www.lmgtfy.com) that pokes fun at people in a passive-aggressive way, letting them know that they could have searched for an answer on their own by saying "let me Google that for you."

The process is similar to those for analyzing how SharePoint manages content, particularly for any exceptions to the model where another system or a manual process manages content. Another system might extend the capabilities in SharePoint, such as when you use a separate system for your records repository, whether because your organization wishes to maintain its investment in the system or because the system provides richer features and capabilities than does SharePoint. Remember, the point is to recognize and analyze the exceptions to the model, not to force everything to fit the model by forcing everything into SharePoint.

■ **Note**   Please see Chapter 16, where I discuss integrating SharePoint with external systems and other records repositories.

So far, I looked at the entry points in the content life cycle model and at how you can apply those to your organization to identify and further analyze any exceptions. Similarly, you can look at the endpoints, where SharePoint disposes of the content. The most prominent question to analyze here is whether the endpoint exists— does your organization dispose of content? You might notice an exception to the model here as well, and it will certainly stand out if you do not have a process for disposing transitory content or official records once they reach the end of their life cycle and no longer offer any value to your organization.

You might also find an exception to the model in manual processes to dispose of content in place of automated system-managed processes. For example, you might host team sites for marketing campaigns, all with a manual process where the site owners are supposed to archive any content they feel will be useful historical references in the future, while disposing the rest. Manual processes are easy to forget as other more urgent tasks vie for a user's attention, but at the same time, your users might not like the idea of the system automatically destroying their content after a set duration, which might be the underlying driver for the process being manual in the first place. To resolve this exception, you might design a workflow with steps for approval or another type of branching logic requiring user input, thus offering you a compromise between manual and automated disposal processes, while still having SharePoint manage the disposal process.

Within the model itself, you can trace the flow of content to identify any gaps. For example, if you have content that persists as transitory content rather than an official record—a likely scenario motivating many readers of this book, I suspect—then this highlights a gap in your organization's content life cycle. Not every piece of content has to go on to become a record, but it either should become a record or be disposed of, as the model indicates. Transitory content should not live on in perpetuity in a transitory state.

You can apply the content life cycle model to validate content processes, identify exceptions and gaps to analyze, or simply to understand a type of content in context. As I started the section saying, it is simply a tool to make the complexity and scale of your enterprise content easier to understand and analyze. This is not a fixed process that you must conform to, nor one you must enforce on every piece of content. You can have many valid reasons to include exceptions to the model, and the model will help you identify and analyze them.

Analyzing the life cycle of your organization's content is a lengthy process, but its outcome produces valuable insights and information for your enterprise content management solution. However, you cannot reasonably scale to analyze every piece of content; instead, you should focus on your main classes of content. I may have gotten ahead of myself here by looking at how to analyze the content before I clarified what content to focus on, but the analysis stays the same whether you analyze individual pieces of content or general classes of content. Let's shift now to look at ways to identify classes of content in your organization that you can apply to the content life cycle model and analyze.

Building an Inventory of Your Organization's Content

Building an inventory of content in any environment except the smallest and simplest may sound like a monumental task, and perhaps it is, especially if you attempt to do this manually. I am not suggesting you create an Excel spreadsheet and begin on the journey of itemizing each piece of content wherever it might be within your organization. I imagine there is probably just too much content, and chances are it changes too quickly for you to have any hope of keeping up. Besides, that kind of detailed raw data does not have any practical use.

Nonetheless, understanding what content you have is useful and you can use this information to design the rest of your enterprise content management solution. You do not need to know each individual file, but knowing an aggregation of the type and number of files will prove to be invaluable. As such, I am really talking about building an inventory of the *kinds* of content within your organization—everything from the file formats to the broad categories of content types users create and work with.

There are a few ways you can approach building such an inventory. For example, from more elegant and prepackaged to cruder and improvised, you can

- Procure a tool specializing in analyzing directory contents and file structures.

- Use an enterprise search engine to crawl content, and then analyze its reports or run custom search queries.

- Write a script to enumerate the contents of storage drives and aggregate the results.

- Eyeball the contents of storage drives and estimate the most common kinds of content.

I like automating the task myself, whether with a specialized tool or another option. Computers are great at parsing mass amounts of information, and collecting and aggregating data about it, the output of which enables you to analyze your inventory of different kinds of content. Some tools work better than others do, but even the most rudimentary custom PowerShell script can get you started. Your challenge will be to segregate the content into *kinds* of content, not simply by file extension or directory.

Identifying kinds of content is the primary objective for an inventory, but you might also find other metadata information interesting and useful. For this reason, a tool that offers a comprehensive report with different attributes for the content might be more valuable for you. You will find the tool especially useful if you can use these attributes to filter or group the content in a custom view, allowing you to answer other questions, such as how many Word documents your organization has that are over 5MB, or even better, what is the monthly growth in number of documents or corpus size.

As you gather data about your content, you should also make note of where your organization stores content. What is stored on shared drives and what is stored in SharePoint or another repository? You should also look at the content's freshness and the ongoing value it provides, if any. How active are users with the content? Knowing this type of information will help give you a better sense about how your organization produces and consumes information.

Knowing the different kinds of content your organization uses will make your later analysis easier. You can reference your content inventory in the next chapter as you build your information architecture. And even better than that, in Chapter 6 I discuss how to design and implement SharePoint content types, making the task quite straightforward when you already have a list of the main types of content in your organization. All of the work you put in early with this analysis to create an inventory of content will continue to make your job easier later, such as in Chapter 9 when I discuss enterprise search, or again in Chapter 15 when I discuss content retention and disposition.

▨ **Tip**   You can use some of the content's attribute information to aid a content cleanup initiative, such as by highlighting potential content to dispose, or for mapping content migration rules.

Capturing information about multiple attributes will help you answer a variety of questions—both those you know about and want to answer today, and those that will come up throughout your ECM program. Once I organize a content inventory into broad classes listing the types of content, I like to add descriptions to each class describing the type of content it includes. I also like to capture other information as well, such as where the class of content fits in the content life cycle and whether it transforms into another content class as it progresses through the life cycle.

Of course, content includes more than just document files; it includes other units of information, such as web pages, list items, and e-mail messages. Be sure to capture information about these other types of content as you conduct your content inventory.

If your organization is new to SharePoint, then some of these other types of content might not be as prevalent as organizations with SharePoint deployments. Alternatively, you might have another system that is similar to

SharePoint or an aspect of SharePoint, such as a wiki. Wiki pages capture blobs of text that users produce while they are collaborating and capturing knowledge. In your content inventory, you might capture details on the different types of wiki pages and the kinds of content they entail.

Articles and web pages published on your intranet and public web sites represent a unit of information you need to consider, whether your portal content managers publish the pages through a content management system similar to SharePoint, or they publish the pages manually by copying and pasting the files onto the server's directory. At this stage, you are taking an inventory about what content you have, so you do not have to get overly detailed here; instead, you can focus on what types of web content your organization uses and where.

▦ **Note**   Please see Chapter 7 for more information on web publishing and web content management.

E-mail messages represent your hardest challenge to describe and class together. People use e-mail for almost *anything* content-related within an organization, everything from sending a traditional letter or memo to a colleague, to sharing and collaborating on a document as users send around different versions. E-mail is generic and multipurpose, making it difficult to generalize and categorize, but at its core, it is an electronic message, a communication transmitting a unit of information between two or more people.

Finally, your organization has physical, nonelectronic content. This is a good stage to start considering that content too. You can include it in your content inventory and begin to look what kind of physical documents your organization produces and consumes in its operations. You do not have to worry so much yet about whether or how you could replace any of these physical documents with electronic content and processes. For now, just take an inventory about what is there.

▦ **Note**   Please see Chapter 16, where I discuss physical documents more from the perspective of managing physical records.

As you read this book, you will expand and build on this list of useful information to capture in a content inventory. I do not want to get ahead of myself just yet, so I will stick with these basics for now. This captures information about the content in your organization, valuable details about what content exists, its characteristics, and how it is used, all serving as your core analysis—it is, after all, enterprise content management. All of your other analysis will build around this core, starting with your business processes within a class of content.

COLLECTING DATA TO DRIVE YOUR ECM PROGRAM

Enterprise content management can feel daunting and intimidating at first glance, and it does involve some complexity with a lot of moving pieces to analyze, but I think most of the unfriendly feelings stem from a lack of information—a black hole of information to guide decisions and implementation designs. You cannot jump in and start building content types without knowing the underlying content, at least not effectively. The same is true with the other aspects of enterprise content management, which can all leave the process feeling unapproachable and intimidating.

You can build confidence and momentum on an enterprise content management implementation by filling those information gaps with raw data, such as a content inventory. ECM projects involve a lot of analysis work, as almost anyone who has done one will probably tell you, but the order of when you perform the analysis tasks can make all the difference. Taking inventories to gather data about your organization's existing state will give you a solid base to analyze and design an effective enterprise content management solution, no matter how complex it is in your environment.

Analyzing Your Content-Related Business Processes

Content does not live in isolation. It usually relates to a business process in some way. With an inventory of content and an understanding for how it fits within the content life cycle model, you can begin to understand what drives the content, process wise, and how the content relates to business processes within your organization. Some of the more valuable aspects of an enterprise content management program relate to identifying and formalizing these business processes that you can associate with different classes of content.

Applying the content life cycle model can help to identify some business processes, particularly those processes that relate to the content's progression through the model. For example, content disposition requires a process to determine when transitory content has reached the end of its life cycle or when a record's retention period has lapsed. Designating a piece of content as an official record also requires a process. These are two obvious content-related business processes visible in the content life cycle model, but a typical organization will also have many more processes underlying the model, some formal and some informal, and they may change depending on the class of content.

To start, take your content inventory and pick a class of content to analyze closer. Look at how the content changes or passes through different phases of the content life cycle model and identify any business processes that you notice. Also, pay attention to where content changes hands to see if there are any processes related to the content transitioning from person to person. I also try to answer the following questions as I analyze content for related business processes:

- Does the content have any obvious or existing processes?

- Are there metadata fields related to tracking the content's status or state?

- Is there an approver for a piece of content or for the phases the content progresses through?

- Do users perform any informal processes with the content inside or outside the system?

Essentially, the trick is to take a close look at the content and consider it from every angle. Through a close analysis, you will get a good sense of the content's related processes, such as how users use it and how SharePoint needs to manage it.

Some of your content-related business processes exist ahead of the content's creation and some trailing from the content's creation—by this I mean that some processes lead into the creation of a piece of content while other processes use the output of a piece of content in the process itself. By thinking about where a process falls in relation to a piece of content, you can uncover those processes that might otherwise be unapparent. You can do this by considering what occurs before a user creates the content, or even more specifically, what triggers a user to create the content.

The processes that come after or from the content are easy for you to identify and capture because you only have to follow what users do with the content. Does the content contain information about a request that other users then reference as they decide whether to approve the request? Does the content become a record of a decision a team made or a team's progress or status at a particular time? What happens to the content afterward?

Not every piece of content has an elaborate business process attached to it. Some processes might be formal, such as an approval process for employee vacation requests. Some processes are more informal, such as a team member updating a wiki page to add new information to their documentation. Generally, I focus most on capturing business process details for anywhere the process matters, and usually these are the more formal ones. If your day is anything like mine, you simply do not have the time to analyze every single process with the same degree of rigor, and so concentrating on the most important processes will help you maximize your time.

Identifying the content-related business processes will help you to analyze and better understand the content and its requirements. Nevertheless, this information continues to be useful after your initial content analysis, particularly when it comes time to design any system-managed workflows you want to associate with the content. For starters, you will have a list of all the workflows you need to design and implement. On top of that, you will have a lot of the workflow analysis and high-level design done already, leaving you to focus on filling in the details and designing the actual implementation.

For example, if you are analyzing the process relating to an electronic form, you will identify the major activities and decisions involved in that process during this stage. Later, when you reach the point where you are ready to design and implement the actual e-form and its related workflow, you already have a good sense of the steps involved and what the process will ultimately accomplish.

■ **Note**   Please see Chapter 8, for more details on designing an e-form approval workflow.

While I write a sentence to describe a piece of content and its purpose, I adopt a different format to communicate any of its related business processes. Describing a business process in one or two paragraphs can be difficult to follow. For those more complex process, it may take you several paragraphs to describe, making it that much more difficult for the reader to follow or grasp quickly. If I do want to use text to describe a process, then I format the text as a use case by creating a numbered list of simple statements describing each of the steps in the process. Alternatively, and more often, I diagram the process.

Diagramming Your Business Processes Using Microsoft Visio

You can use any diagramming tool you prefer to diagram your business processes. Microsoft Visio is one of the primary tools I use as I analyze an organization's content and content life cycle because it can summarize and simplify a lot of complex information, all with the arrangement of shapes in the diagram used to present and communicate the information effectively to many different audiences. Visio has several different diagram templates available for diagramming a process or a state, some of which you will see me use for my diagrams throughout this book.

■ **Note**   To learn more about Visio, please see the Microsoft Office site at http://office.microsoft.com/visio.

There are a few Visio templates that I use most often to diagram details about an organization's content and processes. Each diagrams and presents information in a different way, depending on the purpose of the template. These templates include the following:

- **Process diagram:** A basic flowchart consisting mainly of activity boxes and decision diamonds to diagram the activities and decisions involved in a process.

- **Swim-lane process diagram:** A diagram that builds on the process diagram, with swim-lane rows used to identify the role responsible for the activities or decisions contained within a swim-lane.

- **Workflow diagram:** A diagram that contains icons that visually represent the task in the workflow.

- **Entity-relationship (ER) diagram:** A data design that models the different entities and the relationships between them, often used to model database tables (entities) and the foreign-key relationship constraints between tables.

Visio also includes other templates for other types of diagrams, such as data flow diagrams, UML diagrams, sitemap diagrams, and network diagrams. You choose the appropriate template depending on your communication goal for the diagram. For communicating content-related processes, I find that one of the four diagrams I listed earlier serves my purpose the most often.

One of the challenges with diagramming complex information is deciding what to include in the diagram. If you include too much detail, your diagram will become complex and difficult to follow, resulting in less effective communication. How much information to include or not is more an art than a formula, and it depends on your audience and the purpose of the diagram. A functional specification for a software product requires more detail because developers will code software based on the diagram. Diagrams for content-related processes do not need that much detail, at least not yet. For now, I usually just focus on the main activities and decisions, and I filter out the rest of the details.

I find color helpful as a way to include extra information without complicating the diagram, as I describe in the following sidebar. You may have noticed in my content life cycle diagram that I included dashed boxes to identify the AIIM information life cycle phases, subtly adding this extra information without complicating my diagram. You can experiment with other organizing techniques that communicate extra information, such as boxes or diagram annotations.

FORMATTING YOUR DIAGRAMS

One thing I like to do with my diagrams is to incorporate color whenever possible. I had to omit color for my diagrams in this book because it is printed in black-and-white, but normally I will include a variety of colors in my diagrams. I do this to make them more vivid and more visually appealing, as well as to organize and highlight information within the diagram.

For example, I may highlight important activities and decisions in one color, or I may use different colors to represent different phases or different responsibilities. I adjust the colors, fill, and line format for individual shapes to add emphasis and appeal. Visio 2013 also has some great themes for shapes and it has interesting effects that you can apply to individual shapes within your diagram.

I find the autolayout features in Visio never produce a result I like, at least not yet, so I usually layout my shapes manually and I use the shape alignment and distribution tools in the product to format a professional and polished look.

Identifying Your Information Security Needs

Sometimes security requirements for a piece of content are less rigid, with those security requirements not entailing high-maintenance or requiring too much rigor. Indeed, much of your content may fall into this variety—content that users may or may not restrict and limit access to, being content without sensitive or confidential information, making it acceptable to share with a wider audience within the organization. This type of content still has security requirements, and I discuss how to identify and manage them later in this section. First, let's look at the other end of the scale, content with strict and thorough security requirements.

Certain types of content are so sensitive and critical to an organization that they require detailed and limited security. You manage the access control for this type of content on a need-to-know basis, typically with people who are involved with the content's information, either as the producers of the content or as decision makers relying on the content. More secure content also has a more limited audience.

There are many kinds of content at the more secure end of the scale, including the following (in no particular order):

- **Intellectual property (IP):** From scientific patients to video game algorithms, an organization's intellectual property helps them compete for research funding or sales prospects by differentiating them from other firms.

- **Research and development:** From mining companies conducting feasibility studies to pharmaceutical labs testing new drug treatments, firms want to protect their data and prevent other firms from stealing their ideas.

- **Personally identifiable information:** From government agencies with private citizen data to credit card payment gateways with transaction information, organizations require extra diligence in protecting personal information.

- **Tactical and strategic plans:** From militaries to corporations, their plans of attack or plans for competitive advantage benefit the organization the most when the plans remain a secret from outside adversaries.

These are just a few examples to get you thinking. A firm will have all kinds of content that they want to keep out of the public domain, and they will probably want to keep it contained within a limited group of people within the firm. You can contrast this with an article posted on a firm's public blog—obviously the security requirements for a public blog post will not require any of the confidentially restrictions since it is publicly disclosed, although it will still have some security requirements, such as who can edit the post.

To complicate matters, a unit of information can transition through different levels of security as well. For example, a press release announcing a public company's earnings for the previous quarter will have a specific date and time when the company will make the information public. Before that time, the financial information must remain secure and secret; otherwise, disclosures would give an investor an unfair advantage and thus would be subject to an inside trader investigation by the securities commission. However, eventually the press release will become public knowledge and its security requirements will change.

Knowing your content will help you plan and identify your security requirements along with any information architecture and business processes. If you built an inventory of your content as I discussed earlier, now you can go through and think about the range of security each type of content requires. Think about whether the security requirements change for a unit of information of a particular kind of content. What triggers the change and have you captured the trigger in the business processes that relate to the content?

Just as managing permissions for each individual user will not scale or manage well, managing security levels for individual pieces of content equally will not scale well. If you become overly granular in your security management, you risk applying missing or inconsistent permission settings to content, resulting in possible security holes. Security works most effectively when you generalize settings into groups, and then apply the group to individual items, such as applying permissions to security groups for several items to share, and then adding users to the group to grant those permissions. Incidentally, security also works more efficiently when you manage it through security groups, because groups will simplify and centralize the administration of security.

Similar to groups, you can use categories to design your security solution and establish consistency across your organization. Broad content classification categories allow you to generalize content into one of a few sensitivity levels. This eases the burden for training users because users will only need to know a few different information classification levels, the ways to decide between them to classify content, and an understanding for how users should treat content classified at each level. A well-understood and communicated classification level in turn reinforces security by ensuring users are aware of how to treat a piece of content and who they can share it with, ultimately reducing the occurrence of accidental disclosure of private information.

For example, when working in the federal public sector in my country, the Government of Canada will first conduct a security screening and then assign a security clearance level to an individual—both for outside consultants and for government employees. An individual then has clearance to access information classified with a clearance level that matches his or her own, with a caveat that they also need to have a valid business reason to access the information. Users must classify all information within the Government according to its security or sensitivity level; otherwise, the information is public. The following lists the Government of Canada's information classification levels:

- **Protected:** Designated information that applies to sensitive personal, private, and business information.

- **Confidential:** Classified information that when compromised could cause limited injury to the national interest.

- **Secret:** Classified information that when compromised could cause serious injury to the national interest.

- **Top Secret:** Classified information that when compromised could cause exceptionally grave injury to the national interest.

■ **Note**   For more information on the Government of Canada's Information Management policies, please see their web site at www.tbs-sct.gc.ca/pol/doc-eng.aspx?id=16557.

I have seen organizations adopt the Government's information classification levels and I have seen others design their own or adapt some hybrid. For example, the following lists some other self-descriptive information classification levels, each of which can come with a set of restrictions:

- Employee Personally Identifiable Information (PII)

- Protected Health Information (PHI)

- Customer Identifiable Information

- Confidential—Full Time Employee Only

- Confidential—Internal Only (Employees and Contractors)

- Confidential—Internal and Partners

Of course, you do not have to fit all your content classification needs into this one category. I discuss this more in the next chapter, but at this stage, you might begin to consider other ways you can classify content in common groups. The following lists a few examples:

- Sensitivity Level

- Business Impact

- Regulatory Association

Just as with any other metadata, utilizing multiple categories will leave your information design with multiple ways to classify content, making it that much more self-descriptive for users; plus, multiple categories offer additional dimensions to organize and filter lists of content. Having multiple categories to classify your content facilitates advanced information management scenarios as well, such as enabling sophisticated workflow logic and e-discovery queries.

You can implement these content classifications in SharePoint as part of the metadata you associate with a piece of content. You will continue to identify different classification categories in the next chapter as you design your enterprise taxonomy, and in Chapter 6, I discuss how to configure metadata for content classification. For now, start to consider some of the categories you can use to classify your content.

■ **Tip**   The more content classification you can automate for your users, the more effective your information management strategy will be. You can also increase its effectiveness by making content classifications more prominent and noticeable for users, such as adding information to a Word document's notification bar or changing the display color of a SharePoint list item to reflect its classification.

As you work through your inventory of content and you start to identify general classifications to group different kinds of content, you will begin to get a sense of how complex your information security requirements are. If you generalize your security requirements enough for each similar kind of content, as I mentioned, you will simplify your security requirement into a few broad and manageable categories. From there, you can begin to look at these categories to consider the appropriate scopes of security, and you can use these scopes to identify how you will implement the different kinds of content and security in SharePoint.

▓ **Note**   Please see Chapter 12, where I discuss different options to secure content in SharePoint.

In short, look for ways to group and generalize your security requirements to cover similar kinds of content. This strategy will allow you to scale and it will ease the burden on users to implement and follow the security policies. You achieve this when you avoid getting overly caught up in the particulars of each individual piece of content, and instead focus on major categories to group content within. Focus on the forest, not the trees.

Documenting Your Content Life Cycle Requirements

Documenting these requirements is not the same as creating a functional specification. A *functional specification* describes the system and its functions. Conversely, a *requirements document* describes the interaction with content, the content life cycle phases, and the business rules or events (those rules and events outside the system) that trigger a change or progression through the life cycle.

I stress this because too often I see people jump straight into a functional specification, attempting to describe the process from the perspective of the system; but this is premature at this stage because you have to understand the business and the business problems before you can determine the most effective solution and implementation details. Let the business analysis and the use cases you identify guide you toward the solution, not a list of product configuration options.

I confess that I slip and look at functional specifications prematurely sometimes myself. With prepackaged products, it is easy to accidently skip the business analysis and jump right into the solution—the functional implementation details. It happens sometimes on software development teams too when a team is building an entirely new system. I find it is particularly easy with a packaged software product like SharePoint because the system exists; you are not inventing it, all you are doing is configuring it.

Hence, it can be tempting to jump right into those implementation details by skipping to the function specification. I notice that I am especially prone to this if the project feels like a routine one (or at least routine to me— the outside consultant who repeats many projects with different clients, but there is probably nothing routine about it for the client). I try to stay conscious of this behavior to avoid skipping the business requirements and use cases, and I focus on staying disciplined to understand the business needs first. I encourage you to do the same: understand the problem thoroughly from the business's perspective first before you start deciding on implementation details and functional specifications.

Jumping right into a functional specification does not automatically lead to a project failure, although it may and frequently does, but it usually at least challenges a project. The main challenge it causes is it introduces design constraints much too early. These constraints come from making system decisions early before you understand all the use cases and before you have thoroughly analyzed the problem space. These constraints also often come from people other than the solution architect, people who are not qualified to make design decisions.

I see constraints come up related to all sorts of SharePoint functionality early in a project, such as deciding to do any of the following before conducting any analysis:

- Lock down the user interface

- Implement a specific number of templates

- Decide on universal workflows

- Limit privileges and functionality

These all tend to come up as an overreaction to overly limited and narrow or even nonexistent or misunderstood requirements, and in most cases someone inexperienced with ECM solutions drives these requirements forward. Avoid slipping into this danger zone yourself, and do not let stakeholders or teammates drive premature implementation designs based on faulty perceptions, inaccurate requirements, and missing business analysis.

■ **Note**   Simply calling a premature system implementation constraint a "business requirement" does not make it a business requirement. The business users and the project manager are not the SharePoint experts, nor are they the solution architect. Keep them focused on articulating business processes and business problems, not on designing solutions that introduce implementation constraints.

I refer to this process as introducing implementation constraints because it steers a project and the project team off track toward a direction, one that the team has to then work around, and it may cause them to compromise an aspect or add complexity into the solution design, usually without reconsidering a premature constraint. These constraints lead a team down a more challenging path, or worse, the wrong path, a path stemming from making the wrong decision too early in the process before you analyzed the requirements and understood the problem space. This is the danger I want you to avoid, and I want you to avoid it by focusing on your content requirements from the perspective of the business and the business user's purpose.

I have already set you up with many of the tools you need to document your content requirements effectively, particularly with the content inventory, the content process diagrams, and the content security needs. At this stage, you can put these things together and describe the main classes of content in your organization. You do not have to focus on the hierarchy details for the content at this point, but if you notice any candidates as a more specialized class of content, you can note the potential relationship. However, you should avoid getting caught up on this analysis just yet, because your main goal is to understand and describe the content.

■ **Note**   Please see Chapter 4, where I look at when and how to identify relationships between classes of content.

Next, I find it useful to give a brief sentence that describes the general purpose of a class of content. I write this from the perspective of the business, and to help write this sentence, I ask different types of questions about it, such as the following:

- What purpose does it serve?

- How does it benefit the organization?

- What contribution does it add?

- Where does it fit with the business strategy?

- What are its objectives?

- Why is it useful to users?

After describing its purpose, I then describe the content's security details as I described in the previous section. I like to indicate the sensitivity and privacy for a class of content, including classifications, such as whether it is confidential or whether it contains personal information. Along with these attributes, I indicate the intended audiences for the content as well as any security restrictions I identified during the content analysis phase. If security aspects relate to a state change at some point in the content's life cycle, I like to capture that here as well, along with the details about what triggers a change. For example, as when the security restrictions change after a small group finishes collaborating on a piece of content and publishes it into the public domain.

The next thing I include in a content requirements document is any policies associated with the content that I identified during the analysis, particularly for any retention or disposition policies. These policies can relate to approvals required in the content creation process or to other types of workflows or restrictions that relate to a particular class of content. If you have the details about any process involved with a policy, you can capture that here as well; otherwise, I discuss workflow and other policy aspects later in this book.

■ **Note**   Please see Chapter 6 for more on creating document management workflows.

Finally, I like to include the content process diagram I mentioned previously with the requirements document so people can see where the content fits within the content life cycle model, and what phases apply to it. If I were documenting the content requirements in a Word document, then I would include an image of the process diagram in line with the requirement details of a content class. If instead I am documenting the requirements using a tabular format such as an Excel spreadsheet, then I usually just include a hyperlink reference to the diagram, typically linking to the item in a SharePoint site. The process diagram shows the content in context, and it helps to summarize a lot of additional information that will be useful to you and your project team as you design an enterprise content management solution.

With all of this information, you can work toward understanding your enterprise content, an understanding that will serve as a key component in designing your ECM solution. This approach designs and builds your solution starting from the content and working outward, which helps you to better understand how your organization uses enterprise content, leading you to solve the right problems with an elegant solution.

This requirements document will serve as your knowledge of the problem and it will provide input into the rest of your solution design activities. Content and information about content is core to any enterprise content management initiative, returning your investment in this phase to benefit you again and again throughout your ECM program. If you find yourself stuck or struggling with an aspect of an enterprise content management solution, return to your requirements and process documentation that you produce in this phase to determine whether you were thorough enough with the content analysis. Often revisiting and extending this analysis will resolve issues and remove blockers stalling an enterprise content management initiative.

SAMPLE CONTENT REQUIREMENTS DOCUMENT FRAGMENT

Content Class: Expense Reimbursement Report

File Type: InfoPath Web Form

Description: A form containing employee information and tabular data about business-related expenses the employee is submitting for reimbursement.

Privacy Categorization: Personal

Content Classification: Confidential

Retention Policy: 3 Years

Other Attributes: Project reference, cost center, attachments of scanned receipts

Related Business Process: The following illustration provides an example of the related business process, specifically, an expense reimbursement approval process.

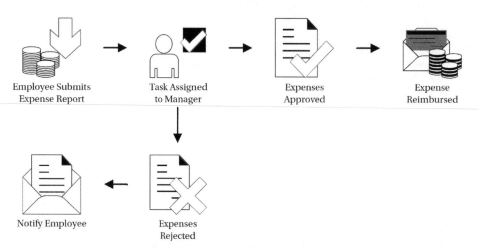

Employee Submits
Expense Report

Task Assigned
to Manager

Expenses
Approved

Expense
Reimbursed

Notify Employee

Expenses
Rejected

Other Details: For billable expenses to clients, the system transforms a copy of the approved expense report into a PDF file to e-mail to the client.

Wrapping Up

Your organization probably has mass amounts of content, each piece of which serves its own purpose. Identifying and understanding general classes of this content and its related business processes is the first major step toward designing an effective enterprise content management solution, and this is done through analyzing the content itself, seeing how users use it, and recognizing its purpose. In this chapter, I provided an approach to identifying and understanding your content by applying the content life cycle model to your different kinds of content. By looking at your content within the context of the model, you can uncover and analyze any gaps or exceptions from the model for a particular kind of content. I then provided guidance on how to take an inventory of the content in your organization and analyze the business processes related to different kinds of content. Finally, I described how to identify your information security needs and how you can document your content life cycle requirements.

Knowing your content, its processes, and any other of its requirements, all form a foundation for your enterprise content management initiative, because the rest of your ECM program will utilize and build upon whatever information you capture. With an understanding of your organization's content and some preliminary ways to classify it, you can begin to organize and structure additional ways to categorize content and the relationships between different kinds of content. In the next chapter, I build on your analysis of the content itself and provide you with tools you can use to design hierarchies and patterns for categorizing and organizing your content, ultimately leading you to produce your information architecture.

■ ■ ■

CHAPTER 4

Designing Your Information Architecture

There is no "top" to the World Wide Web.

—Tim Berners-Lee

How do you organize information when a typical organization contains multitudes of content, ranging from related content to independent, relevant, and active content to historical and horded? This diversity and volume presents a challenge when designing an enterprise content management solution, a challenge you can diminish with your information architecture on hand to support your efforts. In this chapter, I provide guidance on analyzing and designing an information architecture. I share techniques on how to create a data dictionary and how to perform a card sort to analyze and organize information. Finally, I walk you through how to implement an enterprise taxonomy to define the metadata that your organization will use for categorizing and classifying its content.

After reading this chapter, you will know how to

- Describe information architecture and its purpose.

- Analyze your organization's existing information architecture.

- Create a data dictionary to define data fields and their source.

- Perform a card sort exercise to organize information.

- Build your information architecture.

- Implement your enterprise taxonomy design.

- Design your site structure.

- Design your navigation.

Understanding Information Architecture

Information architecture as a discipline concerns itself with the organization of information. This applies anywhere you want to organize information, not just for enterprise content management within an organization. Nonetheless, information architecture is particularly relevant for an enterprise content management initiative because its core purpose is the process of organizing information for better management throughout the information life cycle.

A typical organization contains a lot of information and its information may be growing at an exponential rate, leading to management challenges and the need for an effective enterprise content management solution. You can organize information by its physical location or by the metadata that you associate with it. Organizing a piece of content by physical location is helpful, but it only provides a limited range of organization, mainly the folder structure's single dimension of grouping content together in a single directory structure. This is more of an archaic way of organizing content, and it is largely a legacy process carried forward from physical document storage, back when a physical document could only exist in one physical place and so it made sense to use location as the primary organizing method.

Although organizing by location still provides some use, metadata provides a much richer set of capabilities to organize information by abstracting away the single dimension of a folder structure and enabling the multiple facets available to organize information with metadata. Metadata provides the fundamentals of any modern information organization system.

Metadata is information about information; it provides the vehicle for a unit of information to self-describe itself. When you tag a piece of content with metadata, the term also provides a reference pointer to the content, empowering you to associate several different metadata terms with a single piece of content, unlocking the multidimensional power of the potentially multiple reference pointers. You can categorize metadata into the following three general categorizes:

- **Descriptive:** Metadata describing additional aspects of a unit of information, such as its subject, relevant keywords, and classification.

- **Intrinsic:** Metadata describing a unit of information's anatomy and makeup, such as its file type and file size.

- **Administrative:** Metadata describing how to manage and process a unit of information, such as who created it, whether it is in a draft or published state, and its approval status.

I mention these categories just to help you think about the different types of metadata that you can collect. The categories themselves are not important, and unless you find it useful, you do not have to categorize your metadata with them. As you design your information architecture, you identify a list of metadata that you can use to organize and manage information in your organization. The process of identifying and listing metadata eventually builds out your enterprise taxonomy.

Your enterprise taxonomy creates an index of information within your organization, similar to the index in this book. For example, you might find several different terms in my book's index that all point to the same page, depending on the topic I am discussing. I call this the multidimensional or multifaceted view for finding content. In contrast, a single-dimensional view is the table of contents and chapter structure: a chapter only points to one specific chapter, and sections within the chapter only point to those specific sections.

The table of contents and the chapter structure is the physical layout, akin to a directory structure on a file system. This provides you with a way to "click through" in a sense (or quite literally, in the case of e-book versions), allowing you to discover things in context. For example, you will find topics related to information architecture in this chapter, but the individual topics differ between sections. Nonetheless, the information is contained within this chapter. Alternatively, if you looked up a term in the index, you will find some topics point to several containers, spread across sections in different chapters, and multiple terms might refer to the same topic or section.

Similarly, your SharePoint site containers provide a single-dimensional view of discovering content, as I discussed in Chapter 2. The container hierarchy enables users to click through and discover information in context. The Managed Metadata Service, like a book index, provides the multidimensional view, enabling users to discover content across multiple containers using multiple terms. Figure 4-1 illustrates the single-dimensional view of a folder structure vs. the multifaceted view of metadata terms.

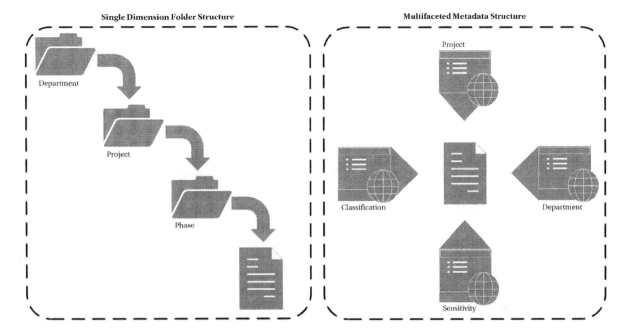

Figure 4-1. *Single-dimensional folder structures vs. multidimensional metadata terms*

When you associate a taxonomy term with a user's profile, you create a link between users and the different units of information that a term references. This helps to facilitate users discovering relevant content based on the metadata tags they associate with topics in their profile. It also identifies topics that relate to the users themselves, in a similar way to how a term can point to multiple pieces of relevant content. This concept of a people index can offer a type of organizational yellow pages, where a term references multiple people and you can find people by topic rather than by name.

Your taxonomy is central to your enterprise content management initiative and it is not something you can fake or omit; everything else in the process really depends on first getting at least a good start with your information architecture. The challenge is in identifying the metadata for your enterprise taxonomy, and often this may feel like a daunting task, but if you follow the process and approach I share in this chapter, you should find this undertaking completely achievable. Start by analyzing the information you already have, your organization's existing information architecture.

Analyzing Your Information Architecture

Back in Chapter 3, I encouraged you to build an inventory of your organization's content. And as I mentioned then, this inventory serves as the core data you can analyze to understand what type of content your organization uses, how it organizes it, and what systems or general storage locations handle the content. This is the best starting place to analyze your organization's information architecture.

You can expand your content inventory by also including articles and other web pages on your intranet, if you have not done so already. This will complete the content picture for you with the text-based web content, and it will also uncover additional information about how your organization structures and manages content, along with the types of web content it publishes. It will start to give you a sense for how simple or complex your web content is, allowing you to start envisioning any opportunities for a web content management solution that you can incorporate into your enterprise content management initiative.

▨ **Note**   Please see Chapter 7, where I discuss web content management in more detail.

In addition to the content itself, you can analyze the folder structures in the content storage locations (or the path structures in the case of web content). Again, this will deepen your understanding of your organization's content and how your users organize it. This in turn will give you insights into how users group content together as well as the folder names that they use to categorize the content.

You can extend your analysis to move beyond the content and capture details about the metadata your organization uses to categorize information. You can learn a lot strictly from analyzing the content and its context, and now you can build on this by studying different ways to describe and classify content. This information will be useful as it provides the majority of your information architecture, at least initially. The tool I use to analyze the metadata throughout an organization is to create a data dictionary.

Creating a Data Dictionary

A data dictionary helps to identify and clarify the different data fields in use throughout your organization, and this will help you to build out the details of your information architecture, similar to how performing a content inventory helped you understand your content's life cycle in the previous chapter. With both a data dictionary and a content inventory available, you will find the analysis and solution design straightforward for the rest of your enterprise content management initiative. The rest of your work will build upon and take advantage of the effort you put in now, and this is because the data dictionary and the content inventory capture the raw data on which you will base your analysis.

I call it a *data dictionary* because the dictionary is a good descriptive metaphor for its purpose: to list and define each data field, and to serve as an authoritative reference source for any future business analysis. It is basically the same as it sounds, a list of data fields that different systems use within your organization to categorize or describe a unit of information. For example, users within your organization can have an Active Directory account to use for logging in and accessing resources on the network. You can identify some data fields by looking at the different attributes for accounts in Active Directory, such as the first name and picture fields.

I also like to identify whether the field is a lookup field to another system or if the field is the source for the data. For example, Active Directory may be the source for those fields, or it may import the users' first name from a Human Resources system and their picture from a SharePoint User Profile Service. Knowing the source for the data field will help you trace the flow of data and its relationships within your organization, and this will help you to design an effective information architecture.

The best place to start is to return to your content inventory, as I described previously. I already pointed you toward some attributes for content classification in the previous chapter, and in particular, for security-related attributes. Another major classification attribute I mentioned, of course, is how you class the type of content itself. Others that I mentioned include the content's sensitivity or business impact. These are useful data fields to include in your data dictionary because this will help you to standardize them and their definitions across your organization.

▨ **Tip**   Unless you already have a system providing lookup lists for the fixed choices in a data field, you will probably identify SharePoint as the source system for these types of data fields, and specifically, the Managed Metadata Service in SharePoint.

Your content inventory will also lead you to additional data fields for your data dictionary. Some fields are obvious, such as the author and the creation date, while other fields are less obvious. However, analyzing each type of content will lead you toward identifying its underlying attributes, and it will help you uncover any gaps or opportunities to capture additional data that you can use to describe or manage a type of content.

Users might not clearly define the attributes for a piece of content or they might not be consistent in the attributes they do define. This is probably one of the reasons behind your enterprise content management initiative, where you ideally want to implement better or more consistently classified content in the future. Nevertheless, even if users have not been working with metadata columns in a SharePoint document library to classify their content in a rich way, and thus make your metadata analysis for your data dictionary easier, they probably still have been using some convention, no matter how rudimentary.

I look at different aspects to identify the different rudimentary attributes and conventions that users tend to use to classify content. Some of the useful sources for this type of information include the following:

- **File names:** Sometimes users will add some classification details to the file name itself.

- **Folder structure:** Often users will organize related information in the same folder, and the folder name might translate well into a metadata field or an option in a metadata field's list.

- **Document information or header information:** Users sometimes classify the document with information inline, such as status, department, and document template or type.

By looking at documents in context and considering any user conventions for classifying and organizing a piece of content, you can gather a lot of information for your data dictionary. Of course, this is only capturing details about what the users are already doing to classify their content. You will also want to identify missed opportunities for how users could be classifying their content. Some of these opportunities might jump out at you while you are analyzing the content and its life cycle, and others will take a little more research and analysis.

I find the best approach for uncovering these other potential data fields is to look at other lists that your organization tracks and uses, fields your organization uses to identify and describe people information, and fields your users would want to use to find and consume information. One approach to discover additional metadata you might want to capture is to involve the users. My favorite tool to involve and facilitate users to organize information is to perform a card sorting exercise.

Facilitating a Card Sort to Organize Information

Card sorting offers you a low-tech way to organize information and design effective information architectures by grouping like topics together. The exercise entails using a series of regular index cards, each card with a specific label for an information container or topic, and a user then sorts them into a pattern of information, grouping some cards together in a way that is intuitive to the user. At its essence, this is the gest of card sorting, and it is what makes it a powerful tool—its simplicity enables its effectiveness.

Using a card sort to design your information architecture results in intuitive designs for end-users, and this is because end-users drive the information architecture by organizing the information in ways that are intuitive to them. It is not a technical analyst inferring how the business might organize information; instead, the business users themselves actually organize the information in a way that makes sense to them. This is a significant difference. Technical people like fitting technology to solve business problems, but they are not necessary domain experts in how the business interacts with information, at least not to the same extent as a regular user from the business.

In some cases, you might want the users to identify the terms they find relevant for labeling or describing an item. This can be terms users would tag a unit of information with, or terms that users would identify in a navigation node, or even terms the users would associate with stages in a business process. For these cases, one of your objectives is to capture a vocabulary of terms that the users would use. You can facilitate this by starting with blank index cards and having the users write down the terms that make sense to them, a term based on a description of the term or its context that you identify for them.

Alternatively, you might already have a list of terms you want to use and you are using the card sorting exercise to analyze how the users group and organize these terms. In this case, you would start with the terms already wrote on the index cards and you facilitate the users sorting and grouping the cards in a way that makes sense to them. This approach helps when you have a range of known topics and you want to discover how users sort and group them.

Whichever approach you take, once users sort topics and group them together, I then ask them to name each group by labeling a sticky note that they then attach to each pile of cards. This helps to identify key categories for organizing and applying metadata and it reveals the general context the users consider for different topics. You might also collect additional details about relationships between groups or the individual topics, but at its most basic level, sorting topics into groups and then labeling the groups is the essence of a card sorting exercise.

■ **Important**   Your job is to facilitate and gather information during a card sorting exercise. For the card sort to be effective, you must remain neutral and not influence the user's decisions.

Once a user has finished the card sorting exercise, I ask them to explain the logic behind the groupings they chose. This can provide valuable insights into any assumptions that a user has about a topic or how it relates to another topic. This is particularly valuable if you discover that the user misunderstood the meaning behind a topic, possibly indicating a poor topic label that you might consider revising.

Sometimes, I conduct a card sorting exercise with groups of users to collaborate on a single card sort. This allows me to observe their conversation and general sense of agreement on relationships between topics, which provides further insights into how users interact with information. It also helps to resolve any inconsistencies between how users sort and group the topics. I use the group sorting sparingly when I want to generate discussions and collaboration in a card sort; otherwise, I have individuals each conduct their own card sort and I aggregate the results for analysis.

After all the users have performed their card sort, I look for patterns shared among the different users, particularly for any prevalent ways to organize topics and label groups. I then look for possible consistency across the different users' card sorts and for common ways to organize the card sort results. When you are searching for a consistent grouping, you can review the logic and reasoning that your users mentioned in making their decisions and this should help you to reconcile any variances.

You can use a card sort to organize a variety of different types of information in your organization, from types of content to different terminology labels, from content relationships to people's roles, and from metadata terms to site navigation. This provides you with a simple, yet empirical way to gather data on information structures and relationships, and then analyze the results to design an information architecture. Users, the domain experts of the information, can reveal relationships and groupings that otherwise might not be apparent, but that a card sorting exercise can quickly uncover.

Of course, users are not information architects and every user will have their own results, but the exercise should reveal patterns in how the users structure information and in how they perceive a topic relates to other topics. You can gather and compare the different ways that your users sorted and grouped topics, noting common patterns and differences, all to look at the different ways that you can organize information. With the results from this analysis, you can begin to design and build your information architecture.

Building Your Information Architecture

Building out effective and efficient information architectures is not simply an engineering exercise where you can apply formulas or a crawling agent to calculate and autogenerate your taxonomy. If you have tools of this type, this might give you a start with how different kinds of content relate to each other and your overall organization, but this should merely serve as a guide. You can also purchase some prepackaged taxonomies, particularly industry-specific taxonomies. Again, you should use these to gain a start, where you can take advantage of common patterns and structures, but you will still need to plan for your own analysis and design activities to move beyond the autogenerated or prepackaged taxonomy solutions.

Information architecture is not so clear-cut; it is an art where you make design decisions based on trade-offs and your organization's priorities. What is true for one organization is not necessary true for another. Any insights will be helpful, such as outputs from automatic tools that crawl your content or from results of a card sorting exercises, but the information architect's job to take all that information in and translate it into the information architecture.

In my process, I like to drive my information architectures by focusing on how the organization will use a piece of content in the future. Metadata enables a piece of content to self-describe itself, to provide additional details beyond the unit of information's contents, all of which provides value toward some future usage. I analyze and consider this future value and future usage by asking the following questions for a piece of content:

- What terms will users use to search for the content?

- What metadata will help users determine the relevancy of the content?

- What categorizations will guide users toward proper use and handling of the content?

- What metadata will the system use to process the content?

- What additional information do regulatory agencies require?

One challenge with metadata is its delayed value—the user tagging a piece of content creates future value by associating a richer set of information to the content, providing information that other users can take advantage of when accessing the content in the future. However, that future value comes with a present cost in terms of the time a user spends tagging his or her piece of content as they add it to the system. To complicate this matter further, the user may never realize that future value him or herself, so they are really investing their time today to provide future informational value for their colleagues.

This present cost vs. future value concept is a trade-off between efficiently capturing content and effective discovery and long-term use of content. Users may not want to have an excessive amount of required metadata slow them down and burden them as they create a new piece of content. They may even feel that a records manager or librarian should be responsible for categorizing content rather than burdening the content producers.

If you require too many metadata fields for a piece of content, then users may end up inputting faulty information to satisfy whatever required field constraints you associate with a type of content. Although the idea of capturing and using a range of metadata might sound appealing in theory, if the end result is users entering garbage data just to work around the constraints, then including this metadata does not benefit the information architecture.

To ease the data-entry burden of metadata, I investigate each individual metadata field that I want to include for a type of content and I look for opportunities to reduce or avoid the user's involvement with categorizing and classifying the content they are capturing. I use the following questions to analyze ways to simplify the process of capturing metadata:

- Can the system infer the metadata field's value rather than require user input?

- Can the system delay or defer collecting the field's value?

- Can the system autopopulate a field's value during a workflow process?

- Can the system capture a field's value inline within the document, such as through a document field in the body of the document?

This chapter focuses primarily on the types of metadata that you can use to categorize and classify content, ultimately organizing your organization's content. However, you will also capture metadata to self-describe content, to support managing its life cycle, and even to meet regulatory compliance, none of which may relate to how users interact with the content. Where possible, I prefer to autogenerate those metadata fields as well, using the same process and questions as the categorization and classification metadata.

You can look for opportunities to autopopulate metadata in a few different ways. The content type itself can have some logic to infer certain fields based on things such as who creates the content, what location the user creates the content in, what values he or she sets for other metadata settings, and the like. You could even analyze body copy of the content itself and attempt to infer metadata values from it. This takes some upfront planning and design, and often it will require a third-party component or some custom development to implement, but its value balances the cost of capturing content with the value of later retrieval and consumption.

A couple of ways that you might approach autopopulating metadata include developing a custom component with the logic. You can hook the custom component's logic into the process with an event on the list or library, or through a workflow that you associate with the content type. Whatever creativity and effort you invest now will add to the effectiveness of your enterprise content management solution by reducing the burden on users having to enter a lot of metadata as they capture content. Alternatively, you can also look for ways to delay capturing metadata until later in the process, such as after content edits or when a content retention workflow initiates.

With your list of metadata you wish to capture, your next step is to organize it into a structure. Some metadata categories or classifications will be simple lists, a single level deep, often implemented in what I refer to as a *closed list*—a list of finite items that users can select an option from to apply to a piece of content, but which a user cannot append items to the list. Some lists may be *open lists*, where users can append items with whatever term they find relevant, such as the "Keywords" term set that users can use to tag content with any term they wish.

▓ **Note**   Users can associate metadata with content by selecting terms from a hierarchical schema designed in a multi-level structure of terms and subordinate, more specific terms. I refer to this type of metadata as a *taxonomy*. In contrast, users might tag keywords from a single-level list of terms that are user driven in an organic fashion. I refer to this type of metadata as a *folksonomy*. Please see Chapter 10, where I discuss social tagging and folksonomies in more detail.

The card sorting exercises will give you some indication for organizing and structuring the metadata terms you identified. Some groups of terms will naturally go together and form a term set, while others take some analyzing and reflecting on your design options. I usually experiment with different groupings and structures as I build out taxonomy schemas, some of which I revise later (even after a production deployment), while others turn out to work well.

For those terms that I do not yet have an idea for how to group them, and there are always some, I usually just add them to a generic list, one similar to the Keywords term set. This gives me the opportunity to implement these terms and to make them available for users to tag their content with, even if I do not fully understand the term's purpose yet, since I can return later to analyze how users use those terms. At that point, I can refine my taxonomy schema and place the term in a more appropriate term set.

My point is that you can change your mind and adjust things later; you do not have to get your taxonomy perfect before you can make progress. One beautiful thing about metadata in SharePoint is its ability for you to change and adapt it as you evolve and refine your requirements. You can move or merge terms, depreciate terms, and even rename terms, all without causing major ripple effects throughout the system and without demanding any major rework efforts. Do not get stuck in endless cycles of analyzing and revising your taxonomy, cycles where you try to design the perfect schema—things change too quickly and your organization will always reveal new information. Try out your taxonomy designs and move forward with the confidence that you can make adjustments and fine-tune your schema as you discover what works and what is less effective.

▓ **Important**   As I keep stressing, you use metadata, not structure, to organize your content because this approach offers the greatest versatility and usefulness. This is an important paradigm shift for you to understand before you can design an effective and modern information architecture.

Once you have a design that you are satisfied with, or at least when you have a slice of your overall information architecture ready, your next step is to implement that design in your environment. In SharePoint 2013, you implement your information architecture through your enterprise taxonomy, through the site structure, and through reference links or navigation menus in the user interface. To implement your enterprise taxonomy in a SharePoint environment, you add it as term sets and terms to the Managed Metadata Service, which I walk you through next.

Implementing Your Enterprise Taxonomy Design

SharePoint 2013 provides a service application to centralize metadata management. You can provision an instance of the Managed Metadata Service to store, manage, and provide metadata to SharePoint sites throughout your farm, and you can even share this service across farms, further centralizing your enterprise taxonomy. Metadata is a paramount service in SharePoint as other services depend on it to provide their own service, such as the User Profile Service and the Search Service. As such, implementing your information architecture as managed metadata has a ripple effect throughout your SharePoint deployment as other aspects of the service take advantage of and utilize the metadata.

The Managed Metadata Service also manages the enterprise *content type hub*, a site collection containing the site columns and content types to synchronize with other site collections across a SharePoint deployment. This allows you to standardize and centralize content types for your organization, including the types of metadata you want to capture along with the types of content.

▒ **Note**   For more information on the content type hub and how to configure it, please see Chapter 6.

You will implement your enterprise taxonomy as term sets and terms in the Managed Metadata Service. To start, navigate to the Term Store Management Tool page by clicking the Managed Metadata Service instance on the Manage Service Applications page in SharePoint Central Administration.

1. Create a new term group by expanding the context menu on the Managed Metadata Service root node, and then clicking New Group. For this example, name the new group **Enterprise Taxonomy**.

2. On the context menu for the Enterprise Taxonomy group, click New Term Set. For this example, name the new term set **Departments**.

3. On the content menu for the Departments term set, click Create Term. Enter a department name, and then press enter to create a new term for another department.

4. After creating terms for several departments, create a term for the Information Technology department. On the context menu for the Information Technology term, click Create Term. Create a **Service Desk** and **System Administration** child term for the Information Technology term, as Figure 4-2 illustrates.

Site Settings › Term Store Management Tool

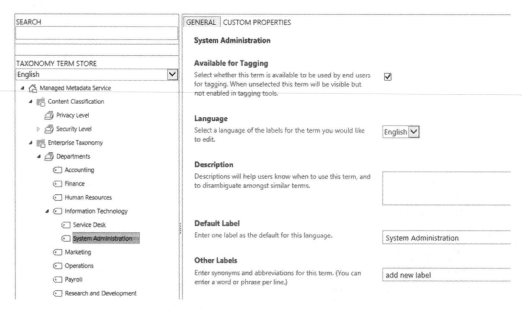

Figure 4-2. *The Term Store Management Tool with a sample department taxonomy*

■ **Tip** Manually inputting the enterprise taxonomy in the Managed Metadata Service for your development, integration, test, staging, and production SharePoint farms is inefficient and risks the challenges and inconsistencies of trying to keep the data in sync. One option is to script and automate the taxonomy data entry, either using PowerShell or a SharePoint feature. For an example, please see my blog post at `http://stevegoodyear.wordpress.com/2011/01/09/managing-sharepoint-2010-managed-metadata`, where I create a SharePoint feature to populate the taxonomy.

Metadata and your enterprise taxonomy serve as the essence of your information architecture. If you do this well, anything else you do related to information architecture merely enhances this core. I come back to the topic of metadata and your enterprise taxonomy repeatedly throughout this book as I discuss many different aspects of enterprise content management. It is important to make a start with a taxonomy and continue to move forward rather than to be stuck in over analyzing and trying to perfect a hierarchy of terms, but at the same time, recognize that this is a foundational piece, central to everything else you do with your enterprise content management initiative. Make a valiant effort on your first pass to design a metadata solution, and then be prepared to come back and continue evolving it.

With the crucial metadata piece started, the next aspect of information architecture relates to the site structure. There was a time when your physical structure was the most important aspect, because that was traditionally the primary way to organize information, but now that metadata should act as your dominant means to organize your content, the site structure details are not as pertinent. In fact, to add precedence and further enhance my metadata strategies, I take an almost *anti-structure* approach to my site structure designs, as I describe next.

Designing Your Site Structure

I spent some time so far in this chapter steering you away from focusing on the physical structure of your information architecture, instead highlighting the role of metadata and virtual structures that you can implement by using reference links or filtered views. However, at some point, you do need to implement the physical storage structure for the actual content containers. As I discussed in Chapter 2, the site architecture does involve a hierarchy of content containers, yet in this chapter I tried to steer you away from building a deep hierarchy.

Having a deep hierarchy of child sites is not horrible, and it certainly does come with some end-user convenience-related benefits, most notably the ability to inherit site settings such as security groups and navigation. This can be attractive, but I prefer to avoid a deep nesting of sites within a fewer number of site collections, and instead I lean toward a flat structure consisting of many site collections, each with a shallow hierarchy of child sites.

I find that the benefits from having many independent site collections loosely coupled together using reference links far outweighs any short-term conveniences with a tightly coupled hierarchy of sites and child sites. For me, the site collection's boundary provides the greatest long-term benefits and flexibility. One major aspect of a site collection's boundary is the ability to move it to a new content database to distribute and level the storage load in your SharePoint farm, offering you an isolated and granular scope of content to move without any complex dependencies or ripple effects throughout the system.

Another operational benefit with a site collection's boundary is the ability to apply a quota to a site collection in a targeted and manageable manner. If you have a massive site collection with a variety of user groups storing their content in it to collaborate, then you will probably find that site quotas will be largely ineffective. I have frequently come across site collections as large as 70 GB or 100 GB with hundreds of users collaborating in different sites within the collection, and the bottom line is that a site quote just will not be effective in these sites for helping to manage system resources. What's the point of even enabling the quota at that point?

Sure, there are valid reasons for site collections of this size, particularly for archival sites or sites that contain a heavy amount of rich media, but I find these are not the rule but that they are exceptions to the rule. If I take the average collaboration-related 100 GB site collection and break it up into at least 10 or 20 or more separate site collections, then I can track the content growth more effectively with site quotas. Best of all, I can spread that content across multiple content databases, thus enabling me with more operational options, such as to target and maximize database system resources to the busiest site collections.

▓ **Tip** I prefer to implement many smaller content databases rather than fewer large ones. I generally target my content database size to between 25 GB and 50 GB. I find this is a great range to support efficient operational tasks, such as with database backups and restores, defragmenting table indexes, and testing for data corruptions or orphaned objects. I also find this is a good size for performing a database attach upgrade. However, I have exceptions to this rule, particularly for archival site content databases, for which my range can increase to as high as 400 GB to 500 GB, depending on the storage requirements.

As you can probably tell, I generally default to a new site collection unless I have a valid reason to go with a child site instead. It is not a golden or blanket rule, but I do tend to encourage more site collections with shallower hierarchies to maximize flexibility in the future. This feels similar to normalizing tables in a database, and perhaps it is my background in database design underlying my philosophy for site structure design. With a normalized database, you have less coupling of tables, as each table serves its own distinct and focused purpose, all using relationships to work together and act as a cohesive unit. This low coupling liberates you because it makes the database less fragile with respect to changes. In the same way, a low coupling of site collections, all independent and self-contained, liberates you because it makes your SharePoint environment less fragile when it comes to future changes and general maintenance.

> ■ **Caution**   Do not let a few convenience factors in the short-term drive you toward an inflexible implementation design. Invest the effort upfront during the implementation phase to develop solutions around a flat site collection model rather than a deep hierarchy of child sites. You will find this investment pays off repeatedly when it comes to your long-term maintenance and the sustainability of your SharePoint service.

In addition to the flexibility with allocating site collections in content databases and applying more granular quotas, your future self will also thank you for the more focused and concise sites. These sites are potentially easier to retire or archive as a unit, and this minimizing the need to manually identify a subset to retire deep within a site hierarchy, a deep hierarchy that likely results in users skipping the manual process to retire their content and instead allowing those areas to persist. You can detect dormant sites easier when they are distinct, as opposed to those that intertwine with a bunch of other child sites, and this detection can reduce the need for manual processes to manage the content life cycle.

One challenge I find with a flat site design that uses multiple site collections is the site provisioning process—once users have a site, they can provision child sites to build out a site hierarchy as they please, a hierarchy that feels natural to them for organizing their content. Users have been conditioned for too long to organize their content using a single-dimensional folder structure, and so this is what will feel natural and make sense to them.

The reality is that content needs a container, so some aspect of a content hierarchy is necessary. On top of that, I do not want to confuse or stress out my users by limiting the content hierarchies they want to work in. Instead, I try to design the solution so that it is easy to create new site collections, and then I promote this process with users through things such as training materials. Inside the site collection, I do not fret too much about the structures and hierarchies that users wish to work with. By designing the site creation process around the main site collections and managed path groupings, for the most part, future sites tend to follow the same pattern.

A good managed path strategy logically organizes common sites under common URL paths. Most users will then notice this pattern and try to follow it for their own site structures. I start with the following managed paths for almost any SharePoint deployment:

- **Sites:** I use the default `sites` managed path that SharePoint adds to web applications, and I plan for the collaboration-related sites under this managed path. These sites types can range from team sites and wikis to community sites and team blogs. You can divide the sites up further under additional managed paths if you think another term will provide a good logical grouping of site types.

- **People:** I change the default `personal` managed path that SharePoint uses for My Sites because I find `people` reads better in the URL to me. If I share the My Site web application with other types of site collections, then I set the My Site managed path as `people`. However, I prefer to dedicate a web application to host My Sites because it enables limiting the scope of settings on the web application, such as the self-service site creation permissions. In this case, I usually have a web application URL with the My Site host at `http://people` and the managed path for personal My Sites set as `sites`.

You might also add other paths to this list with paths for department-related sites. You can also consider paths for specific types of sites, such as a `Projects` path for project sites. I generally keep my list of wildcard managed paths short and simple, but occasionally I do come across requirements to add to the list. For example, with my education clients, I usually add a `classes` path under which to create class sites.

> ■ **Note**   You use *wildcard* managed paths to identify a path to create multiple site collections under and you use *explicit* managed paths to identify an explicit path location to create a single site collection.

You can add a managed path to a web application by navigating to the Manage web applications page in SharePoint Central Administration, selecting a web application, and then clicking Managed Paths in the ribbon. This will open a Define Managed Paths modal window similar to the one in Figure 4-3.

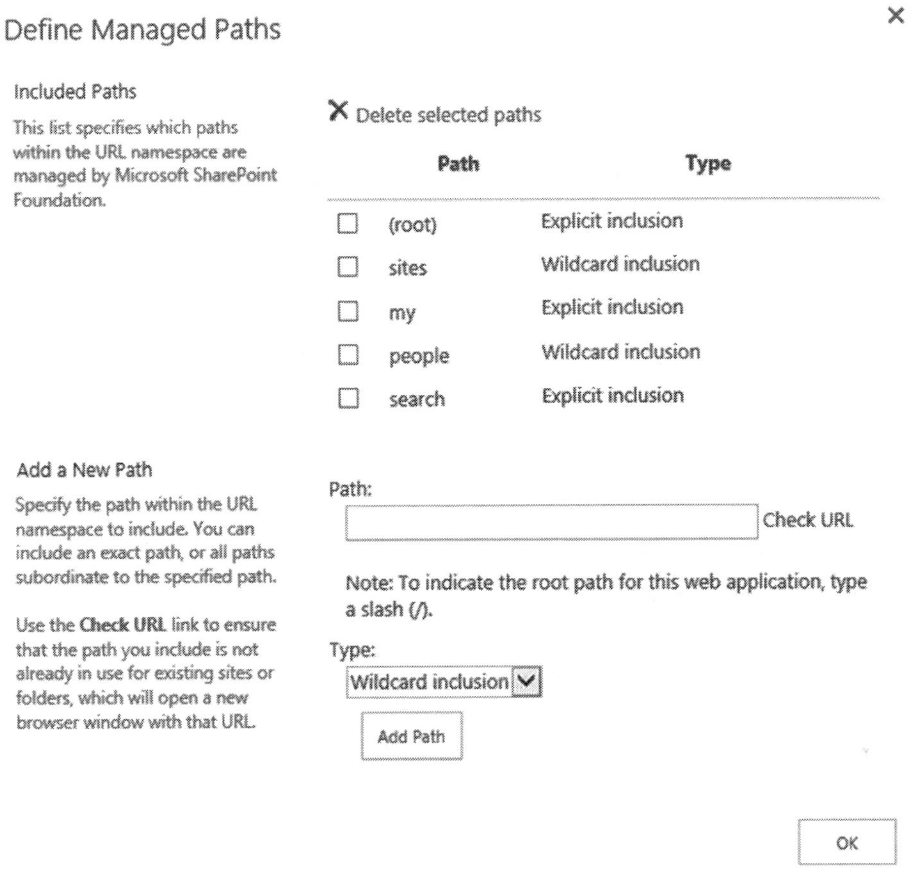

Define Managed Paths ✕

Included Paths

This list specifies which paths within the URL namespace are managed by Microsoft SharePoint Foundation.

✕ Delete selected paths

	Path	Type
☐	(root)	Explicit inclusion
☐	sites	Wildcard inclusion
☐	my	Explicit inclusion
☐	people	Wildcard inclusion
☐	search	Explicit inclusion

Add a New Path

Specify the path within the URL namespace to include. You can include an exact path, or all paths subordinate to the specified path.

Use the **Check URL** link to ensure that the path you include is not already in use for existing sites or folders, which will open a new browser window with that URL.

Path:

[   ] Check URL

Note: To indicate the root path for this web application, type a slash (/).

Type:

[Wildcard inclusion ▾]

[Add Path]

[OK]

Figure 4-3. The Define Managed Paths modal window

▨ **Tip** Sometimes, users desire what I refer to as *vanity URLs*, those short and friendly URLs pointing to a root site. In a large organization, offering vanity URLs just does not scale well, at least not justifiably just for URL cosmetics. Instead, I recommend offering a redirector service where users can register vanity URLs that redirects to the SharePoint site under the managed path. You might also consider a URL shortening service with a simple URL such as http://go and appending numbers or letters to identify the site redirection URL.

Publishing portal sites are often at the root or close to the root of a web application. Rather than use a wildcard managed path as I would for a collaboration site, I use an explicit managed path for portal sites to keep the site paths close to the root. For example, with a portal homepage at http://portal and the need for a human resources portal site close to the root, I would create an explicit managed path at http://portal/hr to create the human resources site there.

■ **Note** Please see Chapter 7, where I discuss portal design and web content management in more detail.

For the most part, your site design is a flat structure, consisting of a lot of site collections that you can logically organize under managed paths. Because there are no hierarchies to physically structure your site collections, they do not take a significant portion of your information architecture design efforts. Instead, you can invest that time into designing your navigation strategy, which I discuss next.

CONSIDERING THE FLATNESS OF THE INTERNET

I commonly see clients think and design their site structure in terms of a physical hierarchy. I think this comes from their experiences working with a folder structure to organize information, thus working with a single-dimensional view of information, organizing content into folders, often creating a deep folder hierarchy for files. This way of working has instilled an ingrained habit of using a containing structure as the exclusive means to organize content. I find this can be a difficult habit to break, because people often are unaware or cannot see alternatives such as making use of metadata.

Even on the Internet, web sites *appear* to be hierarchies, but this is an illusion. True, it has some folder structures, but if you think of the vast scale of the Web, then individual folder structures are largely irrelevant. The Web is not a folder hierarchy; the Web is a series of links pointing to each other in a web-like fashion (hence the name). Some sites may be more authoritative and prominent links might refer to them, but they do not *contain* those other sites nor do those other sites contain them. These are simply term-based references (hyperlinks) that point to different resources. The Web has a predominately flat and wide structure, built using a shallow rather than deep hierarchy.

When you think of your own information architecture, and particularly when you design your site structure, try to avoid becoming fixated on this idea of a structural hierarchy for organizing your information. Instead, think about how links use terms to reference different resources. You can place links on a web page so that they resemble a hierarchy, but these are just reference links and you can lay them out to resemble any type of hierarchy you want, all without forcing the structure to resemble the interface. Using reference links enables you to adjust them without affecting the actual structure because they are just references that point to the structure.

Think about how you can use metadata to tag information similar to how the Web uses hyperlinks, rather than thinking in terms of physical hierarchies like you would build a folder structure on your desktop. This perspective will guide you toward flexible and eloquent designs for your information architecture, whereas a folder structure view will limit and constrain you.

Designing Your Navigation

Web site navigation has remained fairly consistent for years now, in SharePoint sites or any other web application. Effective navigation incorporates basic elements such as a global navigation menu and a current navigation menu to simplify the web site layout and user interaction. The navigation serves to guide a user through relevant areas of the site, to provide the user with some context of where they are in the site, and to provide a means to navigate back the way he or she came.

Where I see navigation fail tends to be where designers tried to get too fancy, such as adding some nifty elements to the interface resembling more of an artistic expression manner than a functional and intuitive design. In my experience, these creative navigation attempts rarely succeed nor do they add any value to the user's site experience. My advice is to focus on the basics, make sure you get the fundamentals of navigation right, and look at how you can make the navigation almost transparent.

SharePoint includes a few key navigation areas. First, there is the top bar that includes links to the Newsfeed, Sky Drive, and Sites directory. You can create a custom control to add links to this navigation menu, which I recommend, and this will provide your users with a consistent navigation across the top of every site page in the SharePoint farm. You can add your custom ASP.NET user control to override the `SuiteLinksDelegate` delegate control and implement your own navigation menu on the top bar. I like to add a link to the organization's portal homepage and one to the enterprise search portal. This fills in what I feel is a gap in the navigation architecture in SharePoint 2013, namely the ability for a user to get to these key intranet web properties intuitively, from anywhere, and within a single click.

For portals, you can design the site's global navigation grounded in the results from the card sorting exercise I mentioned previously, thereby organizing the site navigation stemming from what is intuitive for its users. SharePoint manages the current navigation (also commonly referred to as the Quick Launch list) based on the structure of content containers within the site, but you can modify this navigation menu and align it with the results from the card sorting exercise as well.

In collaboration team sites, users will manage their own navigation structures, or more likely, just accept the autogenerated navigation that SharePoint provides. I have had some clients who wanted to control the navigation even at this level, but for the most part, I find this only complicates things and does not seem to provide much added navigational value. Of course, there are exceptions to this rule, particularly for those team sites that more resemble department portal sites, but generally, I focus my efforts on the bigger navigation picture.

The next major navigational area for me is the site directory, accessed by clicking the Sites link on the top navigation bar. This page contains a list of recommended sites for a user based on his or her interests, as well as sites that the user follows. In addition, you can add what SharePoint terms as *promoted sites*—sites you want to promote and display on the site directory page, displaying them as a tile with an icon and title linking to the site. The following steps walk you through how to add a promoted site link.

To add a new promoted site, first navigate to the User Profile Service settings page and then click the Manage Promoted Sites link under the My Site Settings section. This will open the Promoted Sites page, as shown in Figure 4-4. On the Promoted Sites page, click the New Link button and enter the details for the site you wish to promote.

Figure 4-4. *The Promoted Sites page*

Once you create a promoted site, SharePoint displays it on the site directory page that you can access by clicking the Sites link in the top navigation bar. Figure 4-5 shows an example of a promoted site on the site directory page.

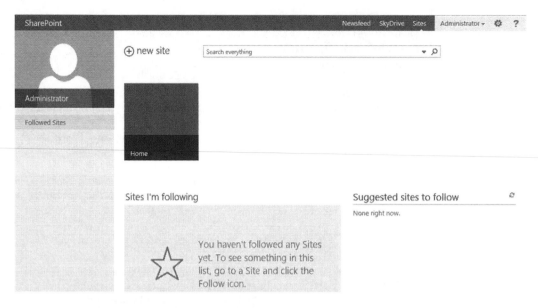

Figure 4-5. *An example of a promoted site on the site directory page*

■ **Note**   You can target a promoted site to specific audiences to increase the relevance of the site directory page.

By taking care of these big picture navigation areas, you address the biggest navigation needs for your SharePoint deployment by guiding users to the key web properties and allowing them to discover the rest organically, or even socially. You can continue to build on your navigation strategy, spending more time on designing your site navigation at a more granular level, but these key areas will provide you with a start and they offer the biggest impact for your navigation strategy.

Wrapping Up

You manage information as part of your enterprise content management solution through your information architecture, which identifies a way of organizing content and its life cycle. You can analyze and design your organization's information architecture by conducting a content inventory, creating a data dictionary, and performing a card sorting exercise with users. As I described, this leads toward the design of your enterprise taxonomy, your site structure, and your site navigation strategy. Your enterprise taxonomy establishes a schema for the hierarchy of metadata that you make available for users to classify and describe their content. You can implement your enterprise taxonomy in SharePoint through the Managed Metadata Service as term sets and terms. I encouraged you to implement a relatively flat site structure, consisting predominantly of site collections, and to focus your navigation design primarily on establishing a consistent top navigation bar and a site directory, both linking to key web properties on your intranet.

This marks a pivotal moment in your enterprise content management solution, because the information analysis and design you do in this chapter establishes the central pieces around which you will build the rest of your solution. An information architecture applies to each aspect of an enterprise content management initiative, from transitory content to official records, and to content discovery in between. In the next part, I shift to focus first on transitory content and the role it plays in your enterprise content management solution, beginning with the next chapter, where I discuss collaboration content and where it fits in the content life cycle model, preparing you with how to plan for and enable collaboration-related content.

■ ■ ■

PART 2

Managing Your Transitory Content

Transitory content represents a significant range and volume of content in your organization. It can vary from teams collaborating on document drafts or departmental portal pages, to electronic forms capturing and processing information as part of a business process, and even to *ad hoc* blog and microblog posts. This diversity can make transitory content feel chaotic, even out of control, all because the content itself is unstructured; however, managing and organizing transitory content generally occurs in the content containers, allowing the content to take whatever shape it requires yet applying order through its container.

The chapters in this part look at how to manage transitory content as I guide you through how to analyze and design solutions for different kinds of transitory content. I start with a particularly popular kind of transitory content in most Microsoft SharePoint environments, where I describe how to enable and manage collaboration content. From there, I discuss how you can classify and organize content, as well as how to implement and configure aspects of your SharePoint environment for content classification and management. Finally, I guide you through how to manage your web content and electronic forms, including sections on how to design and implement approval workflows to formalize the content creation process.

As you analyze and consider your transitory content, remember that just because it is transitory does not mean that it lacks importance to your organization. Some transitory content will progress into official records, preserving evidentiary accounts of transactions, decisions, and historical references; but other transitory content will exist for a period before you ultimately dispose of it. Users likely interact with transitory content more than official records in the course of their job functions simply because transitory content is active and current. Planning and managing your transitory content and its related processes will facilitate effective content use in your organization, and then later, it will transition richer information into an official record. It starts where I start, with enabling effective collaboration.

■ ■ ■

CHAPTER 5

Configuring SharePoint for Your Collaboration Content

A typewriter is a means of transcribing thought, not expressing it.

—Marshall McLuhan

How can you stay ahead of the mass of content, channeling it and organizing it, before it becomes a daunting behemoth? Content all begins somewhere, and in most cases, yours will begin with users collaborating to create new pieces of content, working together or independently, generating reports and documentation, producing artifacts of information as they carry out their job functions. Your task is to design this collaboration process. In this chapter, I provide guidance on how to plan for and manage collaboration sites and how to organize content containers to capture collaboration outputs. I also discuss how to analyze and implement document management capabilities within your collaboration sites.

After reading this chapter, you will know how to

- Describe collaboration and determine your guiding principles for collaboration.

- Design and implement your site creation process.

- Plan and design your content containers.

- Identify and implement your document management needs.

- Review audit and usage reports on collaborative site content.

Understanding Collaboration

Collaboration is one of those almost mythic-like terms people use to fit a variety of situations. Its popularity in business has not died down much in recent years, especially as people discuss SharePoint and the underlying business needs that they want to address with SharePoint. "We need to enable collaboration," or "Collaboration is how information workers work today," or something similar. I just made those quotes up, but I bet they are not far off from some of the collaboration-related platitudes you have heard. I do not doubt the statements' validity, but I do find it more interesting and more useful to dig deeper. I prefer to look at what purpose collaboration serves, and even what collaboration means.

Let's start there—what is collaboration? The *Oxford English Dictionary* defines it as "the action of working with someone to produce or create something." Notably absent from this definition, oddly enough, is any mention of SharePoint—or any mention of any software package or technology solution for that matter. SharePoint is not synonymous with collaboration, and collaboration is not synonymous with SharePoint. Collaboration is much more basic than that.

Collaboration is working with another person or a group of people, each individual adding their part, all culminating into some desired outcome. In the workplace, people collaborate in meetings, over the phone, on physical documents passed back-and-forth, and on and on. SharePoint provides one way to capture the products and output of collaboration and it facilitates one way of collaborating with others. Without SharePoint, users will and do use something else to collaborate with each other, but with SharePoint, they can adopt a standard way to collaborate while also having a consistent place to capture and coordinate their collaboration efforts.

Back in Chapter 2, I listed collaboration as one of the core capabilities for SharePoint, and indeed, it is. The product exposes functionality to support multiple users working together in a variety of ways and in almost every aspect of the product's capabilities. It has a bunch of features that support users to collaborate with each other, from basic things such as a discussion board for teams to discuss and work through a topic together, to advanced things such as sharing OneNote notebooks in a SharePoint site where multiple users can edit and add notes concurrently with each other. It offers features for asynchronous collaboration, such as checking out a document for an individual's exclusive editing, and synchronous collaboration, such as with a team of users adding and editing pages in a wiki library.

Collaboration can take many forms, and depending on the purpose behind a collaborative initiative, you can decide which aspect of SharePoint will best support and facilitate your efforts. You might also use other products to collaborate in ways beyond what SharePoint supports, either to augment what SharePoint offers or to use in place of SharePoint. For example, you might collaborate with peers over e-mail by sending messages as you share ideas and discuss an issue. Alternatively, you might conduct an instant messaging or a web conference session using a program such as Lync, which enables advanced collaborative scenarios with video conferencing or desktop sharing.

For my purposes in this book, I am focusing on the phenomenon of collaboration as it relates to using SharePoint to collaborate on and capture content. However, I wanted to stress that SharePoint is simply a tool in the larger collaboration picture; it is not the picture itself. You can use SharePoint to facilitate and support collaboration among your users, which can help enhance their productivity. SharePoint also provides rich features to capture additional metadata about a piece of content in addition to other aspects that complement a rich and managed information life cycle.

If the value of collaboration is found in the coming together of people to each contribute toward some effort, some new piece of content, some new knowledge, then I find the best way to maximize that value is to reduce any barriers the users face in collaborating together. This includes establishing collaboration tools that support how users work together. But even before that, I find the best results come out of empowering users to create their own collaboration spaces and decide how they want to collaborate together, all with minimal IT involvement (or obstructions) in the process. I refer to this as *liberating collaboration*.

Liberating Collaboration

When I suggest the idea of opening SharePoint to empower users with things such as enabling on-demand site provisioning, there seems to be a general worry with clients in the SharePoint market that their SharePoint environment will degenerate into a free-for-all, users doing what they want, leaving you hopeless and in a chaotic state. Sometimes I even hear archaic terms such as *SharePoint sprawl* to refer to this. Do not let these silly notions distract and scare you into constraining and limiting your SharePoint deployment. You can manage and guide organic growth so that it grows in a sustainable fashion, and you do not have to micromanage or control every little detail to achieve this.

I say *micromanage* or *control* because that is effectively what some SharePoint administrators attempt with their deployment. Let me tell you, unless you have a big team or your user base is small, this idea is just not practical. You just cannot reasonably scale to manage every piece of content your users generate in their sites. There are products out there that may help you audit or implement policies to manage the bigger picture, but this does not change the reality that there is simply too much content to manage at an individual level and still maintain an effective collaboration environment. You will find more success if you look at how you can empower your users and how you can liberate collaboration for them.

Think about those giant network file shares and the amount of content in them. I doubt that anyone manages the masses of files at an individual level for all groups; instead, I imagine that different departments or workgroups have a directory that IT delegates to them, where some users organize an elaborate hierarchy of folders to structure their content, and others simply dump content in whatever folders that IT made available to them. IT generally did not try to control and manage content for users on network file shares; they just provided a platform to store the content. An IT team should attempt to do the same with SharePoint, providing it as a platform and a service to enable users.

For some, their experiences with network shares motivate them to swing the pendulum back the other way, to where they want their SharePoint deployment without an overwhelming repository of content, or content growing out of control without any sense of order. Perhaps your users have a hard time finding anything in the network shares and this is what you want to improve as you transition to SharePoint. I suggest that the problem is not with a lack of controlling this content, but instead the problem stems from letting the content live in perpetuity, all without any classification systems to identify units of information within the content corpus, and all without any way to distinguish between authoritative and obsolete content. The problem is not in users creating chaos and generating SharePoint sprawl, and the solution is not in locking the collaboration process down.

Now, I accept that you might not be able to empower your users and to fully liberate collaboration for them, for whatever reason, and there are many valid reasons for this. I agree there are places for controlling content and its related processes, but I prefer to focus on controlling and locking down content in the records management stage of the content life cycle while liberating the collaborative stages. When I manage this relationship well, between collaborative or transitory content and official records, it becomes a nonissue, liberating me from having to worry about some of those immaterial details.

■ **Note**   Please see the chapters in Part IV, where I discuss records management in more depth.

The trouble or challenge with trying to control content and how users collaborate on it is not only with the amount of content, but also with the variety of different ways that users prefer to collaborate together. Some users are like me, minimalists with the amount of content they preserve and hyperorganized with any content they do retain. Other users are more like my antithesis, hoarders of any and every piece of content that they muddle together without any order or structure. However, most users will be somewhere on the continuum between the ends. This is where those rigid attempts at locking down or controlling the collaborative environment fail, because people collaborate in such diverse ways.

One of my favorite things about SharePoint is its ability to adapt and fit whatever situation you want, to accommodate different ways that users want to work with the system, making it a flexible platform that you can use to meet different business drivers and needs. Its default settings lean more toward a liberating collaborative experience for users, particularly at the site level with designated users as the site collection administrators, delegating full control to them for the site. As I mentioned back in Chapter 2, a site collection is the main container and unit of segregation for SharePoint content—it isolates groups of users and processes while establishing security boundaries. Within the site collection, users can adapt sites, lists, and libraries to fit their needs.

My process for liberating collaboration revolves around the site collection. I use its boundary to manage how users organize content from a global perspective and at the content database level, but I avoid getting caught up in the implementation details of lists and libraries in individual sites. This provides me with the best balance between capturing content for the organization to leverage, and enabling users to work with content and collaborate in ways that they prefer. I then use site quotas to manage the growth and resource usage within sites by establishing thresholds to alert me to revisit a site when site owners request a larger quota, allowing me (or, more likely, the service desk) to assess whether the users are using the site appropriately.

Where this site collection can run into trouble is when users create a deep hierarchy of sites and libraries with a monstrosity of content, resulting in a content repository closely resembling the chaotic file dumping in a network file share that you might have tried to move away from. There are many valid reasons for a deep hierarchy within a site collection, which can work just fine since SharePoint supports them, but I find the undesirable aspects usually stem from not having a fluid enough way for users to create new sites. If you design your site creation process well, you can alleviate many of the issues relating to having content grow out of control.

Designing a Site Creation Process

You have a few options when it comes to your site creation process, and they range from empowering your users to provision their own sites in a self-service fashion, to having the service desk manually provision a site when a user submits a request. There is no right or wrong way to approach your site creation process, but the first step is to determine how open or controlled you want the process to be.

If you want a completely open process where users can provision sites on-demand, then you can simplify your site creation process to focus on decisions such as the default site quota to apply, what information you want to collect from users in a self-service form, and what managed paths you want to provision sites under. Otherwise, you will probably set the process as open and simple. On the other hand, if you want to configure all these settings yourself, you will leave the process closed, though still simple, while addressing similar settings as the more open process.

In between these two extremes is where the site creation process can get interesting. This is where you might automate the process, yet rather than automatically grant every user request for a new site, you can require an approval. The approver might be the user's supervisor, who then becomes the site sponsor. Figure 5-1 illustrates a sample site creation workflow process with an approval step if the requestor is not a manager.

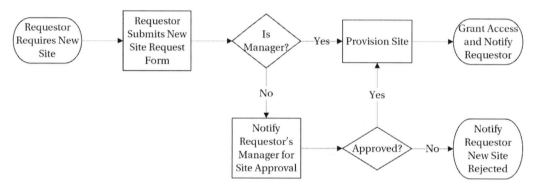

Figure 5-1. *A site creation process with an approval step*

■ **Note** For more on how to create an approval workflow, please see Chapter 7.

I generally design the site creation process in a self-service fashion, and I encourage you to do the same unless you have valid business drivers requiring you to customize or formalize a site request and site creation process. If you do create a custom process, you can implement it in SharePoint by providing your own custom site request page and specifying the URL to that page in the self-service site creation settings. Then, whenever a user attempts to create a new site, SharePoint will direct them to your custom page.

Configuring Self-Service Site Creation

You can configure self-service site creation on a per web application scope. Open SharePoint Central Administration and click the Manage Web Applications link in the Application Management section to navigate to the Manage Web Applications page.

1. Select the desired web application and click the Self-Service Site Creation button in the Security area of the ribbon.

2. Select to allow users to create site collections and select a default quota to apply to new sites.

3. Select how the self-service Start A Site page should work with managed paths, or optionally specify a custom form URL.

4. Click OK.

Figure 5-2 provides an example of the Self-Service Site Creation Management modal window.

Self-Service Site Creation Management

Sites will be created under a shared host name. Read more about security considerations when using shared host names.

Site Collections

Allow users to create site collections in defined URL namespaces.

- ○ Off
- ● On
  Users can create their own Site Collections from:
  http://portal/_layouts/15/scsignup.aspx

  Quota template to apply:
  [Basic Quota ▼]

Start a Site

Give users a shortcut to creating new Team Sites at a defined location

The Start a Site link should:
- ○ Be hidden from users
- ○ Prompt users to create a team site under:
  http://portal/ [   ]

  Use [%userid%] to represent the ID of the user who is creating the site, for example:
  /projects/[%userid%]

- ● Prompt users to create a site collection under any managed path
- ○ Display the custom form at:
  [   ]

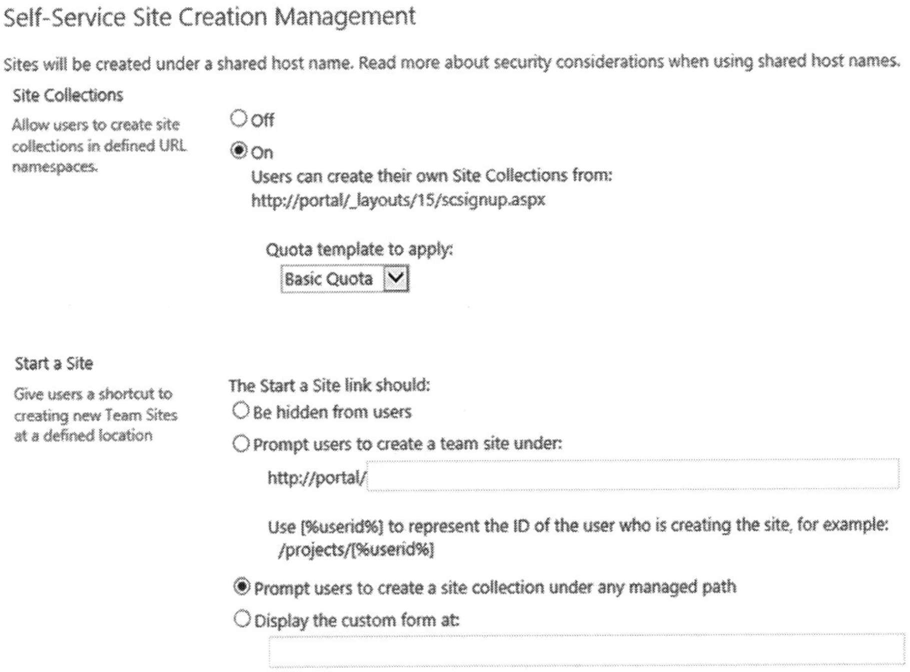

Figure 5-2. The Self-Service Site Creation Management modal window

Designing Your Content Containers

As you might suspect by now, I generally default to a single site in a site collection, and I steer users toward the single site, but I also allow them to extend their sites with child sites to create whatever site structure they need. Nonetheless, I design content containers around a single site for collaborative workspaces, and within those sites is where the containers get interesting.

You can use a SharePoint list or a library to store content. These are the two basic types of content containers that you will use to store the actual content. From there, you can choose a specialized list or library to store and manage specific pieces of content. Ultimately, the type of list or library you choose depends on the type of content you are capturing and the type of collaboration that you want to facilitate. For example, if you want your team to produce documentation, then you might select your content containers from a wiki library, document library, or OneNote notebook within a library. Choosing the type of library you select will depend on the type of user experience you want and on how you want to leverage the content in the future.

___

■ **Note** Please see Chapter 4 for more information on designing your site structure and information architecture.

Within your content containers, you store the individual pieces of content. You can have many different settings to organize and manage your content within a container, and I will return to different aspects of these settings and build upon them in relevant sections throughout this book. For now, I want to focus on managing the size of your content containers, and specifically on how to optimize performance based on the number of items you store in a list of a library.

You may have heard folklore about the number of items a list can hold. In older versions of SharePoint, people talked about limiting a list or a library to 2,000 items; in modern versions, people talk about a threshold of 5,000 items. This is not a list limitation, or more precisely, this is not a storage limitation. You can store many millions of items in a list without issue. The items captured and stored in a list do not have a 5,000-item storage threshold, and because they sit in a list, they do not have much of a performance impact, no matter how many items that list stores. The actual issue relates to querying those list items—it is a retrieval issue, not a storage issue.

These thresholds are important only when you are querying a list to retrieve a set of list items, and they have to do with the algorithm and the processing that SharePoint uses to query and return a set of list items. Remember, SharePoint is an abstraction layer on top of a database; it is not a database, nor does its queries perform like database queries. Because it abstracts away the database implementation details to provide flexible and dynamic columns of metadata and content, it has to translate a flat data structure into its tabular data view with columns and rows in a list or library. SharePoint joins everything together to present a user-friendly tabular view of the data, completely abstracting away the underlying SQL Server storage details. However, the product team optimized SharePoint to perform these data transformations, this abstraction, up to certain thresholds, namely 5,000 items.

SharePoint does not suddenly collapse once you hit 5,001 items. Picture it instead as a performance curve, where around 5,000 items performance begins to degrade at a steeper rate on the curve. This is not terrible or something that should scare you into making absolute decisions along the lines of "every list must contain less than 5,000 items." Large lists generally are not as bad as people often make them out to be. If this were a terrible thing, one that you should always avoid, then the product team would have made it a hard limit built into the product. SharePoint lets you add a huge number of items because sometimes you require this.

As I mentioned, storing a large number of items is not the issue, and when you need to meet these requirements, you can. In those cases, you need to design an effective way to query those items in a large list if you want to avoid or minimize any performance degradation when users query items in the list. Notice that I suggested avoiding any performance degradation might be optional, and this is because every system faces tradeoffs where not everything has to perform lightning fast all the time. You might not need to bother tuning and optimizing performance for lists with queries that perform good enough for your users or with lists your users query infrequently. But with other lists, you will need to optimize the query performance, and those are where you should focus your efforts.

One common solution is to partition the list items in folders, limiting the number of items in each folder to 5,000 or fewer. This is effective, and I suspect this design led to the confusion for some people assuming lists should not store more than 5,000 items. Using folders makes the queries perform better because with the narrower scope of items in a folder, a query affects fewer items, but the issue does necessarily not relate to how you need to *store* the items, only with how you *query* the items.

Segregating your list items in folders is good for automatically managing query performance, but a deep hierarchy gets back to a single-dimensional view of the data, an archaic limitation of the network file share directories. This is not bad, because you can still apply metadata to items and you can use metadata to filter and navigate a document library. Folders present one option, and they work well, but they are just one option. Not every list or library will offer folders, so they are certainly not a golden rule for designing content structures in SharePoint. With some repositories, you may prefer to have them flat rather than in a deep folder hierarchy, or you may find the performance degradation might be so insignificant that you simply accept it and keep your implementation simple. Folders are an option available to you, but they are not mandatory to manage list item limits.

Another misconception with item limits is the assumption that these thresholds only apply to the number of items returned in your query. This is not the case; the thresholds apply to the number of items *affected* by a query. For example, if you have a list with 70,000 items and you apply a filter to your query to limit the results to the first 1,000 items, your query may or may not hit the performance threshold, depending on the query. If you simply select the first 1,000 items without any filters or sorting, then your query will only affect those 1,000 items and you will not hit the performance threshold. If you select the first 1,000 items where say a city column equals "Casablanca" or you want to select the first 1,000 items sorted alphabetically, then your query will need to evaluate each item in the list, affecting 70,000 items, hitting that performance threshold even though your query is only returning 1,000 items.

In this case, you need to optimize your query as best as you can and evaluate whether it causes performance degradations that warrant your efforts to optimize the query or list settings. You can evaluate query performance by manually timing the response time for a list query or by using the SharePoint Developer Dashboard to calculate precise execution times of queries. Here is the PowerShell script to enable the Developer Dashboard on a web application:

```
$content = [Microsoft.SharePoint.Administration.SPWebService]::ContentService
$content.DeveloperDashboardSettings.DisplayLevel = [Microsoft.SharePoint.Administration.
SPDeveloperDashboardLevel]::On
$content.DeveloperDashboardSettings.Update()
```

After executing the PowerShell script, SharePoint will display a button in the top-right area of your site. Clicking it will open the Developer Dashboard window, as shown in Figure 5-3. On the Scopes and SQL tabs, you can review the execution duration information for the different aspects involved with loading and rendering the page. This information can help you identify the poor-performing areas of your site, including those poor-performing list queries.

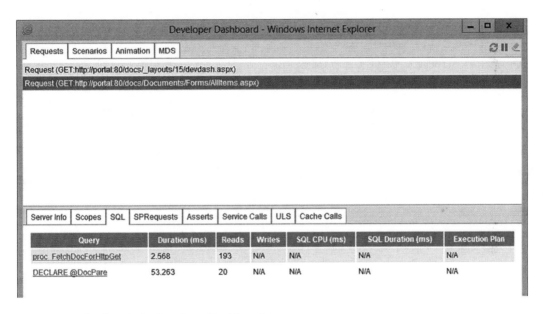

Figure 5-3. The SharePoint Developer Dashboard

■ **Note**   You can throttle the list queries to manage performance for a web application. To set list query throttling, navigate to the Manage Web Applications page in SharePoint Central Administration, select a web application, and select Resource Throttling on the context menu of the General Settings button on the ribbon.

Once you identify lists with queries that perform poorly, you can investigate the list views to analyze the queries and determine what is causing the performance degradation. In most cases, you will identify columns included in the query that cause the query to affect every item in the list, resulting in a query that exceeds the performance thresholds. You identify these columns by looking at queries on large lists that filter or sort on specific columns.

After you identify the columns in the query, you can evaluate whether you want to apply an index to those columns. Indexed columns in SharePoint are conceptually similar to indexed columns in a database: they save SharePoint from having to evaluate every item in a list by utilizing an index instead. Every column involved in the query's sort and filters will require an index to avoid affecting every list item. This, of course, leads to design tradeoffs, because in practicality, you cannot index every column. As you increase the number of indexed columns, you will experience diminishing returns for performance improvements.

Indexed columns have a marginal performance hit when you add an item to a list, because SharePoint will also have to update the index with the new item's data. This means that indices are not a definitive solution, because they require making tradeoffs and design decisions to determine when an indexed column will help. To add an index to a column, navigate to the list or library settings page and follow these steps:

1. Click the Indexed columns link in the Columns section.

2. Click the Create A New Index link.

3. Select the primary column for the index.

4. Optionally, select a secondary column to create a compound index.

5. Click Create.

■ **Note**   You can create a maximum of 20 indices on a list.

Another option is to use the SharePoint search engine to query list items and the refiners in the search results to refine the results by filtering on a particular facet. The performance threshold does not apply to search because it uses its own index to query list items. This is a particularly useful solution when you want to filter and sort on a volatile selection of columns, and it is also useful when you want to aggregate items from multiple lists for your query. Search handles these scenarios well. The product team designed search to execute queries across a large corpus of content, so you will find this is an especially elegant solution for large lists. And if you use continuous crawling for your search indexing schedule, then the query results will include items that users create in near real time.

■ **Note**   Please see Chapter 9 for more information on planning and implementing SharePoint search.

Of course, in the end, you might be better off just accepting the performance degradation as a tradeoff from any added complexity that a folder structure, indexed columns, or search query will entail. These are design decisions that depend on your requirements. More likely, however, these are design decisions that you will leave to your end-users until you identify a list that performs so poorly that it warrants your involvement to tune its queries or columns.

Your content container design first matches the type of content to a specialized list or library for the content, and then you optimize the container for how users query and retrieve content. This design offers valuable settings to capture and manage your content. Lists and libraries have other settings for managing content, and in the next section, I discuss some of those that relate to document management.

COLLABORATING IN DOCUMENT CENTER SITES

SharePoint offers a variety of site templates for different collaboration purposes. There is the team site, a generic site from which you can activate features and build up any other type of site you need. I use the team site most often, but there are other sites I use when they serve a better purpose, such as the wiki site for enterprise wikis or the records center for a records repository. I consider the document center a hybrid between the wiki and the records center. You can use it as a knowledgebase where users continuously add and collaborate on articles and documentation, and you can use it as a document repository.

I use it in a variety of scenarios to support producing and collecting documents, either documents from across the enterprise, such as in a general reference or a knowledgebase, or documents from among a team, such as documentation and reports. A document center is a specialized team site already configured with a document library, document identifiers, document sets, and other document management features.

Identifying Your Document Management Needs

The first thing you need to do to analyze your document management needs is to decide whether content in a library has any special management needs—does the content have any special requirements to manage it, or will a regular library with default settings suffice? Do you want to be bothered with the extra settings and management processes, or do you simply want to provide a container to capture documents?

In most cases, your site collection administrators and site designers will be making these decisions in their own collaboration sites, but you can add a custom SharePoint feature or app to configure a library with standardized settings if you want, and these standard settings will likely utilize a standard set of content types, metadata, and other information management policy settings. In later chapters, I return to these topics and I look at how to centralize or standardize them. For now, I want to focus on document management settings within a single library, because this narrower focus simplifies the introduction to document management settings.

■ **Note** Please see Chapter 6, where I discuss content types and configuring a content type hub in more detail.

You can manage your document management settings at the library through the library's settings page. Click the Library Settings button on the Library tab of the ribbon to navigate to the library settings page, as shown in Figure 5-4.

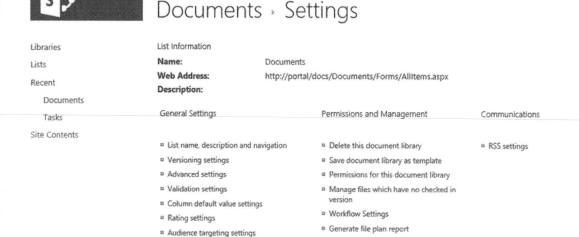

Figure 5-4. *The library settings page*

On this page, you can configure many content management aspects for a library, including the metadata columns you want to associate with content items, document versioning, advanced settings, document alerts, workflow associations, and the document information panel.

Configuring Document Columns

Within a document library, you can configure columns to capture additional metadata for each piece of content. This metadata can help you manage the content itself, such as by enabling you to filter and sort based on metadata, as I described previously. It can also help facilitate collaboration among team members by providing an extra field where they can contribute and collaborate on information. One useful field to add is the Contributor field, which lists the people who contributed to producing the content.

To add a Contributor column, navigate to the library settings page and follow these steps:

1. Click the Add From Existing Site Columns link in the Columns section.

2. In the Select Site Columns From option, select the Core Document Columns filter.

3. In the Available Site Columns list, select the Contributor column.

4. Click the Add button.

5. Click OK.

■ **Note**   Please see Chapter 6, where I discuss assigning columns to enterprise content types.

Figure 5-5 shows the Add Columns page with the Contributor column selected.

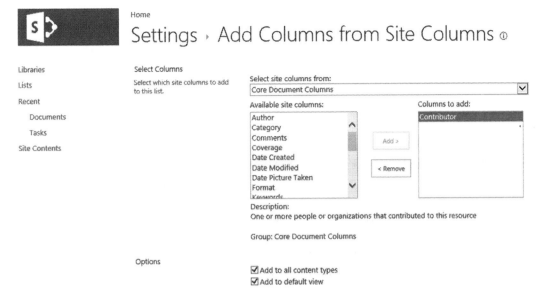

Figure 5-5. Adding the Contributor column

Enabling Document Versioning

Maintaining a history of document changes through previous versions will allow you to review or rollback to previous versions if you do not like a change. Versioning also contributes to other aspects of document management, such as providing the ability to identify who made which change based on the version where a user introduces the change in question. It also enables a publishing process you can perform in-place within a library, where editors can see drafts and contribute changes, while other read-only visitors can only see the latest published version.

To enable document versioning, navigate to the library settings page and follow these steps:

1. Click the Versioning Settings link.

2. In the document Version History, select the type of versioning you desire, consisting of either major versions or major and minor versions.

3. Optionally, select whether to limit the number of previous major or minor versions that SharePoint retains.

4. Click OK.

Document versions can help you keep track of changes that users make, but you can formalize the editing process for users to prevent multiple users from attempting to make the same edits by requiring that a user first check out a document before they can make a change.

Requiring a Check Out for Document Edits

Checking out a document locks the document for exclusive editing by a user; other users can still read the most recent version, but they cannot make changes until the user who checked out the document checks it back in. This prevents users from accidentally overwriting each other's changes. For example, if one user downloads a document to make changes, and meanwhile another user edits the document and uploads their changes back to the document library, then when the first user uploads their changes, they will unknowingly overwrite the second user's changes.

You might want to configure this setting to require a user to check out a document before he or she can edit it if you experience these types of edit overwrites or your users complain that their changes were lost. To require that users check out documents before they can edit them, navigate to the library settings page and follow these steps:

1. Click the Versioning Settings link.

2. Scroll down to the Require Check Out section and select to require users check out documents before they can edit them.

3. Click OK.

Even when you require users to check out a document before allowing edits, a user could still download a copy to edit, and then check out the document later when ready to upload the changes. This is not an ideal habit, and ideally you can encourage users to check out a document as they open or download it, but having to check out a document still draws their attention to information such as when it was last modified rather than having them blindly uploading and overwriting the document, so it should still help.

When users check in a new document or any changes, you might want to know so that you can stay up-to-date with the latest information. Rather than have users notify you when they make changes, you can have SharePoint automatically notify you by subscribing to an alert.

Managing Document Alerts

Alerts can help you and your users keep up with changes in the document library without having to physically check. When a change occurs that meets a set of criteria you are interested in, SharePoint can notify you by sending an e-mail to those subscribed to the alert. This allows you to delegate the task of monitoring changes on a list or library to SharePoint, and the alert will bring any relevant changes to your attention.

Users will generally self-subscribe to alerts for content of interest, but sometimes you may want to subscribe users to alerts when you set up an important document library that you want users to pay attention to. In addition, you might want to manage alerts for a user who previously subscribed to receive alerts, but who now complains that the alerts are bombarding him or her with notifications, yet he or she does not know how to unsubscribe.

To add alerts for users in a document library, navigate to the document library and then click the Alert Me button on the Library tab of the ribbon to open the New Alert modal window, as shown in Figure 5-6.

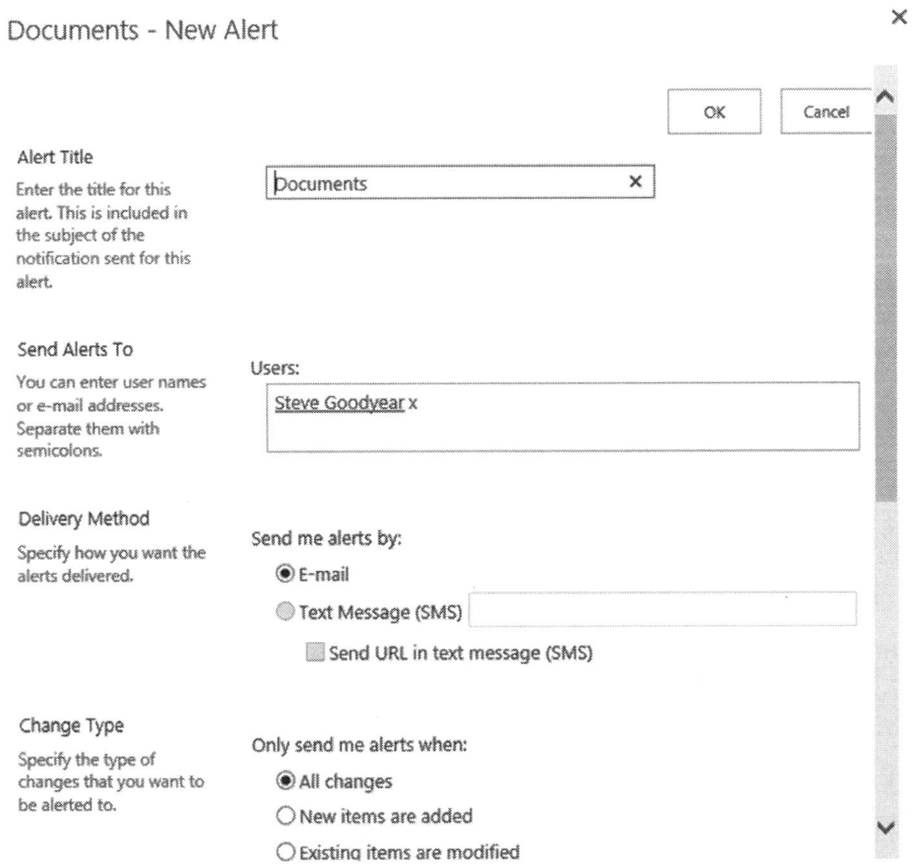

Documents - New Alert ✕

	OK	Cancel

Alert Title

Enter the title for this alert. This is included in the subject of the notification sent for this alert.

Documents ✕

Send Alerts To

You can enter user names or e-mail addresses. Separate them with semicolons.

Users:

Steve Goodyear ✕

Delivery Method

Specify how you want the alerts delivered.

Send me alerts by:

◉ E-mail

◯ Text Message (SMS)

☐ Send URL in text message (SMS)

Change Type

Specify the type of changes that you want to be alerted to.

Only send me alerts when:

◉ All changes

◯ New items are added

◯ Existing items are modified

Figure 5-6. *The New Alert modal window*

You can delete alerts for users by navigating to the Site Settings page and clicking the User Alerts link in the Site Administration section. On the User Alerts page, select the user and then delete any alerts you want to unsubscribe for that user.

Similar to having SharePoint automatically send notifications to users who subscribe to alerts, you can have SharePoint automatically initiate a workflow when users add or change content in a library.

Associating Document Workflows

When you want SharePoint to process logic after a user adds a new item or changes an existing item, you associate a workflow to the library. In the workflow's definition, you can add the logic as steps, either using one of the built-in SharePoint workflow definitions, developing your own custom workflow, or by configuring a workflow definition using SharePoint Designer or Visio. Once SharePoint detects a new or changed item, it instantiates an instance of the workflow for the item.

To associate a document workflow to a document library, navigate to the document library settings page and follow these steps:

1. Click the Workflow Settings link to navigate to the document library's Workflow Settings page.

2. Click the Add A Workflow link.

3. Select to run the workflow on every item in the list or for a specific content type.

4. Select the workflow template.

5. Enter a unique name for the workflow.

6. Select the start options to identify who can start the workflow or whether the workflow starts automatically.

7. Click OK.

▓ **Note**   I discuss workflows more in future chapters. Please see Chapter 6 for more on how to design a content life cycle workflow. See Chapter 7 for steps on how to create an approval workflow.

Setting a Document Template and the Information Panel

By default, clicking to create a new document in a document library creates a blank Word document to start. You can supply your own document template if you want to start users off with a custom template rather than a blank document. For example, if your organization has a standard document format with headers and section structures, then you can specify this as the template that SharePoint will use when users click to create a new document.

To specify a custom document template, navigate to the document library settings page and click the Advanced Settings link to navigate to the Advanced Settings page, as shown in Figure 5-7. In the Document Template section, enter a template URL or click the Edit Template link.

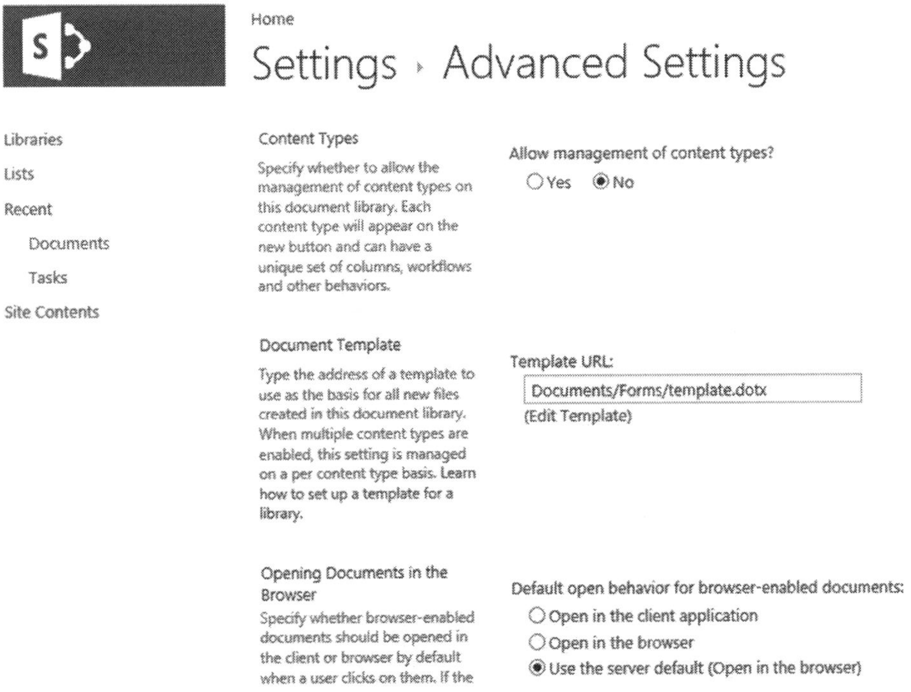

Home

Settings › Advanced Settings

Libraries

Lists

Recent

   Documents

   Tasks

Site Contents

Content Types

Specify whether to allow the management of content types on this document library. Each content type will appear on the new button and can have a unique set of columns, workflows and other behaviors.

Allow management of content types?

○ Yes   ◉ No

Document Template

Type the address of a template to use as the basis for all new files created in this document library. When multiple content types are enabled, this setting is managed on a per content type basis. Learn how to set up a template for a library.

Template URL:

| Documents/Forms/template.dotx |

(Edit Template)

Opening Documents in the Browser

Specify whether browser-enabled documents should be opened in the client or browser by default when a user clicks on them. If the

Default open behavior for browser-enabled documents:

○ Open in the client application

○ Open in the browser

◉ Use the server default (Open in the browser)

Figure 5-7. *The document library Advanced Settings page*

To customize the document template for a content type, navigate to the Site Settings page and click the site content types under the Web Designer Galleries section to navigate to the Site Content Types page. Click the Advanced Settings link and select whether to enter a URL for an existing document template or upload a new document template.

Using custom document templates can standardize the layout and format of specific types of documents, such as a standard functional specification document format for the engineering department or a standard status report document format for status reporting. But hidden within the benefits of a document's standard format and layout, custom document templates also standardize the font face and other typographic styles in the document, enabling you to facilitate brand consistency across documents within your organization, and ultimately moving your users beyond the default fonts and styles in Word to instead produce consistent-looking documents that align with your organization's brand.

Word includes a document information panel to capture metadata properties for the document. You can also provide your own custom document information panel. You can display this panel with the document properties across the top of a Word document. You customize the document information panel by modifying its form using InfoPath. This allows you to capture additional properties and even to link them to SharePoint columns, making the user experience for tagging metadata much more fluid and natural as a user creates and edits a document, rather than troubling him or her for metadata after the fact.

Because document information panels are InfoPath forms packaged with the other assets that make up an Office file, you can standardize on the document information panel to make it consistent across your organization. You can also add custom logic to simplify or automate a business process for an information worker, and you can even pull and integrate data from external systems.

■ **Note**   For more information on designing a document information panel using InfoPath, please see the Office support article at http://office.microsoft.com/HA010201967.

To customize the document information panel, navigate to the Site Settings page and click the site content types under the Web Designer Galleries section to navigate to the Site Content Types page. Click the desired content type and then click the Document Information Panel Settings link to navigate to the Document Information Panel Settings page, as shown in Figure 5-8.

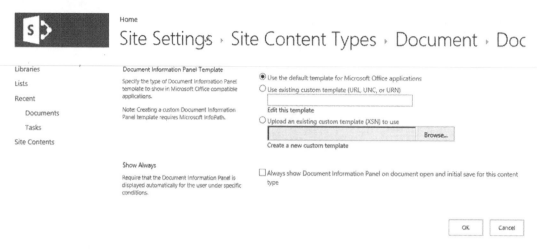

Figure 5-8. *The Document Information Panel Settings page*

If you have an existing document information panel on the site, you can select the option to enter the URL. You can click the Create A New Custom Template link to open InfoPath and edit the document information panel. After you finish editing the panel, save it locally, and then return to SharePoint to upload the custom template. You can also optionally select to always show the document information panel for the content type's document template.

■ **Note**   Please see Chapter 8 for more on InfoPath forms.

Managing Document Information Management Policies

One of the more crucial document management settings in a document library is setting the information management policies. This allows you to configure retention and audit settings most notably, as well as policies for labels and any custom information policies that you develop and define. The following describe each of the standard information management policy settings:

- **Retention:** You can configure retention policies to process a piece of content after a given duration, either from the content's creation date, last modified date, or its record declaration date. You can choose to have SharePoint dispose of the content, declare the content as a record, transfer to another location, delete previous drafts, or initiate custom workflows with more sophisticated logic.

■ **Note**   I discuss content retention and disposition in more depth in Chapter 15.

- **Auditing:** You specify the following audit events to capture the following: open or view, edit, check out or check in, move or copy, and delete or restore content items.

- **Barcodes:** You can have SharePoint assign a barcode to each document or item, or optionally, you can prompt users to insert a barcode before saving or printing.

- **Labels:** You can add a label to a document to print selected metadata information with the document.

To configure an information management policy on a document library, navigate to the document library settings page and click the Information Management Policy Settings link to navigate to the Information Management Policy Settings page, as shown in Figure 5-9.

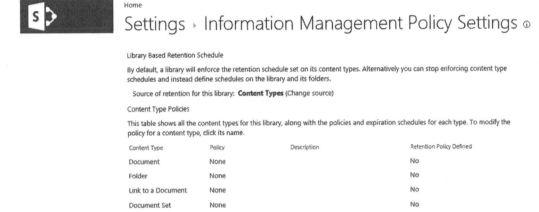

Figure 5-9. *The Information Management Policy Settings page*

Reviewing Audit and Usage Reports for Site Content

If you set an information policy to audit content in a document library, you can review the audit reports to view and analyze audit information about the content. Audit reports can help you track and report on compliance information for specific types of content, such as if you need to audit any changes or access to financial reports in a document library.

You can also review usage reports to analyze the popularity of content and the usage patterns users follow with accessing content. This can help you identify how users search for information and how they are consuming information. You can analyze usage reports to determine your content retention durations or your metadata strategy as you adjust and adapt your content management settings based on how users actually consume the content.

To view site usage reports for all libraries in a site collection, navigate to the site collection settings page and click the Popularity And Search Reports link under the Site Collection Administration section. On the View Usage Reports page, as shown in Figure 5-10, select one of the reports listed in the Usage Reports or Search Reports group.

Figure 5-10. *The site collection View Usage Reports page*

To view the audit log, navigate to the site collection settings page and click the Audit Log Reports link under the Site Collection Administration section. On the View Audit Reports page, as shown in Figure 5-11, select one of the reports listed in the Content Activity Reports group or the Information Management Policy Reports group.

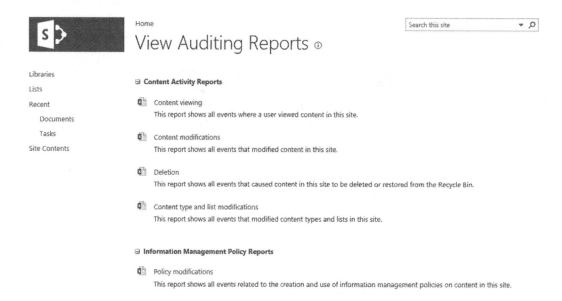

Figure 5-11. *The View Audit Reports page*

Inside Story: Notes from the Field

I once had a client who wanted their IT team to manage every aspect of provisioning and administrating the site collections for their end-users. This, of course, translates to a significant burden on an IT service delivery team that has to respond to every user request, rather than simply delegate those tasks to the end-users to perform themselves. Even though I generally encourage my clients to design their processes around self-service and automation, and I spent some time in this chapter advocating such a position, I know this is not a golden rule that everyone needs to adopt in every situation. In fact, in many situations, just the opposite strategy may be the best one.

Regular users are not IT administrators; they are not experienced with system and security administration. Your users probably have other job functions and their domain expertise focuses on those functions rather than on IT solution design and administration. And so, if your IT operations and service delivery team is resourced well enough and you have a customer service-oriented culture internally, then you may find, as my client found, that performing these functions to service your internal customers can ease their technology burden and enable you to steer the direction for how your users adopt the software.

My client wanted to manage all aspects of the service for their users so that the users would only need to think about the job for which they needed to collaborate with each other. Users consumed the service strictly as contributors to the collaboration process; no one managed their own sites or security. The SharePoint service delivery team created Active Directory groups for every site, they provisioned and configured each site, and they managed every other aspect of the SharePoint service, always masking the administration and management aspects from the users.

I like this level of service because it adds a human element, connecting knowledge workers to real people who can help them and who can answer questions or provide advice. The technology experts, those working in IT, can simplify the process for valuable knowledge workers to focus on carrying out their job functions, supporting the knowledge workers with experts who can best guide the workers on how to optimally leverage the technology. The process can even relieve the stress of a nontechnical person trying to make technology decisions and figure out how best to utilize technology. The trouble is that its budget is expensive and it requires more than adequate resourcing, both of which are often in short supply for many organizations with whom I engage.

Ultimately, this approach does not scale well, because it depends on a central team to provide and manage the service, and the team has to scale with the service's adoption and usage. If you can manage to resource a team well enough to provide this level of service and keep up with scaling it as needed, then this service delivery approach may appeal to you. However, in my experience, these service delivery teams are few and far between the majority who have to compromise by automating many tasks in a self-service fashion, and this is the reason I generally encourage clients to maximize the self-service capabilities that they have available to their users.

My point is that you can tightly control everything for your users, and this might be preferable if you have the budget and resourcing to offer the required level of service. But you realistically cannot have the best of both worlds if you want a functional and sustainable service: either you want to empower your users by enabling self-service functionality, or you want to be like my client and staff a service delivery team to manage the processes on behalf of your users.

Wrapping Up

You can stay ahead of the content masses by planning and designing how you enable your collaboration process to channel and organize content as users create it. You enable your collaboration content by first understanding the nature of collaboration: working with another person or groups of other people to produce or create new content. Collaboration flourishes when you liberate it, empowering users to come together whenever and however they need to as they generate new information in their job functions. In this chapter, I noted how you could liberate collaboration effectively by designing an appropriate site creation process, one that steers users toward sustainable and supportable growth and adoption. From there, I shared different considerations for designing your content containers, particularly as they relate to the number of items you store. Finally, I discussed how you can identify and implement your document management needs, including configuring the library settings to add custom metadata columns, enable document versioning, and setting information management policies.

Enabling collaboration equips users with a productive workspace where they can produce and collaborate on content together. This can generate a lot of content and it is the best opportunity to start classifying and organizing the content, capturing the content with relevant and self-describing information to make future searches and content discovery productive. In the next chapter, I discuss how to move beyond the document library and instead standardize your content management to classify and organize your content at a global level. The primary tool I discuss to achieve this organization-wide standard is the content type, which works closely with the lists and libraries, as well as the content management settings that I have described so far.

■ ■ ■

CHAPTER 6

Classifying and Organizing Your Content

Intellectual property has the shelf life of a banana.

—Bill Gates

With so much content and so many lists and libraries containing content, how can you ever scale to have a useful enough reach where you can guide your users in managing and organizing their content effectively? Rather than finding yourself caught up with individual content containers, or even with individual sites, you can influence how your organization manages and organizes content through a feature in SharePoint called *content types*. In this chapter, I provide guidance on how to use content types to organize and manage content in SharePoint 2013. I also walk through how to configure an enterprise content type hub to centralize and standardize the content types across all sites. Finally, I discuss how to design workflows to manage the content life cycle.

After reading this chapter, you will know how to

- Describe when and how to use content types.

- Analyze and design content types.

- Implement content types.

- Understand and configure document sets.

- Configure your enterprise content type hub.

- Describe the Windows Workflow Foundation.

- Create content life cycle workflows.

- Configure remote BLOB (binary large object) storage for content databases.

Organizing Content

One effective component to organizing content is to dispose of unnecessary content. I am a bit of a minimalist when it comes to retaining content—documents, e-mail messages, notes, et cetera. I save what compliance policies require me to save, what I truly need, or what I may value in the future for sentimental reasons. The rest I dispose of. This minimalism reduces the size, ensuring that the important or valuable content does not get lost in the pile of content. You can dispose of unnecessary content by manually deleting it or by automating its life cycle management with a retention and disposition policy.

▓ **Note**   Please see Chapter 15, where I discuss content retention and disposition in more detail. I discuss it there in the context of records management, but you can apply the same concepts and automation to transitory content.

Before you get overly involved with content organizing and classifying activities, first consider what content you can dispose of and safely exclude from your analysis and design. Do you have content that is so obsolete that it has not been accessed or even been relevant in years? Clearing out this clutter can help jumpstart your content organization efforts. Of course, a significant amount of content providing ongoing value will remain, and organizing *that* content is no doubt your ultimate goal for your ECM initiative.

Organizing content is probably the underlying motive for most enterprise content management initiatives—the content corpus grows at an exponential rate and organizations need a way to manage and cope with this. Back in Chapter 4, I encouraged you to design your structures such that they primarily organize your content through metadata, and then in Chapter 5 I walked you through how to configure document libraries to capture additional metadata. These discussions lead to this chapter and applying those ideas and techniques at a more global and repeatable level, to organize content using SharePoint content types.

Understanding Content Types

When you plan and design your information architecture to organize content in SharePoint, you can approach the design from a storage structure and a folder hierarchy, or you can utilize metadata. I contrasted the two approaches in more depth in Chapter 4 when I discussed how to design your information architecture, and now I apply the concept with how to implement the metadata in effective ways across your organization, and specifically, how to implement and standardize content types.

You saw in the previous chapter that you could apply metadata columns to a document library and achieve the desired effect of organizing content using metadata; however, this approach does not scale very well across a large organization because you may have thousands of document libraries. Any little change you want to make would require a lot of reconfiguring, either manually or with a script, complicating your enterprise metadata implementation. It gets even more complicated if you want to store different kinds of content in the same library, each associated with their own set of metadata. These are exactly the challenges that SharePoint content types solve and the type of complications that they simplify by allowing you to manage the settings for a category of information in a centralized and standardized way.

A list or library can have multiple content types, and each content type can have its own set of metadata, workflows, and information policies. This allows you to manage the information you associate with individual types of content, regardless of the storage location and the other types of content you also store there. Furthermore, you can associate a content type to one or more lists or libraries, enabling you to reuse the content type across your information architecture. You can also centralize your organization's content types in a designated site collection—a content type hub—for SharePoint to replicate across all site collections, as I discuss later in this chapter.

Content types can include the following attributes in their definition:

- Columns (metadata)

- Custom New, Edit, and Display forms for managing an item

- Workflows

- Information management policies

- The Document Information Panel to display in compatible Microsoft Office programs

- The document template for new items in document content types

- The document conversions available in document content types

You can design and configure your own custom content types, extend another content type, or use a built-in one. SharePoint includes several content types in a default team site, and you can activate site features to add several other content types to a site. The following include some of the popular default content types in a site:

- Document

- Wiki Page

- Form

- Event

- Issue

- Announcement

- Contact

- Discussion

- Task

- Folder

- Document Set

- Master Page

- Rich Media Asset

SharePoint provides a sort of inheritance capability for content types. I say *sort of* because it is not true inheritance. The base content type does not provide any implementation details for any inheriting content types when users use them on a page, and instead SharePoint *copies* the implementation details from the base content type to any inheriting ones. SharePoint is aware of the inheritance relationship, but if you change any implementation details on a base content type, you can then *optionally* copy those changes to any inheriting content types. The copying of implementation details and the ability to change a base without affecting an inherited content type is why I say it is not a true form of inheritance.

Nevertheless, SharePoint refers to this content type reference and structure as *inheritance*, because conceptually, that is what the content type hierarchy is doing. Underneath, SharePoint manages the inheritance references through the content type identifier. Content types that include the identifier of another content type and then append their own unique identifier inherit from that other content type. For example, the Item content type ID is "0×01" and the Document content type ID includes the Item's ID and appends a hexadecimal "01" to form its "0×0101" identifier, establishing its inheritance from Item.

All content types inherit from the Item content type. Content types with BLOBs of content such as web pages and pictures inherit from the Document content type, which in turn inherits from Item. Figure 6-1 illustrates a conceptual hierarchy of some of the base content types built in SharePoint, starting with the Item content type.

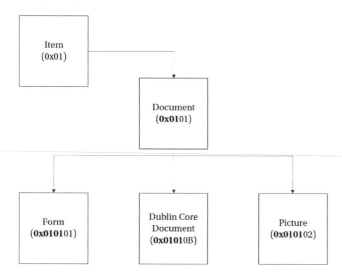

Figure 6-1. *Conceptual hierarchy of content type inheritance*

Content types categorize a piece of content as a specific type of content. Your information architecture can use this categorization to apply policies, to optimize eDiscovery, and to route records effectively in your file plan. Configuring content types at the site level for end users simplifies the content life cycle and how much you can automate as pieces of content progress from transitory through to becoming official records. It also provides a richer user experience by enabling users to manage the content in a collaborative context.

After you associate a content type with a list or library, the content type appears on the context menu under the New Item button in the list or library. When a user clicks the menu item for a content type, then SharePoint opens a new item form for list item content types or a new document based on the template associated with the content type. This offers users a way to create pieces of content based on a centrally managed template, all in the context of the list or library they are working in.

Users can associate content with a content type if they create content on their desktop or offline, and they later upload it to a list or library in SharePoint. When a library has more than one content type associated with it, it will prompt the user to select the content type during the document upload sequence along with other required metadata. For certain documents, such as Office documents, SharePoint stores the content type identifier as a document property, allowing users to create new documents offline with the content type already identified.

SharePoint maintains a gallery of content types in a site, accessed by clicking the Site content types link in the Web Designer Galleries section on the Site Settings page. In this gallery, you can review what content types are available in a site, including those default content types available in a basic team site, content types added after activating a particular feature, or any content types that you create. Figure 6-2 shows a default view of a site content types gallery.

Team   ✏ EDIT LINKS

Site Settings › Site Content Types

Home

Documents

Site Contents

✏ EDIT LINKS

🖳 Create

Show Group: All Groups

Site Content Type	Parent	Source
Business Intelligence		
Excel based Status Indicator	Common Indicator Columns	Team
Fixed Value based Status Indicator	Common Indicator Columns	Team
Report	Document	Team
SharePoint List based Status Indicator	Common Indicator Columns	Team
SQL Server Analysis Services based Status Indicator	Common Indicator Columns	Team
Web Part Page with Status List	Document	Team
Community Content Types		
Category	Item	Team
Community Member	Site Membership	Team
Site Membership	Item	Team
Digital Asset Content Types		
Audio	Rich Media Asset	Team
Image	Rich Media Asset	Team
Rich Media Asset	Document	Team

Figure 6-2. *The site content types gallery*

In the site content types gallery, by default, the page groups the available content types by the following general categories:

- Business Intelligence
- Community Content Types
- Digital Asset Content Types
- Display Template Content Types
- Document Content Types
- Document Set Content Types
- Folder Content Types
- Group Work Content Types
- List Content Types
- Special Content Types
- SQL Server Reporting Services Content Types

You can filter the view of content types by a specific group using the drop-down menu in the top-right area of the page. Groups can help you find the appropriate content type you want to work with quickly and efficiently. When you create your own custom content types, you can assign them to an available group or add your own custom group to better organize and make your content type easier to find.

Content types provide the most granular building block for any enterprise content management implementation within SharePoint. They capture the required information, apply the relevant policies, and manage the retention and disposition. Their effectiveness comes from analyzing your information architecture and thinking through the user experience that you want to provide—information that guides your implementation design and drives much of your enterprise content management solution.

Analyzing and Designing Content Types

Whenever I approach a content type design, I rely primarily on a content inventory and an information architecture in addition to the content life cycle and the desired user experience to manage the content. This provides a holistic view of the content and its value to the organization. It also provides source information to identify the content types and their attributes, especially if you have already grouped your content inventory into different kinds of content, as I mentioned in Chapter 3.

One danger I noticed with designing content types is a tendency to focus on hierarchies and inheritance rather than on metadata and policies. It is true, SharePoint content types support a type of inheritance, but it is not true inheritance in the object-oriented sense, and I find this idea of seeking designs based on inheritance structures becomes more of a red herring, distracting some design teams, leading to an overly complex and bloated content type implementation.

Focus on identifying the content types first—what are the core types of content in use and how do you want to group them? Plan to group main pieces of content together *after* identifying core content areas and the types of information in your organization. From there, abstract the content groups to generalize the content and look at ways to order and organize it.

A deep hierarchy of content types may confuse or overwhelm users with too many options. I try to be mindful of guarding against drifting into some engineering exercise to design an overly complicated information structure, or into some engineering quest to optimize or normalize the content type design. This is not a database design exercise and there are no execution efficiencies for you to gain simply by normalizing how you structure your content types, because underneath, SharePoint does not care about these details. The important thing is to focus on how users use the content types and on the user experience that you want to provide.

Your content type design needs to come out of business analysis and business process design, not from laying out a fancy hierarchy of related groupings of information. You may, and in many cases probably will, find inheritance relationships useful, leading to an enviable hierarchy, but that does not mean your design has to incorporate a hierarchy. Wait until the process leads you into the hierarchical design, and specifically, it will be your business process design activities as they relate to the content life cycle.

On its own, reusing column definitions does not provide a useful driver to inherit from another content type. The column is a site column, so the site defines it once and then reuses the definition. Content types merely reference a site column through a field reference, and since all you are doing when inheriting a content type is copying the field references, you do not gain much beyond the ability to push a copy of the reference when you update the base content type.

Inheritance becomes useful later in the content life cycle because you can configure rules to route items derived from a particular content type to a specific area in your file plan. These types of routing or processing rules are what I use to drive requirements for any hierarchical structure. This is where the content life cycle model can help you design your content type hierarchy as you analyze how you want to process the pieces of content.

Your content life cycle model can also help you decide when to separate a general content type definition into more granular content types where each have a different processing, retention, or workflow requirement. For example, the Image, Video, and Audio content types all inherit from the Rich Media Asset content type, each adding specialized attributes for their particular content, such as resolution information for images and frame rate information for videos, but they all share the commonalities of being a Rich Media Asset that a rich media library can manage.

My point is to think about the user experience for content types in lists and libraries, both during the collaborative stage in the content's life cycle and when users or processes designate the content as an official record. This analysis will reveal the hierarchy and inheritance relationship among content types, as well as the requirements for information policies and workflows, along with having your content inventory identify the required metadata attributes.

I like to start slow, and then gradually increase or continuously improve my content type design, expanding the number and the granularity of content types as I evolve the requirements and use cases. This approach could potentially lead to reworking some of the content classifications in production or to accepting that some content will be classified in less specific or less granular categories down the road as I add additional content types, but this is a trade-off that I am usually happy to make because it avoids risks associated with over-architecting a solution. As with every solution architecture activity, my preference is to put working software in the hands of users and then reevaluate assumptions as I take smaller steps to fine-tune the design based on how users interact with the solution.

Whether you take the iterative approach to your content type design or you prefer to go through a more exhaustive exercise upfront, eventually you will take your designs and begin to implement content types.

Implementing Content Types

You can implement a content type by creating one through the web interface or by activating a feature with a content type manifest definition. To create a content type through the web interface, navigate to the site content types gallery by clicking the Site content types link in the Web Designer Galleries section on the Site Settings page. Click the Create button to then open the New Site Content Type page, shown in Figure 6-3.

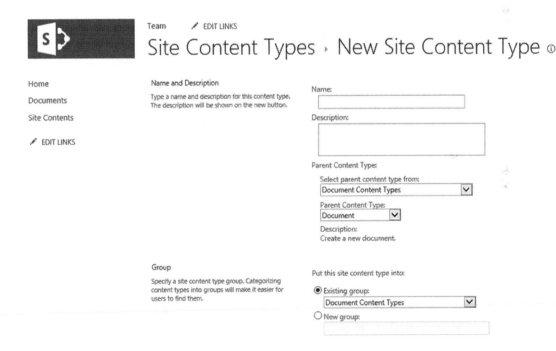

Figure 6-3. *The New Site Content Type page*

Enter a name and optionally a description for the new content type and select a content type to inherit from. As I mentioned earlier, Item is the base content type for any other content type. You can inherit directly from Item or any other content type that derives from Item. Finally, set the group for organizing the content type and click OK to create it. After creating the content type, SharePoint will redirect you to the Site Content Type page, similar to the page shown in Figure 6-4, where you can configure additional settings.

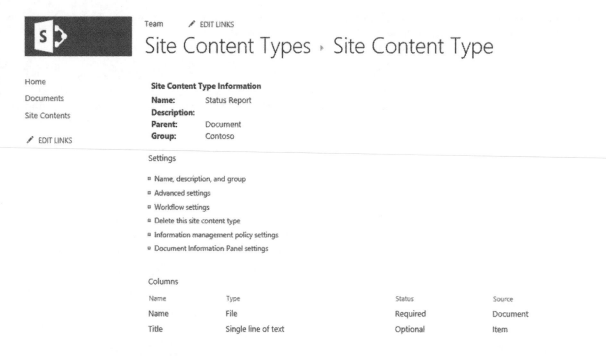

Figure 6-4. *The Site Content Type settings page*

Click the Advanced Settings link to navigate to the Advanced Settings page shown in Figure 6-5. On this page for document-related content types, you can specify the document template for the content type. This option will specify the default document that will open when a user clicks the New button in a document library. You can specify a URL for a shared document template on your network or you can upload a document template specifically for the new content type. In addition, you can specify if the content type is read-only, which prevents any changes to the content type's settings. For list-related content type items, the Advanced Settings page does not have the document template option.

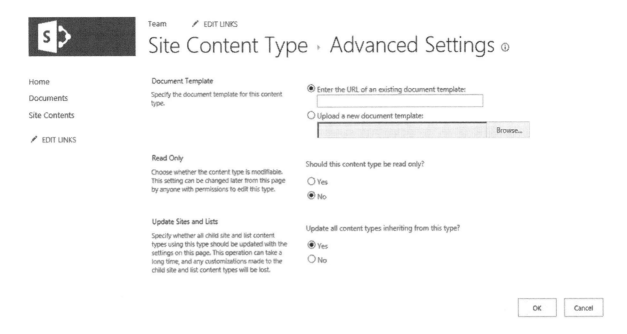

Figure 6-5. *The content type Advanced Settings page for document content type items*

Below the Advanced Settings link on the Site Content Type settings page is the Workflow Settings link. You can associate any workflow template available in the site with the content type through the workflow settings option. I return to discuss workflows later in this chapter and at points throughout the book.

In addition, you can also delete a content type and configure the information management policy or document information panel settings. The information management policy settings work in the same manner as I discussed in the previous chapter. The document information panel settings work in a similar way as the document template where you can provide the URL to a shared template or upload one for the specific content type. You create a custom document information panel template using InfoPath. For list-related content type items, the content type settings page does not have the document information panel settings option.

■ **Note**   Please see Chapter 5, where I discussed information policy settings in more detail.

Under the content type settings section is the columns section, where you can configure the columns associated with the content type or add new columns. Unlike when managing columns in lists or libraries directly, content types only use shared site columns. You can choose to add an existing site column if one is available, or you can create a new site column and add it to the content type.

When you click to add existing site columns, you can add multiple columns from the available columns list, as shown in Figure 6-6.

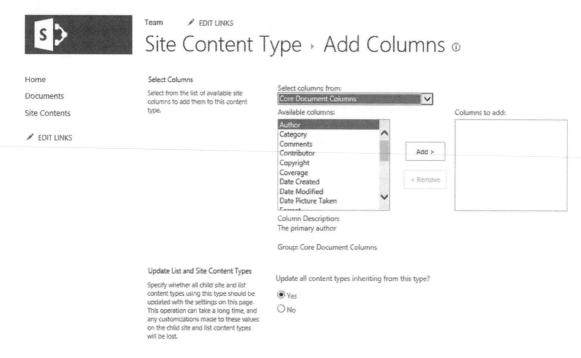

Figure 6-6. *The Add Columns page*

You can also create a content type by activating a SharePoint feature with a content type definition included with its manifest. The following code snippet provides an example of the XML in a content type definition. In this example, the feature would create a Status Report content type that inherits from the *Document* base content type.

```
<!-- Parent ContentType: Document (0x0101) -->
  <ContentType ID="0x0101000fd9bd65db50444a9a660d8a6bb3c7ea0"
               Name="Status Report"
               Group="Status Report Content Types"
               Description="" Version="0">
</ContentType>
```

■ **Note**　For more information on the content type definition XML schema, please see the MSDN article at http://msdn.microsoft.com/ms463449.

Understanding and Configuring Document Sets

A typical content type holds a single unit of information within a package, usually a single document relating to a topic. However, in some circumstances, you may want to manage multiple documents in a single package, treating them all together as a single unit of information.

For example, a purchaser might want to capture all the documents relating to a particular procurement purchase and treat them together as a unit. He or she starts with a requisition from a requestor within the organization, then progressing to collect a number of quotes from vendors, issuing a purchase order, and then ultimately receiving an invoice. The package may include contracts, warranties, and service terms, all of which are relevant to and provide evidence for the purchase. If procurement wants to package these documents together, they can capture them within a document set.

A document set is a special kind of content type, one that acts as a folder for other content types while managing metadata and policies for the items within the set. Document sets provide a page that you can customize to manage the contents and metadata within the set, enabling you to customize the user experience for capturing and managing content within the set.

You can configure a document set content type to

- Specify the allowable content types within the document set.
- Specify any default documents the document set automatically generates with a new instance.
- Specify the metadata to synchronize with all documents in the document set.
- Customize a welcome page to display information about the document set.
- Configure workflows associated within the document set.

After you configure the document set content type and associate it with a document library, you can

- Create new multidocument work products effectively and manage them as a unit.
- Capture the version history of the document set's properties and documents.
- Start workflows for the entire document set or individual items within the set.
- Use the SharePoint Send To command to move or copy the document set to another location.

You can enable document sets for a site collection by activating the Document Sets site collection feature. Once activated, you can create a new document set content type in the same fashion as other content types. To create a new document set, follow these steps:

1. Navigate to the Site content types library in the Galleries section on the Site Settings page.
2. On the Site Content Types page, click Create.
3. Enter a name and description for the document set.
4. Under Select Parent Content Type From, click Document Set Content Types.
5. Specify the group to categorize the new document set content type or select an existing group.
6. Click OK.

After you create the document set, SharePoint will redirect you to the Site Content Type settings page. This page is similar to other content type settings pages, except it also has a Document Set Settings link that accesses the Document Set Settings page shown in Figure 6-7.

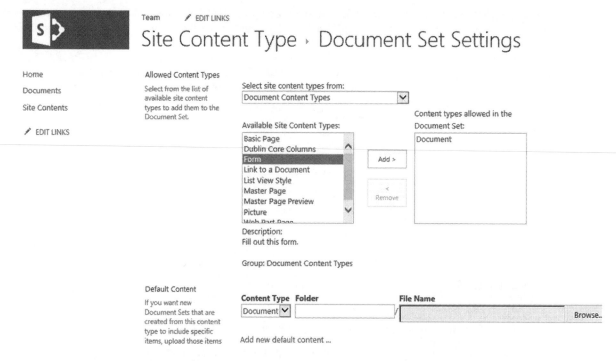

Figure 6-7. The Document Set Settings page

On the Document Set Settings page, you can configure which content types you want to allow users to create within the document set. You can also specify default content to generate when users create a new instance of the document set by specifying the content type and folder, and uploading the file template in the Default Content section.

In the Shared Columns section, you can identify any document set columns that you want to synchronize and include with all the documents contained in the set. This allows users to manage common properties in a single location for the document set and then replicate those properties to each piece of content contained within the set.

Document sets include their own welcome page, an ASP.NET web part page that you can customize. You can choose to show specific columns on the content type welcome page if you want to provide your users with a quick view of certain properties and their values. You can also customize the welcome page by clicking the Customize The Welcome Page link. Figure 6-8 shows the default Document Set welcome page where you can click the Edit Page button on the ribbon to add additional web parts or customize the page's user experience.

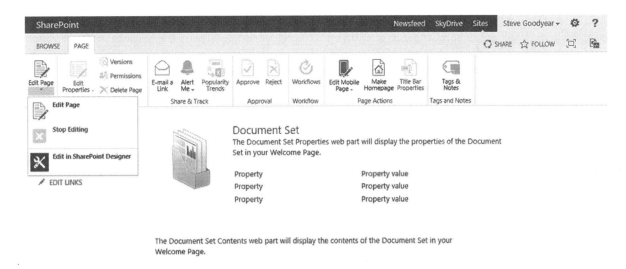

Figure 6-8. *The Document Set welcome page*

Configuring Your Enterprise Content Type Hub

An enterprise content type hub is simply a designated site collection with the Content Type Syndication Hub feature activated, enabling the site to be used as a centralized content type repository. When you specify the site collection URL as the content type hub in a Managed Metadata Service, SharePoint replicates the site columns and content types to all the other site collections, synchronizing configuration settings, workflows, and policies for use in every site consuming services from the same Managed Metadata Service.

While you are provisioning a new instance of the Managed Metadata Service, SharePoint prompts you to specify a URL for the site collection to use as the content type hub, as shown in Figure 6-9.

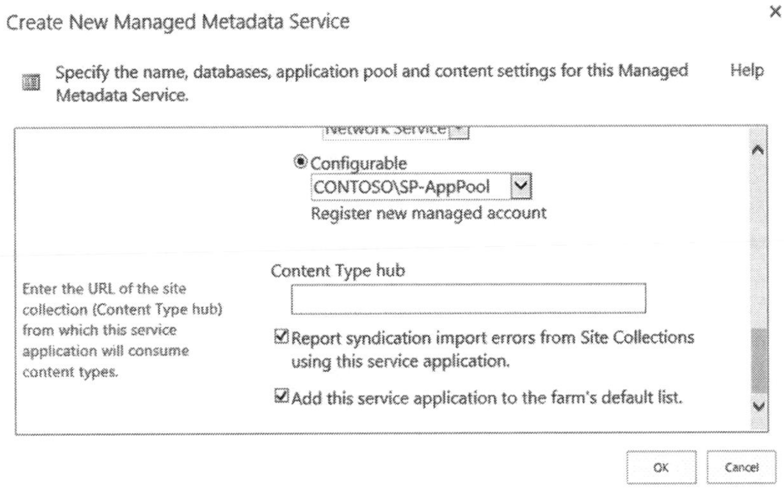

Figure 6-9. *The content type hub URL setting on the Create New Managed Metadata Service window*

Once you provision an instance of the Managed Metadata Service, the content type hub URL field becomes read-only and you can no longer change the value through this web interface. Figure 6-10 shows an example of the read-only content type hub URL on the Managed Metadata Service properties.

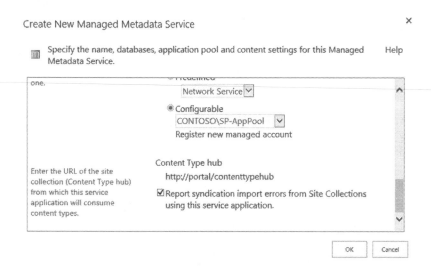

Figure 6-10. *The content type hub URL on the Managed Metadata Service properties*

If you need to change the content type hub URL property for a Managed Metadata Service, then you can accomplish this using the following PowerShell script, substituting the new site collection URL for the HubUri value.

```
Set-SPMetadataServiceApplication -Identity "Managed Metadata Service" -HubUri
"http://portal/contenttypehub"
```

For site collections configured as a content type hub, the Site Content Type settings page I discussed previously and shown in Figure 6-4 will contain an extra option to manage content type publishing. To view this option, navigate to the Site Settings page of your content type hub and then click the Site Content Types link. Click a content type to navigate to the Site Content Type settings page, and then click the Manage Publishing For This Content Type link to navigate to the Content Type Publishing settings page, as shown in Figure 6-11. From this page, you can publish, unpublish, or republish a content type.

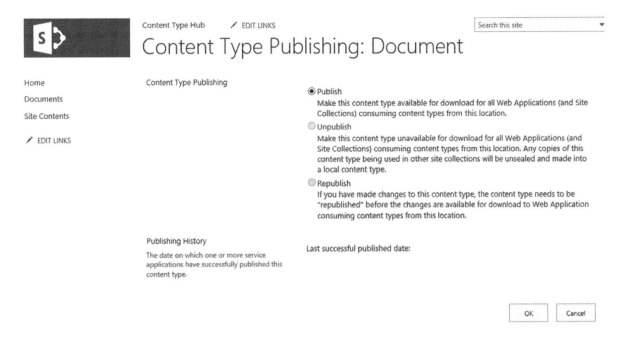

Figure 6-11. *The Content Type Publishing settings page*

Windows Workflow Foundation Overview

Workflows model business processes, breaking them down into a series of activities organized in an order of execution and with dependency relationships between activities as the workflow progresses as people or system functions perform activities or trigger events.

SharePoint 2013 exposes workflow capabilities through its implementation of the Microsoft .NET Windows Workflow Foundation (WF). Before I get too into the SharePoint implementation details, I want to step back and provide an overview of the underlying workflow capabilities built into the .NET framework, capabilities that SharePoint exposes and extends.

Windows Workflow Foundation is a framework that enables developers to create system or human workflows in the applications that they develop on the .NET framework. Microsoft designed Windows Workflow Foundation to provide a consistent and familiar development experience with other .NET technologies in developing solutions for the following scenarios:

- Enabling workflow within line-of-business applications

- User-interface page flows

- Document-centric workflows

- Human workflows

- Composite workflows for service-oriented applications

- Business rule-driven workflows

- Workflows for systems management

Windows Workflow Foundation installs with modern versions of the Microsoft .NET framework, enabling you to incorporate sophisticated workflow applications along with any .NET application that you are developing.

The workflow engine executes and processes a workflow model from start to finish, all within the .NET runtime. However, if you want to pause and save the state of a workflow, such as when your workflow has to wait on input or an event trigger before it progresses to the next step, then the workflow engine depends on storage technology such as SQL Server to maintain the state for a workflow instance.

■ **Note**   For more information on the Windows Workflow Foundation, along with tutorials and samples, please see the MSDN site at `http://msdn.microsoft.com/jj684582`.

Creating Content Life Cycle Workflows

The work you did modeling your content life cycle in earlier chapters translates well into workflows. If you have analyzed your content life cycle and designed your procedure to process content from creation through to its disposition, now all you have to do is implement your model as a SharePoint workflow.

For example, Figure 6-12 shows a simplified sample of a content life cycle workflow that processes transitory content by assigning a task to a user to acknowledge whether the content is still in use. To implement this process as a SharePoint workflow, you would use one of the tools available to create a workflow and add actions or conditions that correspond to each step in your process model.

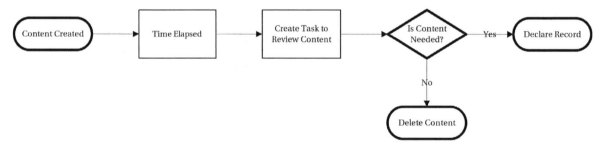

Figure 6-12. *Sample transitory content life cycle workflow*

■ **Note**   Please see Chapter 15, where I discuss content retention and disposition workflow designs in more depth.

You can create workflows in SharePoint in a few different ways with a few different tools. Later in this book, I describe how developers can use Visual Studio 2012 to create custom actions and workflow definitions. Visual Studio offers the greatest availability of custom development and extensibility in your workflows. It is a powerful developer tool, but it might be overkill for what you need if another one of the more end-user-friendly tools will do the job.

Microsoft provides other more end-user-friendly tools for creating and configuring sophisticated workflows without requiring a developer or any specialized knowledge of the underlying .NET framework. These tools are Microsoft Visio 2013 and SharePoint Designer 2013. Visio is a diagraming tool that business analysts have long used to model business processes for workflows, but now it contains a template specifically for SharePoint workflows with shapes relating to different actions or conditions in SharePoint. Figure 6-13 provides an example of creating a SharePoint workflow using Visio.

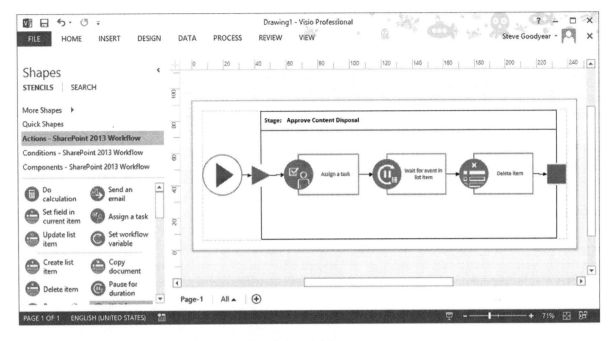

Figure 6-13. *Using Microsoft Visio to create a SharePoint workflow*

Where Visio provides a visual layout and flowchart view for designing and creating workflows, SharePoint Designer provides more of a rules-based view for creating workflows. I find that workflow creation in SharePoint Designer is a similar experience to creating e-mail rules in Outlook. Figure 6-14 shows some of the different workflow steps available for creating a workflow in SharePoint Designer.

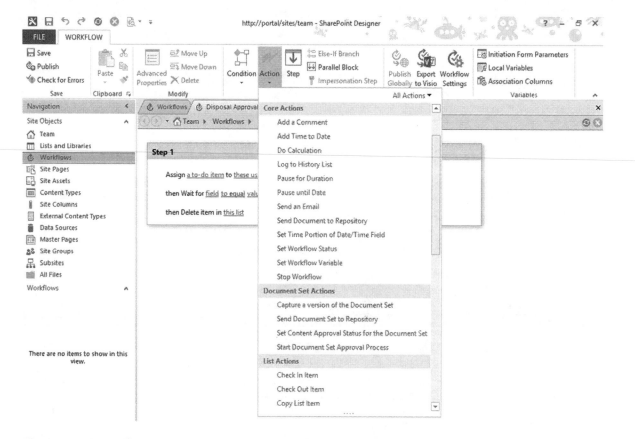

Figure 6-14. *Using SharePoint Designer 2013 to create a SharePoint workflow*

One handy outcome in the compatibility between Visio and SharePoint Designer is the ability to import and export workflows between the two applications. Your business analysts can design a workflow in Visio in the same manner that they are used to working with process models, and then your SharePoint administrator can import the Visio diagram into SharePoint Designer 2013 to finalize any workflow details and publish the workflow to a SharePoint site. Figure 6-15 shows the Workflows ribbon in SharePoint Designer 2013, which includes the button to import from Visio.

Figure 6-15. *The SharePoint Designer 2013 Workflows ribbon*

■ **Note**   Please see Chapter 8, where I step through the process of creating a workflow using SharePoint Designer 2013.

Optimizing Databases with Remote BLOB Storage

I noted earlier in this book how important it is to use multiple content databases to segregate segments of your corpus of site content and spread its load over several smaller databases rather than one massive content database. Multiple content databases addresses the physical organization of content at the underlying storage layer, but you can manage this one step further by organizing how SQL physically stores the BLOB content within a database.

By default, SQL Server stores BLOB content directly in a database table with all the other content. In most cases, this performs very well, particularly for small strings of text or numbers. However, when you add large BLOBs of content, such as with the large files users might upload to their SharePoint site, the database performance can begin to degrade. The large BLOBs of content can affect how well SQL performs with querying other content or managing table indices. One option to avoid the performance challenges with storing many large BLOBs of content in a database table is to enable remote BLOB storage.

Remote BLOB storage (RBS) offers the capability to store BLOBs such as documents and pictures as an individual file on the database server's file system. SQL Server manages storing and retrieving the files, and it includes the files as part of any backup job it runs on a database. Configuring remote BLOB storage is a multistep and somewhat convoluted process.

To configure remote BLOB storage, first you need to enable file stream access on your SQL Server instance. To do so, open SQL Server Management Studio and execute the following SQL statement.

```
EXEC sp_configure filestream_access_level, 2
RECONFIGURE
```

Open SQL Server Configuration Manager, click the SQL Server Services node, right-click the SQL Server instance in the main panel, and check Properties on the context menu. Click the FILESTREAM tab and ensure the file stream access options are checked as shown in Figure 6-16. Click OK to close the properties window, and then restart the SQL Service.

Figure 6-16. *The FILESTREAM tab in the SQL Server instance properties window*

Now return to SQL Server Management Studio and execute the following SQL statements for each content database. First, this ensures that there is a master encryption key (you should substitute your own password for the key generation for the one in my example). Then, it adds a file group for the remote BLOB storage before adding the remote BLOB storage file (directory) to the file group.

```
use [ContentDb]
if not exists
 (select * from sys.symmetric_keys where name = N'##MS_DatabaseMasterKey##')
   create master key encryption by password = N'[PASSWORD !2#4]'
if not exists
 (select groupname from sysfilegroups where groupname=N'RBSFilestreamProvider')
   alter database [ContentDb] add filegroup RBSFilestreamProvider contains filestream
alter database [ContentDb] add file (name = RBSFilestreamFile, filename =
   'c:\Blobstore') to filegroup RBSFilestreamProvider
```

■ **Note** Download the SQL Server 2012 RBS client and install it on each SharePoint server. The RBS client is included with in the Microsoft SQL Server 2012 Feature Pack at

http://www.microsoft.com/en-ca/download/details.aspx?id=29065.

Once you have installed the RBS client on each SharePoint server, you can execute the following PowerShell command to configure SharePoint to enable RBS for a web application.

```
$webApp = Get-SPWebApplication -Identity <Web Application>
$db = Get-SPContentDatabase -WebApplication $webApp
$rbss = $db.RemoteBlobStorageSettings
$rbss.Installed()
# $rbss.Installed() should return true. If False, you haven't installed the RBS client
$rbss.Enable()
$rbss.SetActiveProviderName($rbss.GetProviderNames()[0])
#MinimumBlobStorageSize is in bytes (1048576 = 1MB,
# 2097152 = 2MB, 3145728 = 3MB)
$rbss.MinimumBlobStorageSize = 2097152
```

Notice in the final PowerShell command that I set the `MinimumBlobStorageSize` property. This is important because the remote BLOB storage performs best for larger file sizes. Smaller files generally still perform better by storing the BLOB in the SQL table rather than remotely. I find setting a threshold of 2MB is where SQL performs best, with files larger than 2MB stored and managed in the remote BLOB storage, and files smaller than 2MB stored directly in the table. The ability to set this threshold offers you the best of both storage performance levels.

■ **Note**   For more information on configuring RBS for SharePoint, please see the TechNet article at
http://technet.microsoft.com/ee748631.

Wrapping Up

You implement your content's core information architecture through content types, which offer a means to group information and policies about a particular kind of content and then ensure users apply the information and policies consistently to each piece of content classified with a particular content type. A content type groups metadata fields for collecting information about a piece of content, as well as other policies, such as content retention policies. You create content types in a site's content type library and you can associate the content type with a container through the list or library settings. Content types can include workflows to process the content or manage state information, such as its approval status. You can centralize the management of content types by configuring a content type hub, which then replicates the content types across site collections.

Content types can relate to a number of different kinds of content, from streams of text to Microsoft Word or Excel files, and even to web pages on a portal. Publishing web pages to a portal offers a special form of transitory content because it typically involves communicating articles and other units of information with a wider audience. In the next chapter, I shift to focus specifically on publishing web content and the role it plays in your enterprise content management solution.

CHAPTER 7

■ ■ ■

Publishing Your Web Content

The single biggest problem with communication is the illusion that it has taken place.

—George Bernard Shaw

How do you handle content not contained within a file, not in a discrete unit? Not all enterprise content exists within a document; pieces of content can also be strings of text published on a web portal. In this chapter, I provide an overview of web content management (WCM) concepts and I walk you through how to configure WCM in a SharePoint 2013 publishing portal. I also discuss how to model and configure a publishing approval workflow and how to manage the content deployment settings and schedules.

After reading this chapter, you will know how to

- Explain web content management concepts.

- Analyze your web content management requirements.

- List web content management features in SharePoint 2013.

- Create and configure a publishing portal.

- Model and configure a publishing approval workflow.

- Manage content deployment settings and schedules.

Overview of Web Content Management

A popular way to publish content to a large audience is to post an article or a similar type of web page on a web site, such as an intranet portal or a company's public web site—a process known as *web content management*, or WCM. This concept has been around for years, as organizations have maintained internal intranet portals to communicate with their employees, and external public web sites to communicate with customers, investors, and other stakeholders. Companies with products for sale have also maintained e-commerce sites with product catalogues, shopping carts, and credit card processing capabilities.

Over the years, these types of web sites have become both more sophisticated and more feature-rich. This has been partly enabled by the enhancements and technological advances in the underlying web technology and its supporting programming languages. It has also been fueled by the organization's desire for competitive advantage through leveraging the technology along with custom application development, driven by creative ideas and solutions.

At its essence, web content management has always involved publishing a web page to a web server. Some web sites still post individual pages manually by copying an HTML file to the site's directory on the server. Other sites include a system-managed or data-driven way to publish pages to the web server, especially with modern web applications and large sites. In either case, the process is the same: someone authors the content and then the content is published to the web server where users can access and consume the content. Figure 7-1 illustrates the process of web content publishing.

Figure 7-1. *Web content publishing*

Whether done manually or through a system process, this is the essence of web content publishing. Not too long ago, it used to be so common for people to manually manage their sites and all its pages. So much so that I would often see sales and marketing material promoting web content management systems with concepts such as the ability to standardize page layouts and the publishing process, all with minimizing IT involvement while removing the need for specialized web designer skills to post content. This exciting transformation empowered regular users to manage web content for their own sites. As a testament to how quickly technological advances become commonplace, now rarely do I hear these benefits stressed.

Nevertheless, these end-user productivity and empowerment features are still beneficial, and they form the basis of any quality web content management system. Organizations have leveraged and built on each other's ideas, ultimately evolving WCM into an industry with mature software products providing a platform for standardizing and automating many of the functions in a web content management solution.

Microsoft developed SharePoint 2013 to provide one of those platforms. As I mentioned in Chapter 2, one of its core capabilities is web content management. The product team solidified and matured this capability back in SharePoint 2007 when Microsoft retired Microsoft Content Management Server (MCMS 2002) and consolidated its capabilities within SharePoint, and the product team has continued to enhance this capability with each major release.

The tool exposes these page-editing features with a rich user experience, one consistent with the Microsoft Word text editing experiencing, including a ribbon with a range of formatting options. It also enables end users to select from a range of different page layouts available to manage the format and design of the overall page by simply selecting options in a drop-down menu.

SharePoint leverages its WCM capability to support a variety of features, including article and portal pages, welcome pages, and wiki pages. It also includes, among other WCM features, content deployment capabilities, which copy and deploy content from a draft state in an authoring environment to a published state in a production environment. Figure 7-2 illustrates a typical content deployment process involved in a SharePoint WCM solution.

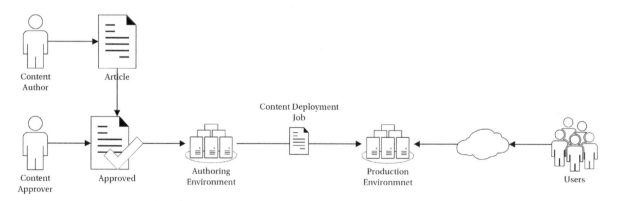

Figure 7-2. *SharePoint content deployment publishing*

Content deployment is useful because it separates the domains of content authoring from content consumption. Users who consume published content access read-only pages, while content authors collaborate on pages in a read-write site. This separation enables you to focus each environment on a variety of options that are specific to the content authoring and consuming experiences, including:

- Targeting high-performing hardware for the published content and its larger number of users.

- Processing a publishing workflow with steps such as editing reviews and approvals.

- Testing and validating content prior to making it available to a wider audience.

- Scheduling the release of published content.

- Managing content translation processes for each locale site with alternate languages.

- Segregating security for the content authors and draft content from the published content.

This last point on security is particularly interesting, especially if you have two different environments for your draft and published content. You can lock down your environment with read-only published content, limiting privileged access and adding an extra layer to defend against potential attacks since the farm would be a read-only copy of content authored elsewhere—an especially valuable aspect for public internet-facing web sites. Your authoring environment then can be behind firewalls in a more controlled and secured area of your network.

I also like having the ability to schedule the publishing of an article or web page. This alleviates the need to remember and make someone available to manually publish a page at a desired time. Many pages will be relevant right away, and so you will not have a need to schedule them because you are publishing them as soon as the page is ready. For those other pages, such as organizational announcements that you want to prepare ahead of time but schedule for release at a particular time in the future, then you can schedule a time to publish them as part of the content deployment process.

Another characteristic of web content management is the automatic management of navigational elements and the aggregation of content. Previously, a webmaster would have had to manage and update these links manually. Then eventually software began to offer easier or more productive ways to approach this, such as using templates or reusable widgets shared across several pages. As web sites became more and more data-driven, sites could also keep track of structures and relationships between pages, enabling pages to query this data to automatically show navigational menu items, all without requiring a webmaster to manually maintain a list of navigation items.

Although WCM is nothing new, it has grown increasingly sophisticated in its capability, particularly as the management of web content has become less and less centralized with users directly creating, editing, and publishing their own content. Despite the ease of content authoring, web content can and does still contain units of information that are just as relevant to archival, legal, and regulatory compliance requirements as the documents I discussed in previous chapters. You can organize and manage the different types of pages and their life cycle by treating them as yet additional kinds of content, managed through SharePoint content types.

■ **Note**   Please see Chapter 6, where I discuss content types in more detail.

Because you treat web content no different than any other piece of content in your enterprise content management solution, I am not going to repeat the details of those concepts I discussed in the previous chapters. It is just another unit of information that you can associate metadata, workflows, retention policies, and the like as part of your organization's content life cycle. This is an important point and I am stressing it here because web content such as simple department article pages or *ad hoc* wiki pages are easy to overlook when analyzing an enterprise's content life cycle.

■ **Important**   WCM is an aspect within ECM that you need to include in your enterprise content management solution.

Web content management is a concept, the essence of which is making content available for users to consume through a device over the network. A web content management system automates and simplifies a lot of those management activities while enhancing the experience for end users to author and publish their own content. As I already mentioned, a core capability in SharePoint is a web content management system, but before I cover its features in more detail, I want to look at how to analyze your WCM requirements.

Analyzing Your WCM Requirements

There are certain considerations to designing any web site, such as how to structure it, how to lay out the pages, what color palette and fonts to use, and the like. These are useful and worthwhile activities for SharePoint portals as well, and I have already discussed how to plan your site structure back in Chapter 4. Your portal site structure is just an extension of the content containers—the sites, lists, and libraries—to also consider the different pages that will display content and communicate information. I drive my structure and other design decisions based on my purpose for the portal site and the user experience that will support that purpose.

This is not a book on web design, so I will leave that to one of the many other books on the topic. However, a couple design elements are important to enterprise content management. In particular, I am thinking of the different web parts that you may include on a page to aggregate content, providing recommendations for related content or other content discovery scenarios. I discuss content discovery more in Part III, but for now, it is important to consider site pages for their content as well as the different page elements that you can add to the user experience, creating a sort of mash-up with feeds and other assets such as images and video.

■ **Note** For more commentary on web site design considerations through examples of bad design, you may enjoy Vincent Flanders' Web Pages That Suck blog at www.webpagesthatsuck.com.

Other elements that you can add to pages include reusable or catalog content. This allows you to use metadata not just for organizing the structure, but also for rendering the content itself. You can implement this through the SharePoint 2013 feature, *cross-site collection publishing*. I discuss this feature more toward the end of the chapter where I note how to configure catalogs and I share examples of web applications that you can create using cross-site collection publishing.

The elements on the pages and their relationship with each other represent the user experience in your design. For web content management applications, this represents a major portion of your design requirements. As you conduct your analysis, you can begin to identify different page elements in your requirements along with details about the source of the content. As I collect this information, I like to create diagrams or mockups to get a general sense of how a page functions and how the different elements interact with each other.

One tool that I find particularly useful for designing layouts of pages is Balsamiq Mockups. Without much designer investment, it offers a quick and visual way to lay out page elements, allowing you to experiment with different designs and user experiences with a low-cost and low-fidelity mockup. Not only can it communicate the essence of a given design experience on a page, but it can also link pages together to mockup the user experience between pages as well.

You can use Balsamiq Mockups or a similar tool to start laying out ideas and to verify design assumptions early on in the process, when making changes is cheap and even encouraged to fine tune and reveal the best design. I use this mockup tool for any user experience I am designing for an application, and especially for portal applications. Figure 7-3 shows an example of a SharePoint portal page mockup with video page elements. As you can see, I have the gist of the page mocked up where users can get the sense for what will be on the page and how it works together. It is not an exact representation, and visually, it looks quite a bit different from a SharePoint page; nevertheless, I bet it looks familiar to you as a SharePoint page. It has enough of the elements there to communicate the design and gather feedback without over-investing in the design activity.

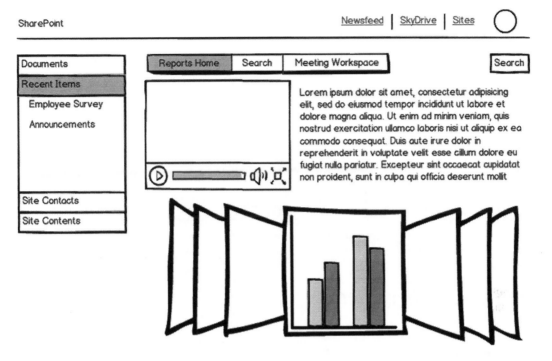

Figure 7-3. *An example of Balsamiq Mockups*

■ **Note**   To learn more about Balsamiq Mockups, please see their web site at `www.balsamiq.com`.

I like to start with analyzing any existing sites and portals. This review gives me a sense for how my clients have organized their portals in the past and the types of content they publish there. I keep an eye out for both things that have worked well and things that have been more problematic. This can reveal clues about what the new portal should continue to build upon and what it should improve. Some questions I like to ask during this review and analysis include

- What are the different areas within the portal?

- What types of pages are in those areas?

- What kinds of content do those pages contain?

- Who authors and publishes content?

- Are approvals required, and if so, who approves content?

- Is content regularly updated?

- What areas are the most popular?

From an enterprise content management perspective, you will also need to consider how to classify the web content if a classification system does not already exist. A classification system includes metadata from your enterprise taxonomy and keyword metadata in a folksonomy, where appropriate. This can help you design how to organize your pages in a similar fashion as I discussed for documents, but it can also help with designing your web content's life cycle.

As you analyze the content life cycle for portal pages, you need to identify their retention and disposition requirements. You may have completed this as part of the content inventory I discussed in Chapter 3, but if not, it is important to start grouping web and article pages into common content types just as you would for other kinds of content. This allows you to generalize and manage metadata, workflows, and other policies for groups of content rather than for individual pages.

■ **Note**   For more on designing content types, please see Chapter 4.

Ultimately, as with any application, you want to answer the question of what purpose does it serves. What is the main goal the portal seeks to achieve? What is its vision? Shaping your requirements around a higher-level purpose will steer your designs toward delivering the value that relates to the purpose.

Rather than looking at product features and finding ways to enable them, I always like to start with requirements and make feature and implementation decisions from them. With a general idea about the web content management application's purpose and design structures, you can begin to consider what aspects and features in SharePoint can support your portal. Let's shift now to look at those WCM-specific features in SharePoint.

SharePoint 2013 WCM Features

Along with all of its collaboration features, SharePoint 2013 also includes a rich feature set for publishing web content, whether for internal intranets or for public web sites. Web content can include rich media assets, such as video or images, the same as collaborative content. It also includes text-based content, which has traditionally made up the bulk of a web site in the form of HTML pages. SharePoint can store and host entire HTML pages in a site, but much more commonly, it stores the text for the page's body content and it merges the text with template-like files to render the resulting page output.

By separating these into multiple files, SharePoint separates the content from the layout and design. The page itself includes the body content and any other header or metadata information. SharePoint then merges the page content with a page layout, which specifies the layout on the page for content and any web parts. SharePoint also merges an ASP.NET master page, which specifies the overall page structure. Figure 7-4 illustrates the relationship of these page elements in rendering a publishing page.

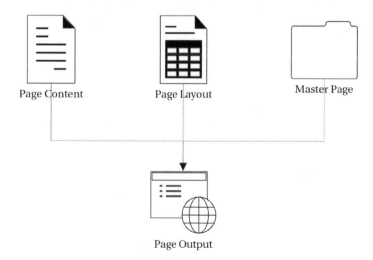

Page Content   Page Layout   Master Page

Page Output

Figure 7-4. *Elements involved in rendering publishing pages*

Page rendering is the core publishing feature in SharePoint. Indeed, posting pages with web content on the network for users to access and consume is the essence of web content management, as I have mentioned. But SharePoint does not stop there, as it also includes a bunch of additional features to enhance the user experience, including:

- **Navigation:** A global navigation that can infer the navigation nodes from the site structure or a site administrator can customize the menu items through the site settings. You can also configure managed navigation for a site, which associates a site's navigation nodes with a managed term set and allows you to manage navigation structures from a centralized location.

- **Pages library:** A site library the portal site uses to store and manage web pages and their content life cycle.

- **Site columns and content types:** Special site columns are added to support publishing features, such as Page Content, Scheduling Start Date, and Scheduling End Date. Special content types are added to support creating publishing content, such as Page Layout, Article Page, and Wiki Page.

- **Design Manager and design packages:** This enables designing and editing custom design assets in HTML and then having SharePoint convert them into SharePoint resources. The design manager provides an interface for managing all aspects of branding your site. Figure 7-5 shows the Design Manager option to select a preconfigured look.

Portal

Site Settings › Change the look

Current

Orange

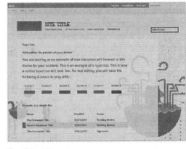

Sea Monster

Figure 7-5. *Design Manager preconfigured looks*

- **Template files:** Master pages, page layouts, and display templates all allow you to customize the overall behavior and appearance for the site. These elements represent the core of the implementation details for your site branding assets. Figure 7-6 shows the ability to manage master pages through the design manager.

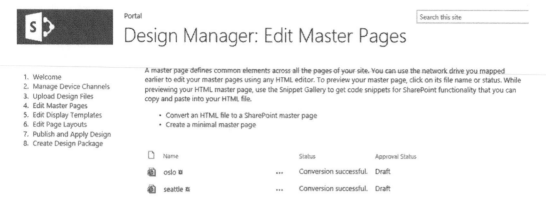

Figure 7-6. *Editing master pages through the Design Manager*

- **Device channels:** This allows you to target rendering a particular user experience for different devices (such as iPhone, Android, or Windows Phone) or to groups of devices (such as all smartphones).

■ **Note** For more information on device channels, please see the MSDN article at `http://msdn.microsoft.com/jj862343`.

- **Publishing web parts:** This includes web pages to support the display of publishing-related data and portal-related user experiences, such as Content and Structure Reports, Content Search, Content Query, and Taxonomy Refinement Panel web parts.

- **Variations for multilingual sites:** This supports creating multilingual experiences by targeting content to specific audiences on different sites. You can use machine translation to translate page content or another translation service, including human translation processes.

■ **Note** For more information on variations, please see the TechNet article at `http://technet.microsoft.com/ff628966`.

- **Approval workflows and publishing scheduling:** Approval workflows enable you to route content to stakeholders for review and approval before publishing it to the portal. Scheduling functionality allows content authors to create content and schedule its release to the portal for a future date and time.

- **Caching:** The page output cache stores page outputs and frequently accessed content in memory to improve processing performance and load times for pages by reducing the amount of content SharePoint needs to retrieve from the database.

▦ **Note**   For more information on caching and performance in SharePoint, please see the TechNet article at
`http://technet.microsoft.com/ee424404`.

All of these features work together to provide a rich user experience with cohesive WCM publishing capabilities. I wanted to provide you with a highlight of the key WCM features in SharePoint to give you a sense of what is happening in SharePoint publishing sites. Now you are ready to create a publishing portal.

▦ **Note**   For more information on SharePoint 2013 WCM, please see the TechNet article at
`http://technet.microsoft.com/jj635881`.

Creating and Configuring a Publishing Portal

Publishing portals are SharePoint sites with publishing features activated. Activating the necessary publishing features will equip your publishing site with those features I noted in the previous section. The product team has made this easy for you by offering a few site templates on the Create Site Collection page, as shown in Figure 7-7. You can create your publishing portal with one of these templates and SharePoint will activate the required publishing features for you.

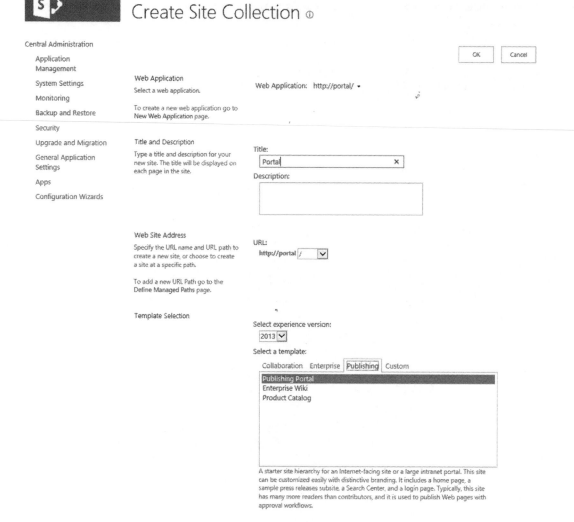

Figure 7-7. The create site collection page with the Publishing template tab highlighed

The three built-in templates for publishing sites are:

- **Publishing Portal:** A portal site with the SharePoint publishing features activated and an approval workflow enabled. You can use this site collection as a starter portal and then add custom branding to customize the look and feel of this site.

- **Enterprise Wiki:** A wiki site with easy content editing and co-authoring to capture and publish knowledgebase articles.

- **Product Catalog:** A site with list or library catalog data to share for cross-site collection publishing and administrative pages for managing faceted navigation for catalog items.

The Publishing Portal template provisions a general publishing site. Figure 7-8 shows an example of the default welcome page for a site created based on this template. This welcome page is meant to guide you through setting up your publishing portal with links to the most common tasks. After you create and configure a site based on this template, you should edit this page's content to make it more appropriate for end users.

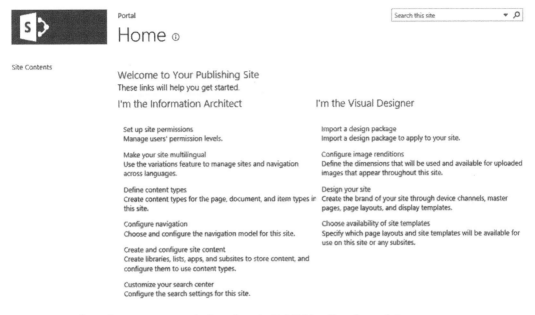

Figure 7-8. *The welcome page on a site based on the Publishing Portal template*

Of course, you do not have to start with any of these templates in order to create a portal site. As I mentioned earlier, every site is merely a team site with additional features activated, and a portal site is no different. You can create a portal site out of a default team site template by activating the following publishing features:

- SharePoint Server Publishing Infrastructure (site collection feature)

- SharePoint Server Publishing (site feature)

After those features are activated, either manually on a regular site or as part of a site provisioned based on one of the publishing templates, then you can begin to publish portal pages. As I mentioned, one element involved in rendering a portal page is a page layout. You can select the page layout from the ribbon while editing the page, as shown in Figure 7-9.

SharePoint
Newsfeed SkyDrive Sites
Steve Goodyear
BROWSE PAGE PUBLISH FORMAT TEXT INSERT
SHARE FOLLOW SAVE
Save New Check In Edit
Edit Properties
Page URLs
Page History
Page Permissions
Delete Page
Manage
E-mail a Link
Alert Me
Popularity Trends
Share & Track
Preview
Page Layout
Make Homepage
Incoming Links
Draft Check
Library Settings
Library Permissions
View All Pages
Tags & Notes
Article Page
Body only
Image on left
Image on right
Summary links
Catalog-Item Reuse
Blank Catalog Item
Catalog Item Image on Left
Site Contents
Checked out to you Only you can see your recent
Title
About
Page Image
Click here to insert a picture from SharePoint.
Image Caption
Click here to add new content
Byline

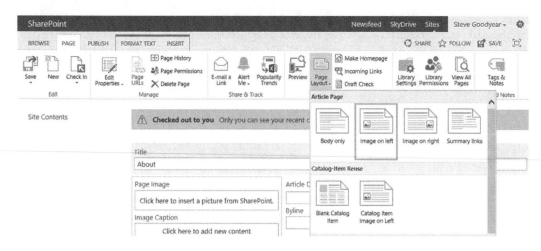

Figure 7-9. *Editing a publishing page and selecting a Page Layout*

You can also edit the metadata to include in a publishing page's HTML head section. Click the Edit SEO Properties option in the Edit Properties menu on publishing tab of the ribbon to open the SEO Properties page as shown in Figure 7-10.

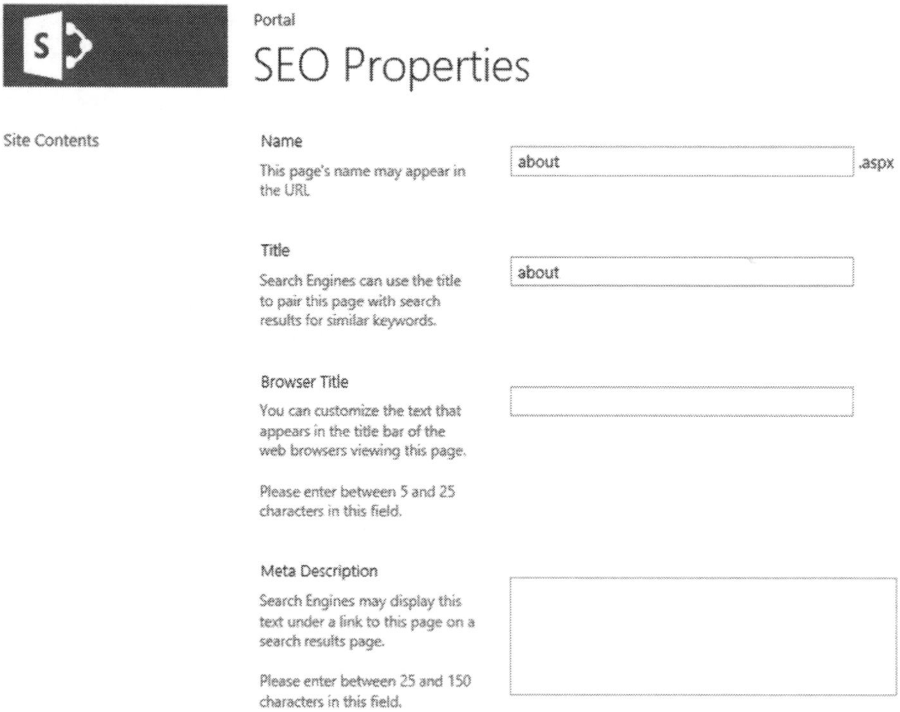

Portal
SEO Properties
Site Contents
Name
This page's name may appear in the URL
about
.aspx
Title
Search Engines can use the title to pair this page with search results for similar keywords.
about
Browser Title
You can customize the text that appears in the title bar of the web browsers viewing this page.
Please enter between 5 and 25 characters in this field.
Meta Description
Search Engines may display this text under a link to this page on a search results page.
Please enter between 25 and 150 characters in this field.

Figure 7-10. *The SEO Properties page for a publishing page*

Publishing pages have several other configuration options available on the ribbon that I will leave for you to explore and experiment with. They can help you enhance or fine-tune the publishing experience for your portal, but one in particular is especially useful for supporting publishing processes: the Publishing Approval workflow.

Configuring a Publishing Approval Workflow

I first mentioned SharePoint workflows back in Chapter 2, and they are certainly common in publishing portals. The most common workflow requirement for publishing portals is approval workflows, so much so that the product team included a built-in Publishing Approval workflow to meet this requirement.

Publishing workflows can grow to be quite complex, depending on your publishing process and other needs. For example, a publishing process might include a series of editorial and copyediting reviews before an article is ready for approval and publishing. You could create a workflow or edit an existing workflow template using SharePoint Designer 2013 to include these additional steps in the workflow.

To illustrate the workflow capabilities and configuration options, I will walk you through the steps for the default Publishing Approval workflow in SharePoint. Although this is a basic workflow template, it does handle the vast majority of approval requirements for publishing sites, particularly for those new publishing sites that have not had any workflow capabilities in the past. In only a few steps, I will walk you through how to configure an approval workflow to handle the process illustrated in Figure 7-11.

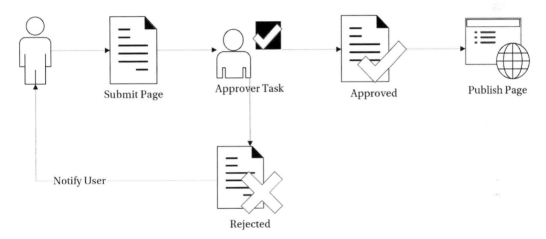

Figure 7-11. *A publishing approval workflow modal*

To add a publishing approval workflow to your publishing site, follow these steps:

1. Activate the Publishing Approval Workflow site collection feature.

2. Navigate to the Pages library settings page.

3. Click Version Settings and select the option to require content approval. Click OK.

4. Click Workflow Settings and then click Add A Workflow.

5. In the Workflow section, select the Publishing Approval workflow template, as highlighted in Figure 7-12.

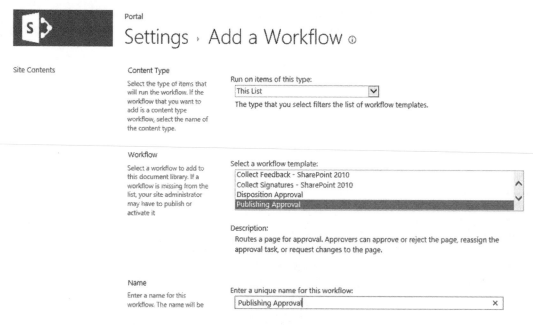

Portal

Settings › Add a Workflow ⓘ

Site Contents

Content Type

Select the type of items that
will run the workflow. If the
workflow that you want to
add is a content type
workflow, select the name of
the content type.

Run on items of this type:

| This List ▾ |

The type that you select filters the list of workflow templates.

Workflow

Select a workflow to add to
this document library. If a
workflow is missing from the
list, your site administrator
may have to publish or
activate it

Select a workflow template:

| Collect Feedback - SharePoint 2010 |
| Collect Signatures - SharePoint 2010 |
| Disposition Approval |
| Publishing Approval |

Description:

Routes a page for approval. Approvers can approve or reject the page, reassign the
approval task, or request changes to the page.

Name

Enter a name for this
workflow. The name will be

Enter a unique name for this workflow:

| Publishing Approval | ✕ |

Figure 7-12. *The Add A Workflow page with the Publishing Approval workflow selected*

6. In the Start Options section, check to start the workflow to approve publishing a major
version. Click Next.

7. Enter the Approvers for the workflow by entering a user or a SharePoint group to the
Assign To field, as shown in Figure 7-13.

Portal

Settings › Change a Workflow › Publishing Approval

Approvers	**Assign To**		Order
	Approvers	👤 🗐	All at once (parallel) ▾
	☑ Add a new stage		
	Enter the names of the people to whom the workflow will assign tasks, and choose the order in which those tasks are assigned. Separate them with semicolons. You can also add stages to assign tasks to more people in different orders.		
Expand Groups	☐ For each group entered, assign a task to every individual member and to each group that it contains.		
Request	Please review and approve or reject this page for publishing.		
	This message will be sent to the people assigned tasks.		
Due Date for All Tasks			📅
	The date by which all tasks are due.		
Duration Per Task	5		
	The amount of time until a task is due. Choose the units by using the Duration Units.		
Duration Units	Day(s)		▾
	Define the units of time used by the Duration Per Task.		

Figure 7-13. *The workflow details page for the Publishing Approval workflow*

8. Configure the other fields as desired and check the option to Enable Content Approval. Click Save.

When authors create a new portal page and submit it for approval, they will see a status on the page similar to Figure 7-14.

Figure 7-14. *A publishing page waiting for approval*

The workflow will create a task for the approvers to review and approve or reject the submitted page. Figure 7-15 shows the task details for an approver to review. The task links to the page itself for the approver to review, and it includes a place for the approver to add additional comments. Approvers have the option to approve or reject the page right from the task details screen, and they can also request changes to the submitter or reassign the task, all as part of the Publishing Approval workflow.

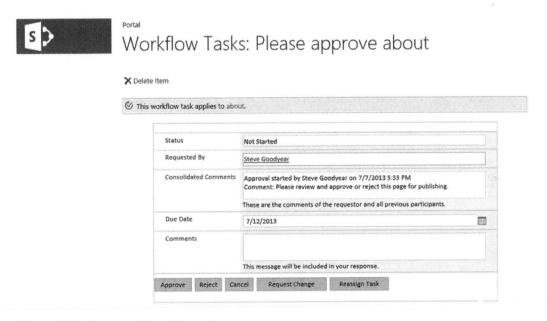

Figure 7-15. *An approval workflow task*

Workflows enable you to automate processes involved with publishing content to a portal site. However, in some cases you may want to author content in an isolated site collection with limited access and then publish the content to another site collection for general access. SharePoint manages this scenario through a feature referred to as *content deployment*.

Managing Content Deployment Settings

You use content deployment to deploy content from one site collection to another site collection. This deploys a *copy* of all the content selected in the source site collection to the destination site collection, and optionally a copy of any security settings. The source and destination site collections can be in the same farm or in different farms.

Two key concepts for configuring SharePoint content deployment are paths and jobs:

- **Paths:** A content deployment path defines the relationship between a source and destination site collection. You need to create a path first, and then you can associate a job with the path to schedule the content deployment.

- **Jobs:** A job defines the specific content in the source site collection that you wish to deploy to the destination site collection. It also includes the content deployment schedule settings.

To enable and configure content deployment for a site collection, follow these steps:

1. Activate the Content Deployment Source Feature site collection feature on the source site collection where you want to deploy content from.

2. Navigate to the SharePoint Central Administration site on the *destination* farm and click the General Application Settings section link.

3. Click the Content Deployment Settings link.

4. Select the option to accept incoming content deployment jobs. Click OK.

5. Navigate to the SharePoint Central Administration site on the *source* farm and click the General Application Settings section link.

6. Click the Configure Content Deployment Paths And Jobs link.

7. Click New Path to navigate to the Create Content Deployment Path page shown in Figure 7-16.

Figure 7-16. The Create Content Deployment Path page

8. Enter a name for the path and select the source web application and site collection.

9. Type the URL of the *destination* SharePoint Central Administration site. This can be for the same farm or for a different farm. Click Connect.

10. Select the destination web application and site collection. Click OK.

■ **Important**   The source and destination site collections must exist in different content databases.

---

11. On the Manage Content Deployment Paths And Jobs page, click New Job.

12. Enter a name for the job and select the relevant path. Check the option to run the job on a schedule and enter the desired schedule.

13. Click OK to return to the Managed Content Deployment Paths And Jobs page, where you should see the newly created path and job listed similar to Figure 7-17.

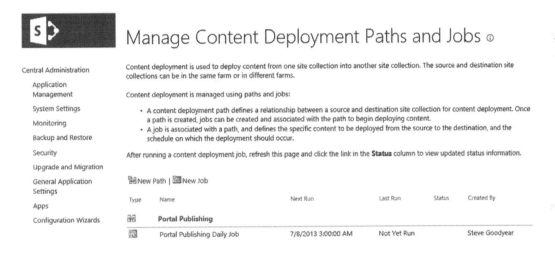

Figure 7-17.   *The Manage Content Deployment Paths And Jobs page*

Content deployment takes a copy of the content and deploys it to another site, which is great in many publishing scenarios, but in some cases you just want to reuse content on different sites. SharePoint enables content reuse through the cross-site collection publishing.

Configuring Cross-Site Collection Publishing

The cross-site collection publishing feature provides you with the ability to use one or more authoring site collections to author and store content that one or more publishing site collections can then display the content. Where authoring site collections are responsible for the content itself, publishing site collections are responsible for the UI and site design to display the content.

Cross site-collection publishing works through the SharePoint search service. The search crawler will crawl the content in the authoring site collection and include it in the search index. Once search indexes the authoring site collection content, then it is available for the publishing site collection to query and display the content in a web part on its page. Figure 7-18 illustrates the relationship of content in cross-site publishing using two separate SharePoint farms (although they could be two different site collections in the same farm).

Figure 7-18. *Cross-site collection publishing*

Authoring and publishing site collections work well with managed navigation. Term sets you use for tagging content in an authoring site can also be pinned to the navigation term set used by the publishing site. With this setup, you can display relevant content based on the navigation node a user selects. This adds to the dynamic and data-driven aspects of your published site and is one of the primary uses of the managed navigation feature in SharePoint 2013. Cross-site collection publishing benefits to your portal site designs by:

- Providing a range of site and information architecture options.

- Separating content authoring from branding and rendering.

- Allowing for content reuse across user experiences.

- Sharing content across site collections, web applications, and farms.

You can author content in one environment and then create a data-driven publishing site to display the content using metadata filters and managed navigation. The following lists some possible scenarios and applications for using cross-site collection publishing:

- Product catalogs to show product information based on metadata

- Job catalogs to show details for available job postings

- Contact catalogs to show individual contact details

- Policies and procedures catalogs to show policy articles

- Knowledgebase catalogs to show knowledgebase articles

- News and announcement catalogs to show news articles

- Case study catalogs to show case study articles

- Location catalogs to show building and office information

By sharing specific lists and libraries as catalogs, you can then reuse the list items on one or more publishing sites. You can share every list as catalogs, but you cannot share every library as catalogs for cross-site collection publishing. The reason for this is because the feature relies on search to crawl and index text and HTML content, rather than BLOBs. The following lists the specific lists and libraries that you can share as catalogs:

- **Pages library:** A pages library can store any HTML content for reuse in publishing site collections. Storing content in this library also enables you to use the approval workflow for list items.

- **List:** A list stores any type of list item that you want to store in a list rather than a pages library.

- **Asset library:** An asset library can store files such as pictures, audio, and video files that contain content to display on the publishing site. These files are stored in the BLOB cache, not the search index, which means that the publishing site will not display them in the same manner as other content. Publishing site users will also need read access to the asset library.

- **Document library:** A document library can store files such as Word or Excel documents that. Because these files are not HTML content, you treat document libraries in the same manner as asset libraries.

▓ **Note**   Only HTML content is indexed and available in the catalog for publishing sites to query. Non-HTML content such as Word and PDF documents are not stored in the index and must be referenced directly.

Before you can reuse content in a list or library in publishing site collections, you first have to share the list or library for use as a catalog. When you share a list or library as a catalog, you can choose to enable anonymous access to the content, which fields uniquely identify the catalog items, and a managed metadata field to use as a navigation term in the publishing site collection. You must add at least one item to the list or library before you can share it as a catalog.

To enable cross-site collection publishing, you must activate the Cross-Site Collection Publishing and Cross-Farm Site Permissions site collection features. Then you can navigate to the desired list or library settings page and click the Catalog Settings link to navigate to the Catalog Settings page, similar to Figure 7-19.

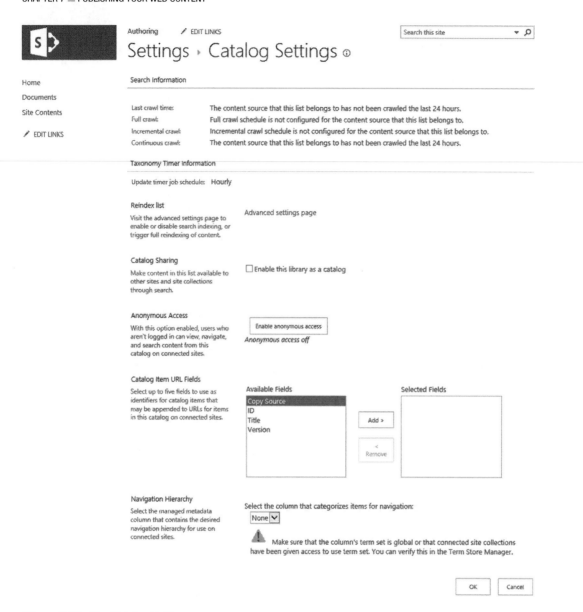

Figure 7-19. *The Catalog Settings page*

Once you have shared the catalog in the authoring site, you can configure a catalog connection in the publishing site collection to consume the catalog. When configuring catalog connections, specify the catalog to use to display content from, the term set used for tagging, and how to construct the category item URLs. You can then display the content using category pages and catalog item pages, which are page layouts used for showing structured catalog content consistently across a site. You can display the catalog content in several ways, including:

- Adding the Catalog-Item Reuse web part to a page and then configuring the web part properties with a custom search query.

- Adding a publishing page using one of the Catalog-Item Reuse page layouts.

▓ **Note**   For more information on planning for cross-site collection publishing, please see the TechNet article at
http://technet.microsoft.com/jj635883.

Wrapping Up

Web content is a unit of information just like a document is, and as such, you treat it the same as any other piece of content when analyzing and designing your enterprise content management solution. Web content management is a subset within the larger scope of enterprise content management, making it important to include in your ECM initiative to prevent any gaps in your content life cycle requirements. In this chapter, I described WCM as the process to author and publish content on an intranet portal or public web site, whether this is an automated or manual process. I then listed the main WCM features in SharePoint 2013 and I provided guidance on planning and configuring a publishing portal. Finally, I discussed specific publishing topics related to approval workflows and deploying content.

Portals contain a significant amount of content beyond the reports and other types of documents that one might typically think of when considering enterprise content management. Articles and other types of information posted on a portal also participate in your organization's content life cycle, and so they need to be managed with appropriate policies and workflows. Similarly, your organization may contain paper or electronic forms to capture information and support a business process, making these units of information critical to consider and include in your enterprise content management solution. In the next chapter, I focus specifically on designing and managing electronic forms using InfoPath, using which can open new possibilities to replace paper-based forms and processes with an electronic form solution integrated with your ECM platform, SharePoint.

CHAPTER 8

■ ■ ■

Designing Your Electronic Form Processes

Knowledge unqualified is knowledge simply of something learned.

—Plato

How do you manage all the content that is not a document or a simple web page? Organizations contain all types of content, from unstructured content such as documents and web pages, to more structured content. One significant category of more structured content in most organizations is forms and their related processes. In this chapter, I provide guidance on analyzing form requirements and form processes, particularly for your existing paper forms. I also share techniques for designing electronic forms in InfoPath with approval workflows you can deploy for SharePoint to host.

After reading this chapter, you will know how to

- Describe the types of forms and form use within organizations.

- Consider the difference between paper-based forms and electronic forms.

- Model paper forms and form processes to transition to electronic forms.

- Analyze and design electronic forms and workflows.

- Build electronic forms in InfoPath.

- Build an electronic form approval workflow in SharePoint Designer.

Types of Forms in Organizations

I would be hard pressed to name an organization that does not rely on forms of some sort in their business processes. Most business processes seem to rely on some type of data entry, whether the process is for collecting data or for tracking the status of a particular transaction.

For example, one process for onboarding a new employee may include a form to collect the employee's contact information to enter into the payroll system; another process may include a form with a checklist for things such as account creation, merely to track that these activities take place. In the first type, the process exists primarily to collect specific data for entry into an enterprise system. Whereas in the second process, the data entry exists to track and support the process.

You can also have a hybrid of these two: some form fields explicitly collect data while other fields manage conditions for what data the form collects or what processes the form spurs. I find this blended type of form is the most common, but there is a place for the two distinct options as well.

Forms support all sorts of operational processes. This can include manufacturing checklists on a production line; product pick sheets in a distribution warehouse; employee vacation requests or expense reports; customer order sheets; and even job candidate applications. Forms exist in some way whenever there is a transaction or data exchange between two groups—whether between two internal departments or externally with customers or partners.

With forms connected to so many interactions, it should be clear that they represent a major portion of data within an organization, and therefore the reason why they warrant coverage and consideration in your enterprise content management solution. Indeed, these forms are a catalyst to some crucial business decisions and transactions, and as such, you need to consider their entire life cycle as you would for any other piece of enterprise content. Forms are just a different kind of unit of information, and as such they still needs to be managed, retained, and then ultimately disposed.

One of the greatest opportunities I find in most enterprise content management initiatives that I get involved in is with optimizing and automating the forms and any of their related processes. Typically, this involves transitioning from paper forms to digital forms. You can either replace the form itself with a digital form for the users to fill out, managing the form as a digital artifact throughout its entire life cycle. Alternatively, you can continue with the paper form but then scan it to transform it into a digital version after a user has manually filled it out and submitted it.

■ **Note**   Please see Chapter 16, where I discuss document imaging in more detail.

Paper Forms vs. Electronic Forms

Paper forms have been around for a very long time. They have been the standard agent for capturing data or processing a transaction. Electronic forms are relatively new in comparison and they essentially serve the same purpose as paper forms, only they are digital. Because the two are so similar, even near perfect substitutes I dare to say, it is no surprise that a general trend to digitize forms has been ongoing for several years now. Yet despite this trend and its popularity, I am often somewhat surprised to discover just how prevalent paper forms can still be in an organization. The reason for this, however, is that paper forms are still useful—they still serve a purpose.

Imagine using forms in places where it is just not practical to use a computing device, or even where digitizing the form would not add any benefits. I mention this because not everything needs to be transformed into a digital state. Some things are fine to continue as a hard copy, maybe for a given duration until it becomes advantageous to digitize it, or maybe indefinitely. The deciding factors are typically things such as identifying and measuring value that outweighs the costs involved with the transformation. These costs can be implementation costs directly, or the impact costs for the users using the form.

I remember when I was a teen in high school working for a pizza restaurant. Part of my job, in addition to washing dishes and making pizzas, was to answer phones and take orders. Now, we had a computer point-of-sale system to enter the orders in an electronic form, but while we were on the phone with customers taking their order we used a pad of paper order forms.

Using paper forms was to simplify the process, allowing for easy changes with the swipe of a pen. It kept order taking quick and easy, and most importantly, focused on the customer rather than a computer, or so my manager believed. After the call, we would then enter the order in the computer. The user experience with their computer system may have improved dramatically since then, making the paper order forms no longer necessary or as helpful, but at the time, they had a legitimate reason to continue using paper-based forms despite the availability of electronic forms.

Some paper-based forms you might dispose of after their use, while others you might scan and capture as digital copies for archival purposes. Still other forms you might use to initiate and feed into an electronic form's process, much like the ordering process at the pizza restaurant I worked at.

I feel that paper forms are already so established and there is already so much written about them that I do not need to go into detail about their advantages and disadvantages. I just wanted to point out that there are any number of valid reasons to continue using paper forms even though I do not go into detail and instead now shift to focus on electronic forms.

Digital forms offer you the options and capabilities to provide richer user experiences, such as with incorporating sophisticated validation logic for any data-entry. Their digital state means that you can control access over a network, allowing you to store and manage the forms within a central location, and this enables you to track the status of forms and any related workflows. They also offer the possibilities to optimize their storage and retrieval, much like any digital document's storage and retrieval strengths over a physical document, as I discussed in Chapter 4.

▓ **Note**   Please see Chapter 9, where I discuss using enterprise search for content retrieval in more detail.

Modeling Paper Form Processes

A large proportion of the forms and business process workflow engagements that I get involved with focus on replacing a paper-based form with a digital one. I think this is such a common scenario these days that I want to spend some time sharing how I approach these requirements.

I begin with the paper form itself. On the form, I analyze the data it collects and I begin to consider these types of questions:

- What is the form's main purpose or goal?

- Who can initiate a form's process or submit a form?

- Are all the fields still necessary?

- Does the data already exist for any field that the form can query or infer to prepopulate?

- Do different users fill out different parts of the form? Who else is involved?

- Where will the form data be stored?

- What systems or processes rely on the data?

- What type of validation rules apply to a form and its fields?

- Does the form require any special security or auditing?

- How is the form stored and for how long?

- Does the form require any formal approval?

- Are there any requirements around how to capture signatures or the types of signatures?

DIGITAL SIGNATURES IN INFOPATH FORMS

One interesting requirement I often come across relates to form approvals. One popular scenario tracks the form approval in a workflow with a timestamp of who approved them. However, sometimes this is not thorough enough. For example, you might have the requirement to apply a digital signature to a form.

Digital signatures use a signer's certificate to take a hash of the form data and sign the form. Only that user's certificate can generate that hash and any changes to the form data will invalidate the hash. Therefore, digital signatures can provide evidence that a form with its data was signed using a specific and private certificate.

You can configure these digital signature options in the InfoPath Form Options, as shown in the following figure.

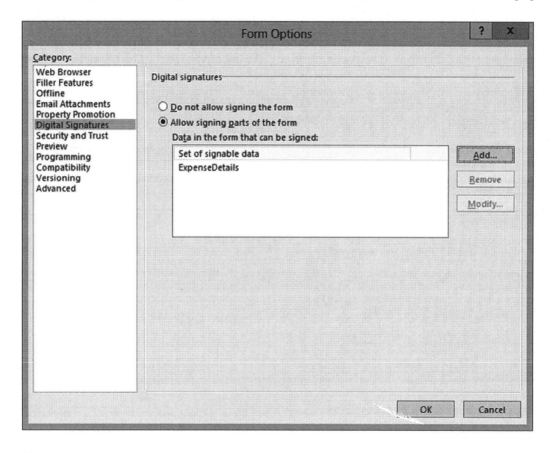

Digital signatures are not always necessary, as a workflow can provide similar assurances by tracking approvals based on a user's credentials and it can track the form's contents. Nonetheless, when you need that extra rigor, the option is available.

The form requirements analysis questions I noted help prod different requirements for an electronic form because they build a complete picture of the form by considering it from different perspectives. With a solid understanding of a form and its purpose, I find that I am in a good position to visualize and model a digital solution.

I start with the forms, and in most cases, a lot of thought has already gone into which questions to ask—or more specifically, which fields to include on the form. I drop any questions that are no longer necessary and I look for ways to prepopulate any fields that can query or infer their data values. For the rest of the form, I generally just copy from the paper form, including details such as the question order and the form layout. Not only are these design decisions already thought through and proven, but they are also what the users are already used to in their experience with the form, making the digital form feel familiar and consistent. Thus, users perceive the electronic forms as a less drastic change from what they are used to using.

■ **Tip**   Make the electronic form's user experience consistent with the paper form's user experience so that users will find the form familiar and easy to use.

Before I finalize the form design, I look at the form from the perspective of the new technology (the digital technology) to consider whether the technology offers any options to improve the user experience with filling out and interacting with the form. Is there anything extra that digital offers over paper to improve the experience for a particular form? This can be things such as showing and hiding sections of a form based on field values that users enter, or even automatically capturing location information from a user's computing device. Digital technology offers a wealth of possibilities like these that paper just cannot offer. I let the desired user experience drive these types of form design improvements.

With a digital rendition of the paper-based form, I then model the business process that the form progresses through. Essentially, this involves tracking all of the different people (roles) who interact with the form to identify what each adds to the form's value-chain and who they hand the form to next.

One thing I watch out for is that with a paper-based form, the form only exists in one physical place at one time (unless, of course, if you photocopy it), so this can make a business process appear to be sequential. Certain tasks may be sequential, but other seemingly sequential tasks may actually be fine to process in parallel—a subtle change that can often dramatically optimize a workflow's productivity since tasks will not have to wait on other tasks unnecessarily.

Let's imagine a simple form and business process to model for an example by taking a simple expense report. The expense report itself contains identifying information for the submitter as well as lines for each expense item. Once submitted, a supervisor approves (or rejects) an expense report, and then someone in payroll issues a reimbursement. Figure 8-1 illustrates this simple expense report example.

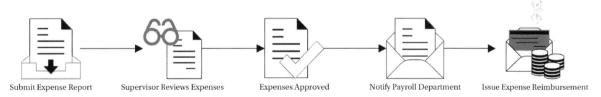

Submit Expense Report   Supervisor Reviews Expenses   Expenses Approved   Notify Payroll Department   Issue Expense Reimbursement

Figure 8-1. *A simple expense report process*

I take these process models to build the actual approver workflow in SharePoint. Using the modeled form, I build an InfoPath form template to also deploy to SharePoint and associate with the workflow. Later in the chapter, I return to discuss how to build electronic forms and approval workflows, but first I want to consider how to analyze and model form processes when you are beginning from scratch, without any existing paper-based forms to analyze and build a model from.

Analyzing and Designing Form Processes

Sometimes, clients want me to help them design an electronic form and a related workflow based on new requirements, rather than based on replacing an existing form and process. I treat the analysis and design process exactly the same as when I am analyzing an existing paper-based form, except I also add steps to determine what fields the form needs to include.

Generally, by going through the form details and its related business process, the fields are often revealed through the analysis. The process—and the details behind the process—lead to information such as what data the form requires at a given step or what values determine different variants in the process.

Overview of InfoPath 2013

Microsoft InfoPath 2013 is a tool for designing sophisticated electronic forms to gather and process information from users. Its entire purpose centers on electronic forms—either providing a tool to design a form template or to fill out and submit a form.

I love InfoPath because it is so focused and specialized on managing forms well. I also love it because of the richness in its form editing user experience and the extensiveness of its form processing functionality. Specifically, I am thinking of these key features built into InfoPath:

- Tight integration with SharePoint, including sharing data fields as SharePoint columns and interacting with SharePoint workflows

- Simplified conditional formatting rules that support complex form designs

- Built in data-entry validation rules and warnings

- Capabilities to include code-behind for custom developed form logic and processing in Microsoft .NET

On this last point, you can programmatically interact with a form, workflow, or external data sources and web services. Although I do not go into detail on this topic in this book, I still felt it was worth mentioning because it opens up a variety of possibilities for custom solutions.

▓ **Note** To learn more about InfoPath 2013, please see the help and resource topics listed on the Microsoft Office support site at http://office.microsoft.com/HA104014266.

When you open InfoPath 2013, you have several options for the type of form you want to create, as shown in Figure 8-2.

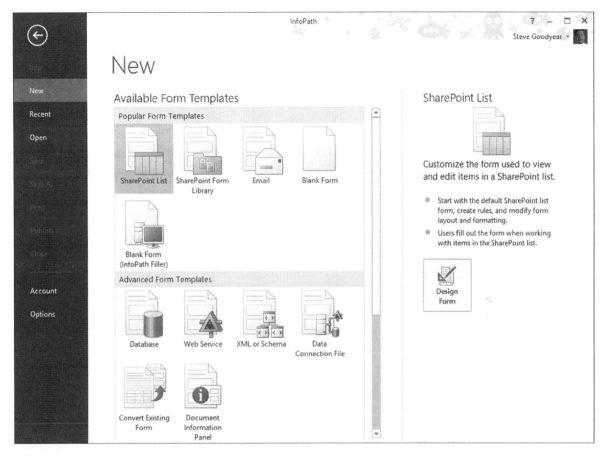

Figure 8-2. *The InfoPath 2013 interface*

InfoPath itself is a simple interface, as shown in Figure 8-3 with a form created using the SharePoint List template. Underneath this interface is an XML editing engine that merges the XSL in a form template with the XML data collected in the form itself, presenting a merged instance with the form structure and data. As you work with InfoPath, remember that it stores data in an XML format and the form template in XSL format, both independent of each other.

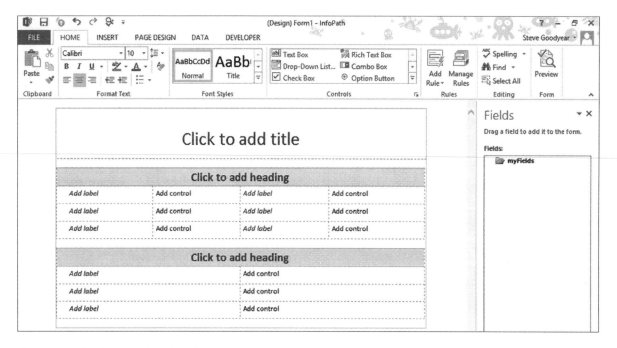

Figure 8-3. *The InfoPath 2013 interface*

The client versions of InfoPath include the form designer and the form filler; the pair separates the design tasks from those related to filling out the form. This separation helps to reduce accidental changes to the form template while providing users with a rich client to use for interacting with forms. There is also a server version of InfoPath called InfoPath Forms Services that renders InfoPath forms as web pages. This allows users who do not have the InfoPath form filler client installed to also fill out SharePoint-hosted forms using their web browser.

I encourage you to explore the tool and all of its possibilities for your electronic forms. Although it sports a simplified interface and the ability to rapidly create electronic forms, it has a lot of functionality and complex processing capabilities. To get you started, I will walk through an example of creating a simple electronic form using InfoPath 2013.

Building Electronic Forms in InfoPath

InfoPath makes the process of building forms easy and seamless. Begin by opening InfoPath 2013 Designer and selecting a template to create a form based on. In this example, I created a form based on the SharePoint List template. You can configure and publish a form by following the steps in this section.

1. Add the relevant fields to the form and rename them to a meaningful name in the field properties window. In this example, I started using the SharePoint List template and added fields related to an expense report, as shown in Figure 8-4.

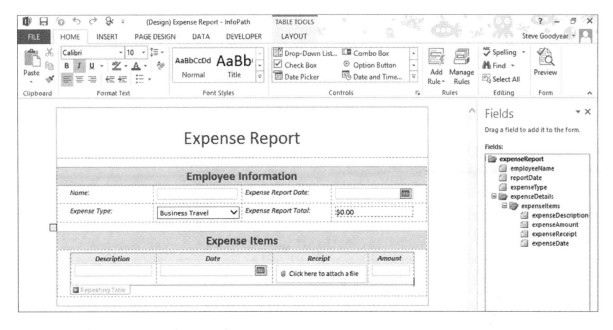

Figure 8-4. *The expense report form template*

2. Add a button.

3. Select the Button Properties menu option form the button's context menu.

4. In the Button Properties window, set the Action to Submit and give the button a label, as shown in Figure 8-5.

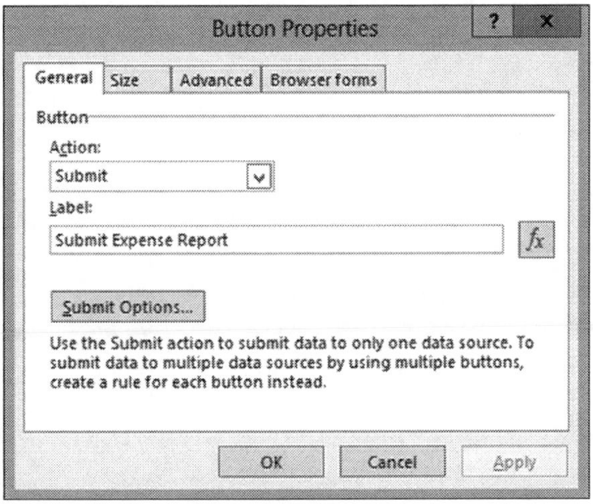

Figure 8-5. *The Button Properties window*

5.   Click Submit Options to open the Submit options window, as shown in Figure 8-6.

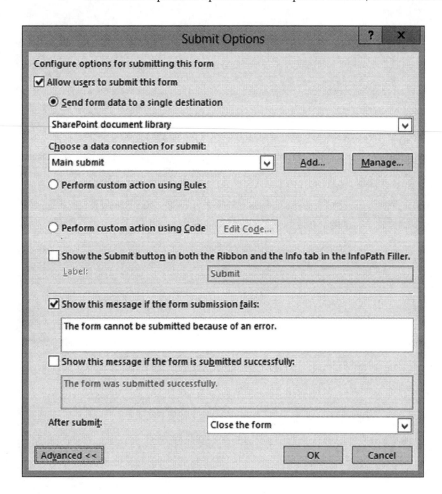

Figure 8-6. *The Submit Options window*

6.   Configure the form submit options by selecting to send the form data to a SharePoint document library.

7.   For the Choose a data connection for submit option, Click the Add button to open the Data Connection Wizard.

8. Enter a document library URL to submit the form to and enter a formula for the file name that ensures forms are submitted to the SharePoint library with unique names, as shown in Figure 8-7.

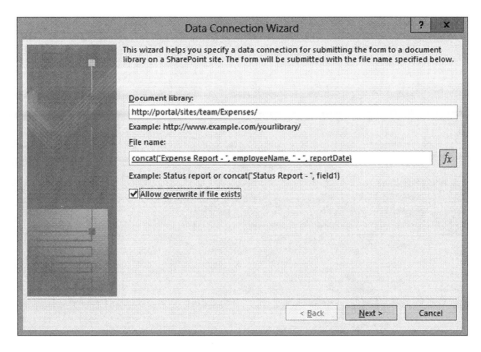

Figure 8-7. *The Data Connection Wizard*

9. Click Next and give the submit connection a name.

10. Click Finish to dismiss the Data Connection Wizard.

11. Click OK to dismiss the Submit Options window.

12. Click OK to dismiss the Button Properties window.

At this point, the form is ready for you to publish it to the SharePoint site. If you desire, you can adjust the submit options and the form options from the InfoPath form Info page, as shown in Figure 8-8.

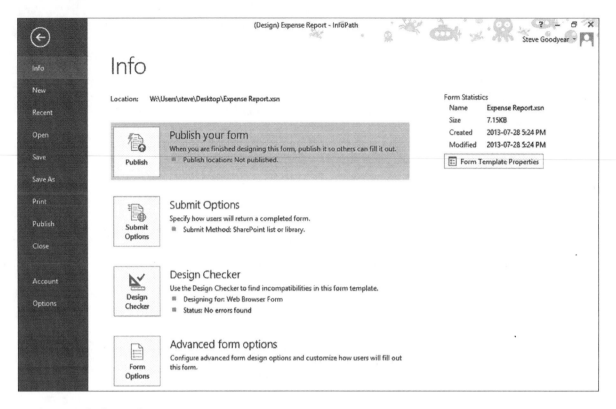

Figure 8-8. *The form info page*

When you are ready to publish, click the Publish your form button and select to publish to a SharePoint library. Enter the URL for the site you wish to publish the form to and click Next. Continue through the wizard setting the appropriate options and finally click Publish.

Once you publish your form successfully, open a browser and navigate to the form library where you published it. Click to create a new form and verify the form opens in the browser. In this example, I clicked to create a new expense report and it opened in the browser as shown in Figure 8-9.

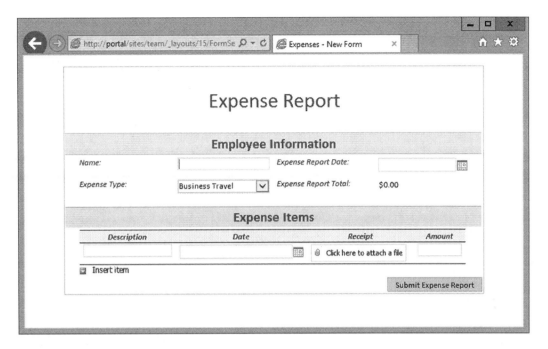

Figure 8-9. *The expense report rendered as a web page*

Confirm that you can fill out and submit the form as expected. Once you are satisfied with the form and how SharePoint processes it, you can release the form for regular users to use in their processes. If you want to associate a workflow to the form to process it after users submit it, then you can also do that at this stage. One tool I use for creating these types of workflows is SharePoint Designer 2013, which I introduce next.

■ **Note**   For more information on developing InfoPath form templates, please see the MSDN site at
http://msdn.microsoft.com/aa945282.

Overview of SharePoint Designer 2013

SharePoint Designer was first introduced as SharePoint Designer 2007. It is the evolution of Microsoft FrontPage 2003, a former web design editor that Microsoft redeveloped and rebranded for the advanced administration and design of a SharePoint site.

You can download and use SharePoint Designer from the Microsoft download site without any licensing costs. Any site administrator or site designer can install the tool to manage advanced aspects of the site, including the site's visual design, forms, and workflows.

■ **Note**   To get SharePoint Designer 2013, please download it from the Microsoft download site at
www.microsoft.com/download/details.aspx?id=35491.

Microsoft developed SharePoint Designer to enable advanced users to rapidly create SharePoint solutions to meet business needs without requiring an extensive custom development effort or specialized web programming skills. The tool enables users to compose no-code solutions for a variety of common scenarios in an easy to use environment.

■ **Tip**   Because SharePoint Designer offers users with advanced site design and management capabilities, it poses the risk of increased support calls if untrained users accidently cause breaking changes in their site and need help to get it functioning properly again. If this is a concern for you, you can disable SharePoint Designer in the general settings for a web application in SharePoint Central Administration.

To open a site in SharePoint Designer, open SharePoint Designer 2013 on your desktop and click the Open Site tile on the Sites tab, as shown in Figure 8-10.

Figure 8-10. *The Open Site tile in SharePoint Designer 2013*

Alternatively, you can open a site by navigating to the site in a browser and clicking the Edit in SharePoint Designer button on the ribbon, as showing in Figure 8-11.

Figure 8-11. *The Edit in SharePoint Designer menu option*

Once you have a site opened in SharePoint Designer, you can manage its different aspects through the tool. For some tasks, the tool will open a browser window and navigate to the relevant site settings page, such as for administering site security. For other tasks, you can accomplish them directly in the tool. To change the design of a page, open the page in SharePoint Designer and then edit its design. Figure 8-12 shows the SharePoint Designer 2013 interface.

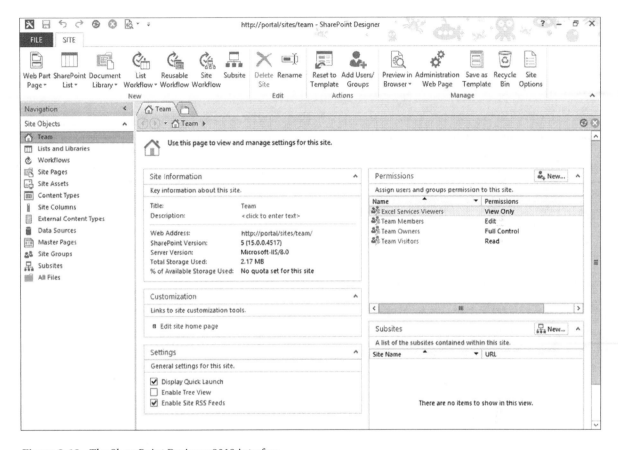

Figure 8-12. *The SharePoint Designer 2013 interface*

The tool exposes several options in its user interface, including managing:

- Lists and libraries
- Workflows
- Site pages and page designs, site assets, and master pages
- Content types and site columns

I will leave the details behind the majority of the features in SharePoint Designer for you to explore and experiment with on your own. However, there is one particularly useful SharePoint Designer feature I want to focus on next: creating and configuring advanced workflows using the tool's built in workflow actions.

■ **Note**   For more information on using SharePoint Designer for developer tasks, please see the MSDN article at http://msdn.microsoft.com/hh850380.

Workflow Actions in SharePoint Designer

Workflow actions consist of a self-contained unit of functionality to execute and process, allowing you add the action in a modular fashion as a step in the overall workflow. When adding an action to a workflow, you can set its variables and associate it with different shared properties in the workflow. This allows you to reuse common functionality in actions for different purposes.

Within a workflow, you model one or more tasks that the workflow needs to process. You can think of these as the steps the workflow needs to complete. For a group of related steps, you can organize them within a workflow stage, which is like a summarizing step containing other steps. Within the steps of a workflow, you configure the actual processes to execute that you require to complete the step. These individual processes within a workflow step are called *actions*.

Workflow actions can consist of actions built into SharePoint Designer as well as custom developed actions or activities that you develop for special purposes. I will refer to those workflow actions that are built into SharePoint Designer as *workflow actions* and to custom developed ones as *workflow activities*.

■ **Note**   For more information on developing custom workflow activities, please see the MSDN article at http://msdn.microsoft.com/ee231574.

You build workflows by adding and configuring a sequence of actions. I find the process is similar to creating rules in Outlook to process e-mail. Figure 8-13 shows the workflow actions menu located in the SharePoint Designer ribbon.

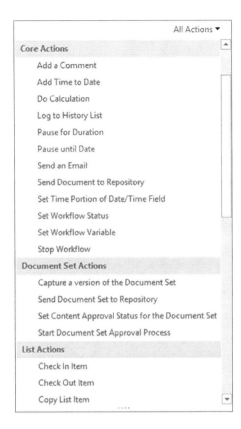

Figure 8-13. *The workflow actions menu in SharePoint Designer*

As you can see, the actions are organized into groups to make it easier for you to build a workflow. These groups are core actions, coordination actions, list actions, project actions, task actions, and utility actions. The following sections list and describe the actions included in each group for workflows you create using a SharePoint 2013 workflow model.

Core Actions

SharePoint Designer groups actions together under *Core Actions* for easy access to the most commonly performed workflow actions. The core actions include:

- *Add a comment*: Allows you to leave a comment in the workflow designer for reference and workflow description purposes.

- *Add time to a date*: Adds a specific time in minutes, hours, days, or months to a date.

- *Build a dictionary*: Builds a dictionary variable of key/value pairs.

- *Call an HTTP web service*: Calls a web service over the network and it returns data returned from the web service in the JSON format.

- *Count items in a dictionary*: Returns a count of the number of items in a dictionary.

- *Do a calculation*: Performs an arithmetic calculation and stores the output value in a variable.

- *Get an item from a dictionary*: Returns a particular item from a dictionary variable.

- *Log to history list*: Writes a message to the workflow history list.

- *Pause for a duration*: Pauses the workflow execution for a specified time interval.

- *Pause until a date*: Pauses the workflow execution until a specified date and time.

- *Send an e-mail*: Sends an e-mail message with a predefined message to a user or group.

- *Set time portion of a Date/Time field*: Creates a timestamp and stores the value in a variable.

- *Set workflow status*: Sets the status of the workflow.

- *Set workflow variable*: Sets a workflow variable to a value.

- *Go to a workflow stage*: Sets the next stage to flow control in the workflow processing.

Coordination Actions

The actions grouped together under *Coordination Actions* relate to invoking a workflow based on the SharePoint 2010 workflow platform. The coordination actions include:

- *Start a list workflow*: Starts a list workflow based on the SharePoint 2010 workflow platform.

- *Start a site workflow*: Starts a site workflow based on the SharePoint 2010 workflow platform.

List Actions

The actions grouped together under *List Actions* relate to manipulating lists and list items. The list actions include:

- *Check in an item*: Checks in an item that is checked out in a library.

- *Check out an item*: Checks out an item in a library.

- *Copy a document*: Copies a document from the current library to a different library.

- *Create a list item*: Creates a new list item in the specified list.

- *Delete an item*: Deletes an item.

- *Discard a check out for an item*: Discards the changes and the check-out status for an item.

- *Set field in current item*: Sets a specified field in the current item to a specified value.

- *Translate document*: Translates a document into a particular language.

- *Update list item*: Updates a list item.

- *Wait for event in list item*: Pauses the current instance of the workflow to await a specified list item event.

- *Wait for field change in current item*: Waits for a field on the current item to equal a particular value.

Task Actions

The actions grouped together under *Task Actions* enable you to create workflow tasks and assign them to users or groups in a SharePoint site. The task actions include:

- *Assign a task*: Assigns a workflow task to a user or group and establishes a due date.

- *Start a task process*: Creates tasks for multiple users and enables the tasks to be taken through a customized process.

Utility Actions

The actions grouped together under *Utility Actions* manipulate strings or calculate intervals between date values. The utility actions include:

- *Extract substring of a string from the end*: Copies a specified number of characters starting from the end of a string and stores the output in a variable.

- *Extract substring of a string from the index*: Copies a substring starting at the specified index in the string and stores the output in a variable.

- *Extract substring of a string from the start*: Copies a specified number of characters beginning at the start of a string and stores the output in a variable.

- *Extract substring of a string from an index with a length*: Copies a string comprising of a specified number of characters, starting at a specified index in the string, and stores the output in a variable.

- *Find interval between dates*: Calculates the time interval between two dates and stores the output in a variable.

- *Trim string*: Removes white space from the beginning and end of a string.

- *Find substring in a string*: Finds a particular substring inside of a string and returns the starting position's index.

- *Replace substring in a string*: Replaces a particular substring with another substring.

As you can see by this list of groups and their actions, SharePoint Designer offers an extensive number of things you can use to configure a highly sophisticated workflow process, all without requiring any custom development. Using any combination of these built-in actions, you can create workflows of varying degrees of complexity. In the next section, I walk through an example of how to create a simple approval workflow.

Building Approval Workflows in SharePoint Designer

SharePoint Designer 2013 makes it easy to create and configure a workflow in SharePoint. I find it is not all that different from creating an e-mail rule in Microsoft Outlook 2013, at least conceptually. In this example, I will create an approval workflow to process the expense reports I created with InfoPath in an earlier section. The steps in this section will walk you through how to create a workflow using SharePoint Designer.

1. Open SharePoint Designer and open a site where you want to create a workflow. Click the Workflows option in the Navigation pane.

2. On the ribbon, open the List Workflow context menu and select the desired list or library. For this example, I selected the expense report library.

3. In the Create List Workflow window, give the new workflow a name and select the platform type.

4. Add the relevant actions and steps that you wish to include in the workflow based on the information you captured in the business process model that I described earlier in this chapter. For this example, I added a few approval-related actions that assign a task for a site owner to approve the expense report, and once approved, declare the expense report as a record. Figure 8-14 shows these actions added to my example workflow.

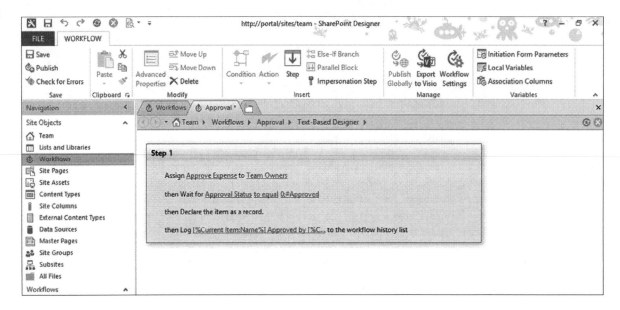

Figure 8-14. *Actions added to a new workflow step*

5. In the workflow ribbon, click Publish to save and publish the workflow to the SharePoint site.

6. Navigate to the SharePoint site and click the item context menu for one of the expense reports. On the item context menu, select Workflows to navigate to the item Workflows page, as shown in Figure 8-15.

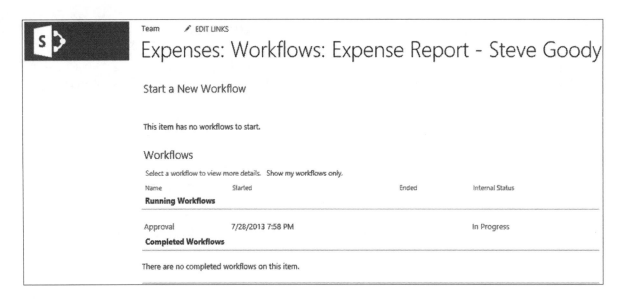

Figure 8-15. *The item workflow status page*

Start an instance of the workflow to test the workflow. Then verify the workflow details for the item by clicking the Completed link next to the item in the library to view the workflow details. Confirm that the workflow processed correctly and ended with the desired results.

> ■ **Note** For more information on developing SharePoint 2013 workflows, please see the MSDN article at
> http://msdn.microsoft.com/jj163181.

Inside Story: Notes from the Field

My timing with writing this chapter is perfect, because I just engaged with a client to advise them on electronic forms and workflow while I was in the processes of writing. They are a nonprofit organization that runs fundraising campaigns, and all of their processes currently revolve around paper-based forms. Their customers, donors, fill out paper-based forms to submit along with their donation. Fundraising groups also fill out forms with organization and fundraising campaign information. Other forms exist to feed into the process for setting up payroll deductions or coordinating how to allocate funds. The process is very form heavy and involves a lot of repetitive data entry.

Data such as contact or campaign information repeats across the forms, causing repetitive data entry during the same process. Furthermore, in subsequent years when an individual or organization launches a new campaign, the data remains largely consistent, yet with the paper-based forms, the users have to repeatedly fill in the repetitive data. This experience of repetitive data-entry left users feeling as if their time was being wasted and some users expressed some discontent with the process.

What made this worse was that the users whose time was being consumed with repetitive data-entry were volunteer fundraisers. These volunteers were having time consumed with those administrative tasks, time where they could better spend doing fundraising activities.

Here we had our business case and the ultimate vision for the project: minimize any administrative burden for any fundraisers or donors so that their energies could be better spent fundraising—in short, to make their lives easier.

By replacing the paper forms with InfoPath forms and connecting those to a database, we were able to eliminate all the duplicate data-entry. We also achieved secondary benefits, such as exposing the real-time status of a fundraising campaign, providing rich reporting of which forms were still outstanding for a campaign, and increasing the overall collaboration and responsiveness between donors, fundraisers, and campaign organizers.

Wrapping Up

You manage your form content in the same fashion as any other unit of information in your enterprise content management solution. SharePoint 2013 offers a rich set of features to manage electronic forms, and specifically InfoPath forms, allowing you to incorporate them as simply another content type. In this chapter, I provided an overview of forms in organizations and I discussed the differences and similarities between paper-based forms and electronic forms. From there, I shared some guidance for modeling and designing your forms and form processes. Finally, I provided you with an overview of InfoPath 2013 and SharePoint Designer 2013, two tools available to help you build your electronic forms and their related processes.

With your transitory content organized along with areas for your users to collaborate on different pieces of transitory content, your next challenge is to help your users discover relevant content, either to collaborate, to reference, or simply to stay current. In the next part, I shift to focus on content discovery and how you can plan your enterprise content management solution around facilitating the discovery of relevant content, beginning with the next chapter where I discuss enterprise search and how a your enterprise search strategy provides the basis for key content discovery scenarios.

■ ■ ■

PART 3

Designing Your Information Discovery

Content has little value if users cannot discover it and then work with it. This can vary from users actively searching for information they know they need as an input to their job function, to content users are unaware even exists but that contains information that a user would potentially find relevant. It can also include a librarian or records manager discovering content in response to a legal or regulatory case. Content discovery is a crucial aspect to your enterprise content management solution because it drives the content's value to your organization by making it available to your users.

The chapters in this part look at different topics related to discovering content within your organization. I start with the concept of an enterprise search service you can provide to your users so they can find any relevant content they need to locate, a service that other content discovery features also depend on to crawl and index the corpus of content. From there, I discuss discovering content through social connections such as social tagging. Then I guide you through how to plan for electronic discovery and discovery case management to support formal and often regulatory-related content discovery requirements. Finally, I contrast content discovery with its counterpart: how to secure content to prevent unauthorized discovery.

As you consider the different information discovery techniques, remember that your ultimate goal is to facilitate users in their process to discover relevant information, while also preventing users from discovering or accessing content that is not appropriate to their role and job function. You build an effective information discovery solution by considering the user experience and paying attention to how you designed your information architecture to organize and classify the content. Your information architecture identifies relationships between content as well as other information, such as stages in the content's life cycle. It also leads to search relevancy and the ability to refine search results, establishing enterprise search to provide the core technical components for information discovery, and the topic I look at first.

CHAPTER 9

■ ■ ■

Implementing Enterprise Search

Knowledge is of two kinds. We know a subject ourselves, or we know where we can find information on it.

—Samuel Johnson

How can users find content if they do not know where a piece of content exists or what a particular file name is? If you know where something is, then you can click into the directory and directly access it; in all other cases, you can use a search engine to quickly connect you to the information you seek. In this chapter, I provide an overview of enterprise search and the search architecture in SharePoint. From there, I discuss how to analyze your enterprise search requirements. I also walk you through how to create an enterprise search application, and how to configure content sources to index and make available for search results.

After reading this chapter, you will know how to

- Explain the importance of search.

- Describe enterprise search.

- Describe the SharePoint search architecture.

- Analyze your enterprise search requirements.

- Create an enterprise search application.

- Configure search content sources.

The Importance of Search

Search has become the centerpiece of any enterprise content management solution. Its criticality relates to all the other features and capabilities depending on search for different aspects of information management, such as content auditing and reporting, but in particular, content discovery.

This chapter focuses on providing a search engine to support users who are explicitly searching for desired information—an aspect of the SharePoint search engine that provides a compelling portion of an organization's content discovery needs. But the search capabilities run even deeper and reach even further than providing search results for a user's query entered into a search box. With the content crawled and included in the index, search provides a foundational service that other capabilities can consume and take advantage of in providing their own content discovery features.

Two capabilities that especially utilize and extend the search engine are social and eDiscovery, as illustrated in Figure 9-1. In the next chapter, I point out areas where SharePoint suggests relevant search results without a user entering a search query, all based on social data and what SharePoint search predicts the user will find relevant. Then, in Chapter 11, I walk you through how search provides the plumbing underneath to make eDiscovery and case management work, and I show how the more extensive the amount of content you include in your search index, the more effective your eDiscovery and case management solution will be.

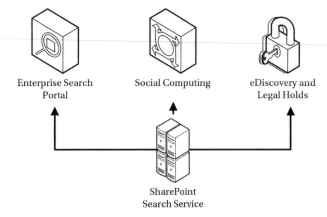

Enterprise Search Portal   Social Computing   eDiscovery and Legal Holds

SharePoint Search Service

Figure 9-1. *Social and eDiscovery leveraging the SharePoint search engine*

My point is that search reaches further and can affect more than what first might be apparent. Maximizing the number of content sources to crawl and include in the index helps to provide a richer search experience for users, providing them with a single place to search for information across a variety of content repositories. A thorough index also increases the range of content you can discover and place on hold in a legal or regulatory case, as I discuss later.

Search crawls content across your organization, indexes it, and then relates pieces of content to each other. It gives you a comprehensive view into information across your organization. I like to think of SharePoint as the glue that holds the different enterprise systems together; this makes search the adhesive part of that glue because its index can hold a global perspective across all the content repositories, no matter how many silos you use to structure your information.

I often hear questions about whether SharePoint should replace different systems, particularly as stakeholders learn about the different capabilities built into the product. SharePoint does not have to replace every enterprise application, and indeed, it should not replace an application when the other application does a better job. Pick the best application for each job, and then use SharePoint search to provide a centralized access point to all of the enterprise data.

Deploying the SharePoint search component adds a wealth of features to support your enterprise content management initiative, and as such, the effort deserves your forethought and attention to think through the possibilities and maximize a search engine's potential in your organization. Most notably, a well-designed enterprise search engine provides your organization with

- An entry-point to discover information in different repositories across your organization.

- A rich drill-down experience for filtering and refining search results.

- Customizable search-result formatting and ranking.

- Document previews to determine result relevancy for supported Office documents.

- A usage analytics and reporting engine to identify popular content and usage trends.

- Secure search results filtered based on what a user has permission to see.

Even though I only focus on the search engine itself in this chapter, know that your work here provides the groundwork for those other capabilities when you are ready to enable them. Investing effort and planning in search now will reward you later as you tackle those other capabilities and leverage the search engine and index. Before I venture into the technical details of search, I want to discuss the conceptual aspects of enterprise search.

Understanding Enterprise Search

The goal of an enterprise search engine is to connect users with relevant information, quickly. People are used to quickly finding information on the Internet using one of the popular public search engines. Enterprise search engines essentially attempt to replicate that experience for users within an organization.

Your ultimate goal for an enterprise search deployment is to provide a search experience where users can find relevant information based on their context and what they are seeking. To achieve this, you need a search engine with sophisticated algorithms to determine the relevancy of each piece of content in a massive corpus of data. You also need a search engine that crawls data in different content repositories, not just SharePoint sites.

The SharePoint search engine crawls content across the enterprise, in multiple repositories and file formats, to then build an index that users can run queries against to find relevant content. As Figure 9-2 illustrates, an enterprise search portal can aggregate search results from a range of content sources, including:

- Local and remote SharePoint sites

- Network file shares

- Structured and unstructured data accessed using Business Connectivity Services (BCS)

■ **Note**   For more information on Business Connectivity Services in SharePoint 2013, including how to create data connections to external data sources for search to crawl and index, please see the MSDN site at http://msdn.microsoft.com/jj163782.

- E-mail and public folders in Exchange or Lotus Notes

- Portals and web sites hosting HTML pages

- People and profile information

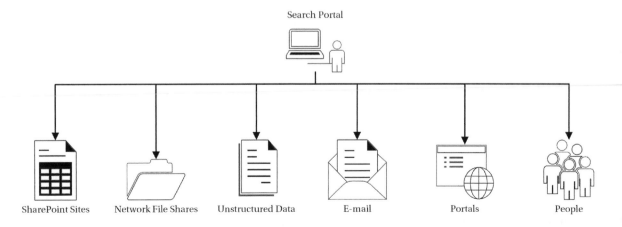

Figure 9-2. *Enterprise search portal with multiple content sources*

Including all the different silos of content across the organization makes the search results more compelling for users—the more content repositories you include, the richer the search experience will be for users because they will be able to search across a more complete range of content. This helps to provide users with search results likely to include the piece of content they are looking for; it also helps the search engine to tune relevancy and build a more complete index of the enterprise's content.

When I think about the search capability in SharePoint, I think about deploying an enterprise search portal—one where users can treat as a web destination to find information anywhere in the organization. To establish it as a destination, it needs to include all of the content repositories necessary to consider the search portal as an *enterprise* portal.

■ **Note** For more information on how to install and configure the search service in a SharePoint 2013 farm, please see the search configuration details in the "Farm Configuration" section of my SharePoint 2013 Build Guide at `http://stevegoodyear.wordpress.com/sharepoint-2013-build-guide`.

SharePoint Search Architecture Overview

Search runs as a service in SharePoint 2013, and Microsoft designed its architecture to facilitate redundancy and scalability in multiple directions. The search architecture consists of components and databases working cohesively to provide the search service.

Microsoft architected the search service across six components, each responsible for processing a specific portion of the search service. A search architecture includes the following components:

- **Crawl Component**: Accesses content repositories and crawls content.

- **Content Processing Component**: Processes crawled items, including document parsing and property mapping.

- **Index Component**: The logical representation of the search index. You can divide the index into discrete partitions, each stored in files on a disk.

- **Query Processing Component**: Analyzes and processes search queries and results.

- **Analytics Processing Component**: Runs the search analytics and usage analytics.

- **Search Administration Component**: Runs system processes essential to search.

Search uses the components to run and process the different aspects of the search service. In addition to the search components, the search architecture also includes the following databases:

- **Crawl Database**: Manages the crawl operations and stores the crawl history.

- **Link Database**: Stores link click-through information as well as link information extracted by the content processing component.

- **Search Administration Database**: Stores search configuration data.

- **Analytics Reporting Database**: Stores the results of usage analytics.

Figure 9-3 illustrates the relationship between the search components and databases in the search architecture. At the center of the architecture is the search index, which is paramount to providing a rich search experience. The search architecture feeds content to the index through the crawl and content processing components. A search portal sends a user's search query to the index through the query processing component.

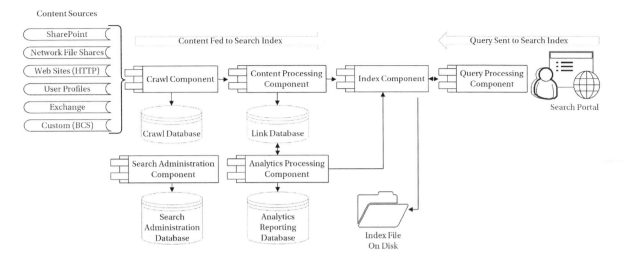

Figure 9-3. *The SharePoint search architecture*

In the smallest deployment on single-server farms, you will deploy all of the search components on the SharePoint server and all of the databases on the database server. As your search needs evolve, you can scale out the farm by adding additional servers to host specific search components. For example, if you scaled from a single-server farm to a six-server farm, you can distribute your search components across the servers with redundancy—two servers handling web requests, two servers hosting the query processing component, and two servers hosting the remaining crawl, content processing, analytics, and administration components.

One of the key benefits this search architecture offers is the ability to scale your SharePoint farm to meet a wide variety of usage characteristics by targeting individual components to specific servers. You can also create additional index partitions to handle a growing number of content items and divide the index load across multiple servers.

■ **Note**   For more information on the search architecture in SharePoint 2013, please see the TechNet site at `http://technet.microsoft.com/jj898538`.

Analyzing Your Enterprise Search Requirements

Search is one of my favorite aspects of SharePoint to deploy. It is like bringing an organization out of the dark ages, mostly because it suddenly makes information available—people can find whatever they want, wherever it is located, with just a few keywords. I might be dramatizing it a little, but at the time, it can feel *that* exciting. It all starts with gathering the requirements and imagining the possibilities.

As you analyze your search requirements, avoid complicating them. Remember: one of the things that Google did well is it created a simple interface with a single text box where users could enter a search query. It made a simple user interface. My best advice to you is to follow that trend and avoid getting too crazy with design activities. Figure 9-4 shows the default search portal page—a simple user interface with everything your users need to conduct a search. This is a good place to start.

Figure 9-4. *The default SharePoint search portal*

The first big requirement to solve is what happens from there, once users submit a search query. Luckily, SharePoint has solved most of the details around requirement. As Figure 9-5 shows, the search results on a default enterprise search portal are already feature-rich. Along the left side of the page, you can see *refiners,* a set of links where users can click to refine the search results. Down the middle are search results, and if you hover over one, you can see a result preview pop up along the right.

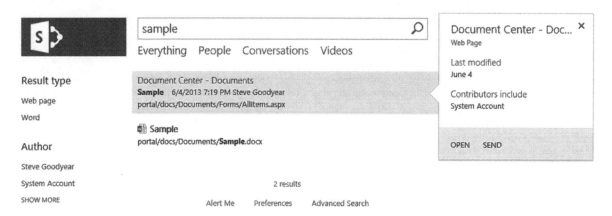

Figure 9-5. *The search results page*

I generally try to start with this experience in the initial phase of the search deployment. Unless you are replacing an existing and well-established enterprise search engine in your organization, these default features will almost always be sufficient enough to generate a *wow* factor for your initial launch. Avoid complicating things in the user interface at this stage unless you have a compelling reason (such as adding functionality to meet a specific and critical requirement).

Hopefully, you can avoid those requirements initially and focus instead on the content. Indexing the right content, after all, is the value of your enterprise search engine. You can always enhance the interface and user experience in the search portal later because this does not have a lasting effect on overall adoption. Having relevant and comprehensive search results, on the other hand, *does* have a lasting effect on overall adoption. This is what attracts users and establishes your search portal as a destination for finding information, but only if it delivers in its search results right from the start. This is the most critical piece.

The essence of your requirements analysis for an enterprise search, at least initially, consists of identifying all of the content repositories available on your network. This includes every SharePoint farm, every network file share, and every other web resource containing information. If there is information contained somewhere on the network that will benefit users with being searchable and discoverable, now is the time to identify that content and consider including it in the search index.

▓ **Important**   Particularly with network file shares, I have noticed some people find themselves practicing something commonly referred to as *security through obscurity*—content the system does not disclose only because others are not aware it exists, even though there are no permissions restricting access to the content. As you analyze requirements for indexing a network file share, look at where you might be missing access control permissions, because otherwise, the search engine will expose the content in related search results.

Think about this: how valuable would Google be if it only contained half of the content on the Web? Google can calculate relevancy based on the number of other sources referencing an item; it can even translate text based on human translations somewhere else on the Web. Having such an extensive and comprehensive corpus of data feeds many of Google's algorithms. The larger the corpus, the more effective the algorithms. But more importantly for our purposes, not only does its underlying engine rely on its indexes having enough coverage of the Web's content, but its users expect results from an extensive and fresh index of content.

Your users will have the same expectation that your enterprise search engine's index adequately covers your organization's array of content. Start with identifying and including the content first, and then build your requirements from there based on the search experience your users desire or the relevancy you need to tune.

Its simplicity is what makes search striking. This does not mean there is no work to do or things to administer; there is. In addition to continuing to refine your search requirements and tune your search engine, you should always start with the content.

Administering an Enterprise Search Service

Administering an enterprise search service revolves around two main areas: indexing content and tuning for queries. The entire goal is to crawl all the necessary content as frequently as needed to provide users with meaningful and relevant search results for their search queries. The majority of your search administration tasks will involve those two areas.

You can administer and monitor search in a similar fashion as other aspects of administering SharePoint, only through the Search Administration page. From SharePoint Central Administration, click the Manage Service Applications link in the Application Management section. Select the desired search service and click the Manage button in the ribbon to navigate to the Search Administration page for the search service, as shown in Figure 9-6.

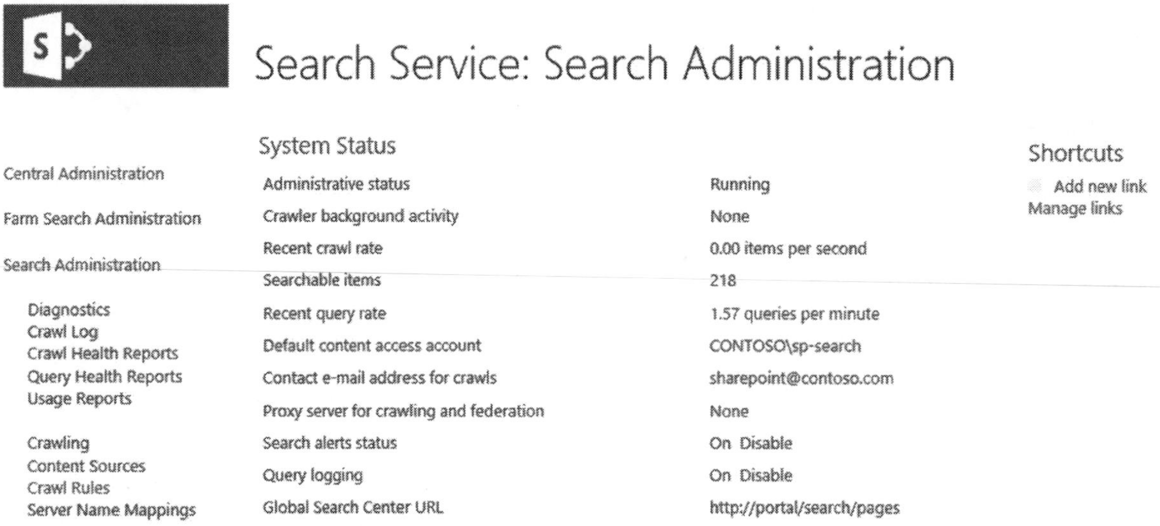

Search Service: Search Administration

Central Administration

Farm Search Administration

Search Administration

  Diagnostics
  Crawl Log
  Crawl Health Reports
  Query Health Reports
  Usage Reports

  Crawling
  Content Sources
  Crawl Rules
  Server Name Mappings

System Status

Administrative status	Running
Crawler background activity	None
Recent crawl rate	0.00 items per second
Searchable items	218
Recent query rate	1.57 queries per minute
Default content access account	CONTOSO\sp-search
Contact e-mail address for crawls	sharepoint@contoso.com
Proxy server for crawling and federation	None
Search alerts status	On Disable
Query logging	On Disable
Global Search Center URL	http://portal/search/pages

Shortcuts

Add new link
Manage links

Figure 9-6. *The Search Administration page*

Notice the different administration options on the left navigation menu. The navigation menu groups the administrative options into three categories: Diagnostics, for reviewing logs and reports; Crawling, for configuring and managing the crawling settings; and Queries and Results, for configuring and managing how the search service processes queries.

In the center area, the page displays the system status. This dashboard includes details about any active crawling activity and the number of searchable items that the index contains. It also includes the content access account and e-mail address for crawls, both of which you can edit by clicking the respective link for the item you wish to change.

■ **Note** The Contact E-mail Address for Crawls specifies the e-mail address that SharePoint will include along with the request header information that the crawler service sends to servers as it requests content from them. The target servers can then log the request, including the e-mail address, so that a server administrator can use it to contact a search administrator if there are any issues with the crawling service, such as the crawler overloading the target server's resources.

Scrolling down on the Search Administration page, you can see the Search Application Topology, similar to the one shown in Figure 9-7. This topology lists the different components configured in the search architecture and which server hosts each component. In my example, I have a single server and it hosts all six components. The topology also lists the four databases in the search architecture and which database server hosts each.

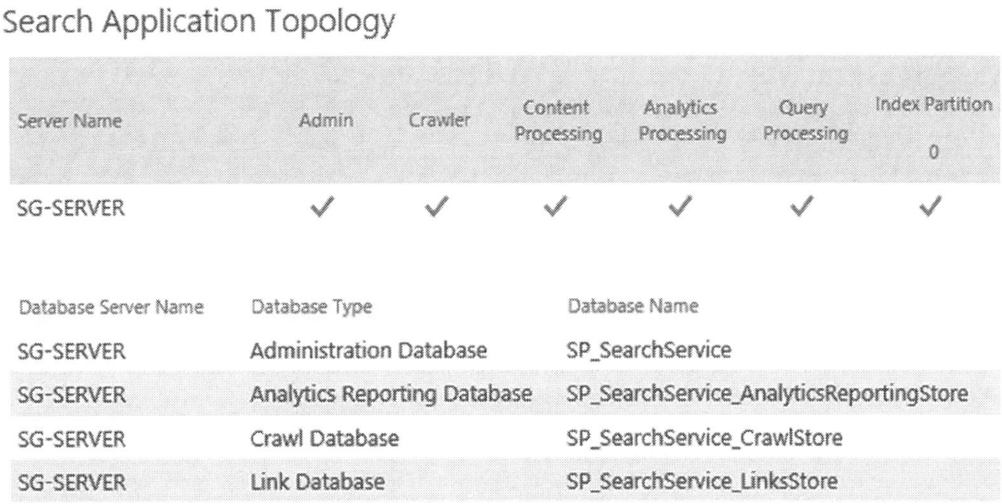

Search Application Topology

Server Name	Admin	Crawler	Content Processing	Analytics Processing	Query Processing	Index Partition 0
SG-SERVER	✓	✓	✓	✓	✓	✓

Database Server Name	Database Type	Database Name
SG-SERVER	Administration Database	SP_SearchService
SG-SERVER	Analytics Reporting Database	SP_SearchService_AnalyticsReportingStore
SG-SERVER	Crawl Database	SP_SearchService_CrawlStore
SG-SERVER	Link Database	SP_SearchService_LinksStore

Figure 9-7. The Search Application Topology section

■ **Note**　Although this is not a comprehensive guide for managing SharePoint search, I wanted to provide you with a brief introduction to the service and the key areas you can configure. For more thorough administration guidance, please see the TechNet site at `http://technet.microsoft.com/ee792877`.

The Search Administration page is the main entry page for administering different aspects of your search service. In the next few sections, I cover the most common tasks you need to perform to administer a search service, starting with configuring a content source.

Configuring Search Content Sources

Content sources in a SharePoint search identify the target locations and the protocol to use for connecting to the target storage location. A content source loosely relates to a content repository; although a content source can include multiple content repository locations in some cases, typically referred to as *start addresses*, as long as they share the same protocol for connecting and accessing the location. A content source also manages the crawling schedule and the account used to authenticate for crawling the content.

Your search engine will not provide any search results if you do not have a content source configured and scheduled to crawl content. As such, this is the most important step for you to complete before you can enable an enterprise search engine. To manage the content sources for your search service, click the Content Sources link in the Crawling section on the left navigation menu on the Search Administration page to navigate to the Manage Content Sources page similar to Figure 9-8.

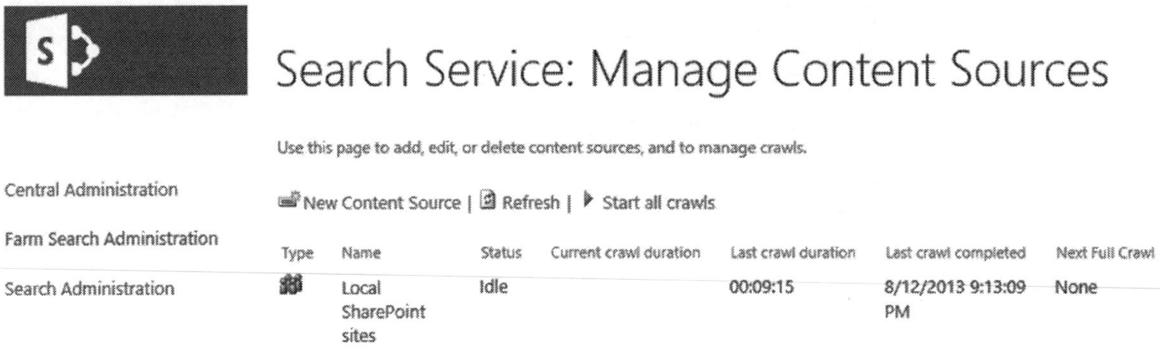

Search Service: Manage Content Sources

Use this page to add, edit, or delete content sources, and to manage crawls.

Central Administration

Farm Search Administration

Search Administration

    New Content Source | Refresh | ▶ Start all crawls

Type	Name	Status	Current crawl duration	Last crawl duration	Last crawl completed	Next Full Crawl
	Local SharePoint sites	Idle		00:09:15	8/12/2013 9:13:09 PM	None

Figure 9-8. *The Manage Content Sources page*

You can manage the settings for an existing content source by clicking the name of the content source you wish to edit. You can also create a new content source by clicking the New Content Source button. If you create a new content source, you have to specify a name for the content source and the type of content to crawl (the protocol to connect with), as shown in Figure 9-9. By default, you can select from the following content source types:

- SharePoint Sites

- Web Sites

- File Shares

- Exchange Public Folders

- Line of Business Data (Business Connectivity Services)

- Custom Repositories

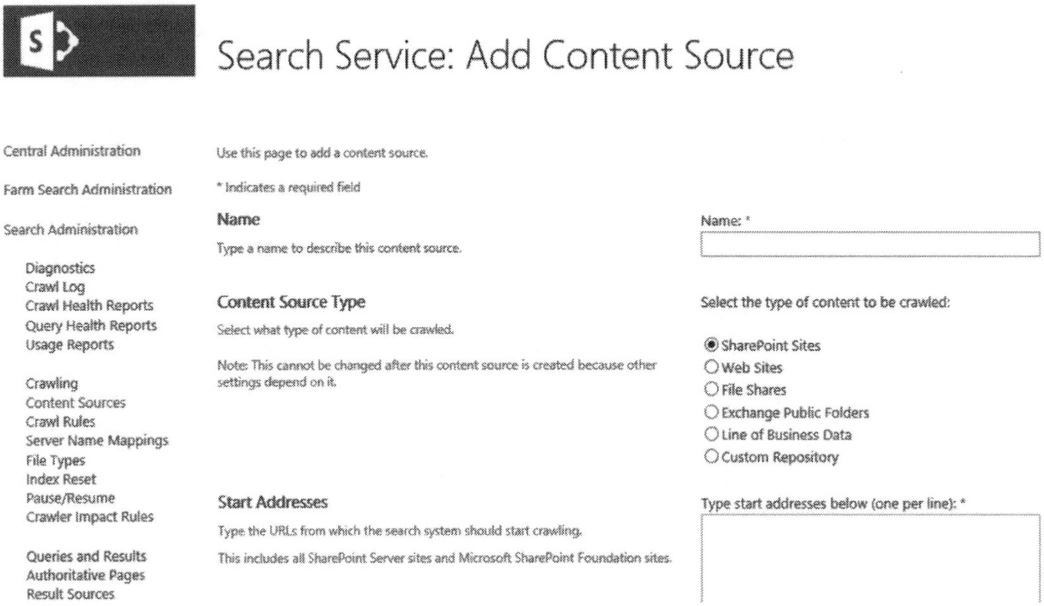

Search Service: Add Content Source

Central Administration

Farm Search Administration

Search Administration

    Diagnostics
Crawl Log
Crawl Health Reports
Query Health Reports
Usage Reports

    Crawling
Content Sources
Crawl Rules
Server Name Mappings
File Types
Index Reset
Pause/Resume
Crawler Impact Rules

    Queries and Results
Authoritative Pages
Result Sources

Use this page to add a content source.

* Indicates a required field

Name

Type a name to describe this content source.

Content Source Type

Select what type of content will be crawled.

Note: This cannot be changed after this content source is created because other settings depend on it.

Start Addresses

Type the URLs from which the search system should start crawling.

This includes all SharePoint Server sites and Microsoft SharePoint Foundation sites.

Name: *

[   ]

Select the type of content to be crawled:

- ◉ SharePoint Sites
- ○ Web Sites
- ○ File Shares
- ○ Exchange Public Folders
- ○ Line of Business Data
- ○ Custom Repository

Type start addresses below (one per line): *

[   ]

Figure 9-9. *The Add Content Source page*

Next, enter the start addresses for the content source. You can include multiple content repositories by adding multiple start addresses—they do not have to be the same host, only the same source type (protocol). You might also separate content repositories into different content sources to specify different crawl schedules for each. Finally, select or create the crawl schedules and click OK.

■ **Tip** For SharePoint content sources, you specify the people profile content as well as the My Site content by specifying `sps3` and `http(s)` protocols for the respective start addresses. For example, you could include `sps3://people` and `http://people` for profiles and site content hosted on that web application.

Configuring Crawl Rules

You can fine-tune how SharePoint crawls a location by creating a crawl rule. Create a new crawl rule by clicking the Crawl Rules link on the left navigation menu on the Search Administration page, and then clicking the New Crawl Rule link. Figure 9-10 shows the options for creating a new crawl rule.

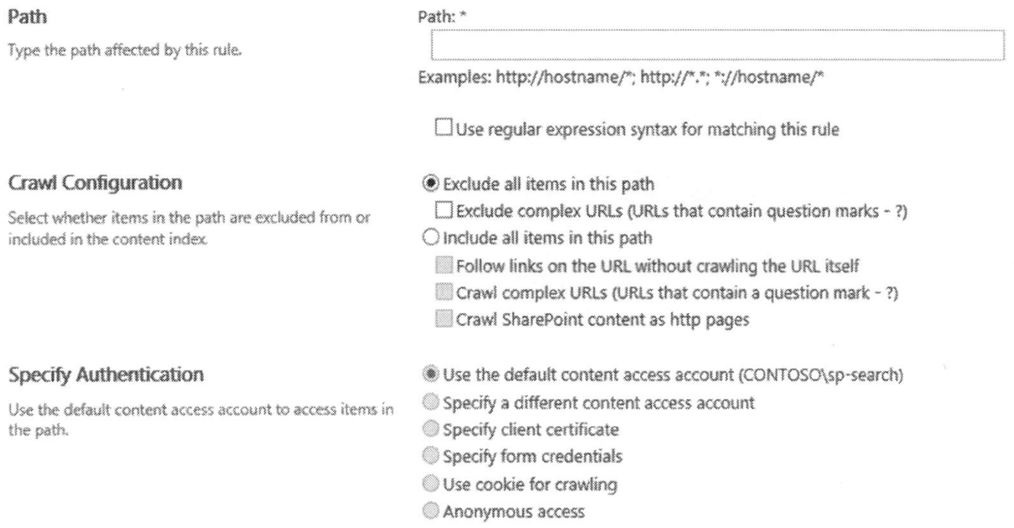

Path	Path: *
Type the path affected by this rule.	[ ]
	Examples: http://hostname/*; http://*.*; *://hostname/*
	☐ Use regular expression syntax for matching this rule
Crawl Configuration	◉ Exclude all items in this path
Select whether items in the path are excluded from or included in the content index.	☐ Exclude complex URLs (URLs that contain question marks - ?)
	○ Include all items in this path
	▨ Follow links on the URL without crawling the URL itself
	▨ Crawl complex URLs (URLs that contain a question mark - ?)
	▨ Crawl SharePoint content as http pages
Specify Authentication	◉ Use the default content access account (CONTOSO\sp-search)
Use the default content access account to access items in the path.	○ Specify a different content access account
	○ Specify client certificate
	○ Specify form credentials
	○ Use cookie for crawling
	○ Anonymous access

Figure 9-10. *The Add Crawl Rule page*

You can apply a crawl rule by following these steps:

1. Specify a path and any wildcards or regular expressions for identifying the location to apply the rule.

2. Select the crawl configuration to specify what to exclude or include in the location during a crawl.

3. Specify the authentication credentials for the crawl content access account.

4. Click OK.

Configuring Result Sources

Use results sources to scope search results and to federate queries to external sources, such as remote SharePoint farms and public Internet search engines. You can specify result sources for the following protocols:

- **Local SharePoint**: Results from the index of the local search service

- **Remote SharePoint**: Results from the index of a search service hosted in another farm

- **OpenSearch 1.0/1.1**: Results from a search engine that uses this protocol

- **Exchange**: Results from an Exchange source

■ **Note**   Result Sources in SharePoint 2013 replace the deprecated Search Scopes in previous versions of SharePoint.

To create a new result source, click the Result Sources link in the left navigation menu on the Search Administration page to navigate to the Result Sources page, and then click the New Result Source button. On the Add Result Source page shown in Figure 9-11, specify a name, description, and protocol for the desired result source. Set any other relevant options and click Save.

Search Service: Add Result Source

ⓘ **Note:** This result source will be available to all sites. To make one for just a specific site, use the query rules page in its Site Settings.

Central Administration

Farm Search Administration

Search Administration

Diagnostics
Crawl Log
Crawl Health Reports
Query Health Reports
Usage Reports

Crawling
Content Sources
Crawl Rules
Server Name Mappings
File Types
Index Reset
Pause/Resume
Crawler Impact Rules

Queries and Results
Authoritative Pages
Result Sources
Query Rules

General Information

Names must be unique at each administrative level. For example, two result sources in a site cannot share a name, but one in a site and one provided by the site collection can.

Descriptions are shown as tooltips when selecting result sources in other configuration pages.

Protocol

Select Local SharePoint for results from the index of this Search Service.

Select OpenSearch 1.0/1.1 for results

Name

Description

○ Local SharePoint
○ Remote SharePoint
○ OpenSearch 1.0/1.1
○ Exchange

Figure 9-11. *The Add Result Source page*

Configuring Query Suggestions

Query suggestions appear when users begin to type a query in the search text box. SharePoint dynamically manages the list of suggestions based on popular search terms and what a user has searched for in the past. You can also manually supply a list of phrases to always or never suggest, depending on your objective.

Configure the query suggestions lists by clicking the Query Suggestions link in the left navigation menu on the Search Administration page to navigate to the Query Suggestion Settings page shown in Figure 9-12.

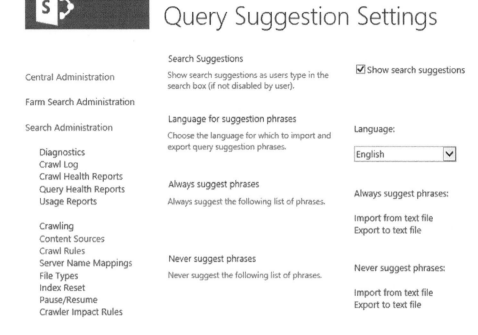

Figure 9-12. *The Query Suggestions Settings page*

If there are phrases you do not want to appear as query suggestions, such as query phrases that users frequently mistype, simply list the phrases in a text file and click to import the text file for the Never Suggest Phrases option.

For those phrases you wish to always suggest, list them in a separate text file and click to import it for the Always Suggest Phrases option. Figure 9-13 illustrates an example of the phrase "practical sharepoint 2013 enterprise content management" I added to always suggest. Now, whenever a user begins to type the word *practical* on this search portal, the search page will suggest the entire phrase.

EDIT LINKS

Search

practical   🔎

practical sharepoint 2013 enterprise content management

Figure 9-13. *Search query suggestion example*

Building an Enterprise Glossary

One common theme running across each and every company I have consulted with or worked for involves a distinct language involving company- or industry-specific terms and acronyms. These are any terms that a regular person outside the organization would be unfamiliar with, such as terms with a specific usage only relevant within your firm or acronyms that outsiders would be unaware of.

To give you an example, years ago, I worked for Pepsi, and a common acronym at the time was *PQI*. It was so common, in fact, that our people would use it as a verb. To an outsider, this would seem foreign and difficult to understand, simply because the letters in the acronym are not obvious, at least not to anyone outside the soft-drink industry at the time. The acronym stands for *product quality initiative*, and it essentially refers to the "best before" dates on the soft drinks.

When private-label soft drinks came on the market and challenged the bigger bottlers and their brand-name beverages with cheaper alternatives, Pepsi responded by adding best-before dates to each bottle and can. The message was that buying the brand-name drink meant you were buying freshness and quality—you could visually verify a bottle or can has not sat on a shelf going stale. In other words, you could visually verify the product quality of the name-brand drinks, but not the no-name alternatives, introducing an initiative to differentiate. Hence, *product quality initiative*.

If a bottler used *PQI* as a verb, as in "these drinks are going PQI," he or she was saying that the drinks were about to expire. Anyone familiar with the anonym, which you now are, would understand; but for everyone else, particularly new employees, this would sound odd and foreign. To compound this, try to imagine just how many different acronyms and terms a typical organization would have (at Pepsi, we printed out a list, and later we discovered we missed a few despite the list spanning nearly thirty pages).

You can solve this problem like we solved this problem at Pepsi back in the day by printing out a glossary booklet. Paper-based glossaries can be difficult to distribute and a challenge to maintain, and let's face it: a bound booklet glossary is not convenient to carry around with you. A better solution is to add a glossary to your SharePoint search engine.

I like to describe this second option in the context of new people joining your organization. As part of their orientation, you could introduce them to the search portal, telling them that when they hear an unfamiliar term, they can type it into search and see a glossary defining it in the search results. Instead of being lost or confused, forcing them to face the embarrassment of asking what a term means, they can inconspicuously search and find out what it means on their own—from the browser on their desktop or even from their mobile device while they are on the go.

A search-powered glossary provides a nice way to onboard new employees and a convenient way to maintain a list of relevant terms in an easy-to-find source. This feature also helps to drive adoption of the search engine, because not only can people use it to find content and other people (as I discuss in the next chapter), they can also find information on terms or phrases used within the organization.

In previous versions of SharePoint, you could add terms in what the product referred to as *best bets*. In SharePoint 2013, the product team made some subtle changes to the idea of promoted search results, ultimately to extend the functionality and add a finer degree of control to how you define the criteria for promoted results. This functionality now found in the *query rules*.

Configuring Query Rules

Query rules enable you to conditionally promote important search results, show blocks of additional result information, and even tune result rankings.

You can create a query rule to provide a glossary item in the search results by following these steps:

1. Click the Query Rules link in the left navigation menu on the Search Administration page to navigate to the Manage Query Rules page.

2. Select the Local SharePoint Results result source from the Result Source drop-down menu. This adds the glossary item to the default result source.

3. Click the New Query Rule button to navigate to the Add Query Rule page.

4. Specify a rule name. In my example, I called the rule *ECM*.

5. Define the Query Conditions that make the rule fire. In my example in Figure 9-14, I specified "ecm; enterprise content management" for the Query Conditions so that the rule would fire and return the glossary definition for when users submit either the acronym or the phrase for a search query.

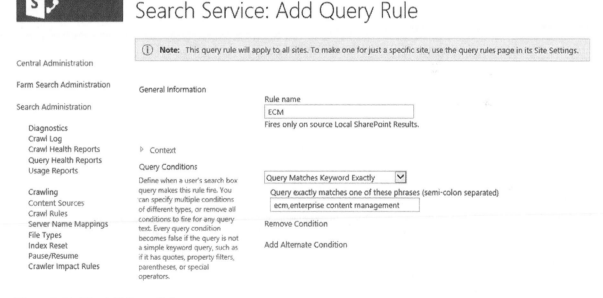

Figure 9-14. *The Add Query Rule page*

6. Click the Add Promoted Result link in the Actions section. Enter the glossary term's title and definition in the modal window, as shown in Figure 9-15. Click Save to dismiss the modal window, and then click Save to create the rule.

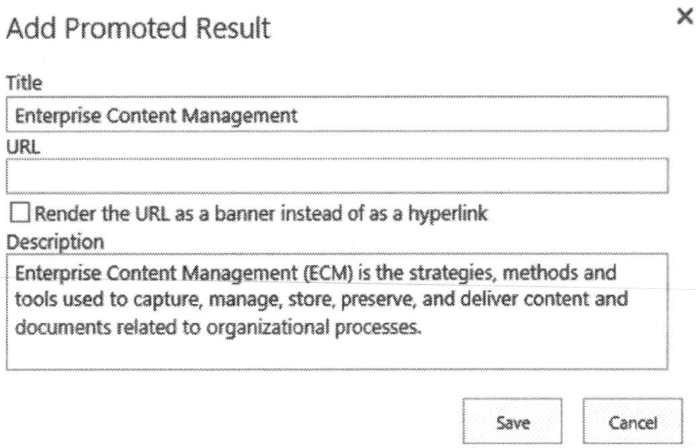

Add Promoted Result   ✕

Title

Enterprise Content Management

URL

☐ Render the URL as a banner instead of as a hyperlink

Description

Enterprise Content Management (ECM) is the strategies, methods and tools used to capture, manage, store, preserve, and deliver content and documents related to organizational processes.

Save   Cancel

Figure 9-15. *The Add Promoted Result modal window*

You can test the query rule by navigating to the search portal and submitting the term as the search query. If you created the query rule successfully, you should see a result similar to Figure 9-16.

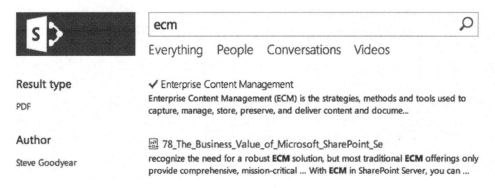

Figure 9-16. *Promoted result example*

Wrapping Up

Users use search engines to find the relevant information that they seek. This makes search an important aspect of your SharePoint deployment, or even as I suggested, the centerpiece of your SharePoint deployment. Enterprise search offers a single entry-point to discover information in the enterprise. Its architecture in SharePoint includes the components that access and crawl the content to build an index, and the components that process search queries by utilizing the index. Your enterprise search solution should start with the content, and design its search experience from there.

People in an organization search for all types of information: sometimes this is content, and sometimes it is other people and their knowledge. Sometimes people discover content through other people and their knowledge. Discovering information through others is the essence of social computing, an aspect of which builds on the SharePoint search engine in addition to other social features. In the next chapter, I discuss the topics relating to social capabilities in SharePoint, including searching for people and for knowledge *through* other people. I also look at other social features, such as profiles, social tagging, and blogging.

CHAPTER 10

■ ■ ■

Planning Social Computing

Everybody gets so much information all day long that they lose their common sense.

—Gertrude Stein

Knowledge in an organization centers around people, the organization's people who possess the expertise or who can reference the information somewhere on the network. But if one is not the expert, how can he or she discover and access this knowledge? In this chapter, I provide an overview of the social computing capabilities in SharePoint, including how to deploy a people search and how to manage the My Site features. I also discuss social tagging and how tagging can help users to discover relevant content. Finally, I walk you through how to configure blogging settings and manage ad hoc blog content.

After reading this chapter, you will know how to

- Describe the social computing capabilities in SharePoint.

- Analyze your social computing requirements.

- Deploy a people search portal.

- Manage My Sites features and configure profile synchronization.

- Configure audiences and audience targeting.

- Create a personal blog.

Understanding Social Computing

Somewhere along the way, *social* became a scary word for folks. Not that they are antisocial or anything like that, they just hold a misguided notion that the idea of social is somehow bad. I believe this discomfort with *social* comes out of equating social computing with social networking—the two terms are *not* synonyms. But if one does think about social networking when presented with the prospects of social computing, then he or she might begin to picture things such as Facebook, possibly along with the aspects of newsfeed streams filled with irrelevant posts—at least irrelevant to the organization and its function.

Let me clear some of this up and tell you unequivocally, SharePoint is not *Facebook for the enterprise*. If the term *social* scares you or some of your stakeholders because of a mental block that cannot move past such an idea, then choose a new term—interpersonal computing, perhaps. These are important and valuable concepts, ones you can use to make knowledge more discoverable and accessible in your organization. Social computing exposes knowledge through people, either directly through your immediate network of colleagues, or, and even more valuably, through your extended network, tapping into your colleagues' network, or your colleagues' colleagues' network.

I can usually articulate the value and business case of a social computing initiative by asking a single rhetorical question: How do you find people in your organization when you do not know their names? The value of social computing is tangled with the answer—the people and metadata about them and the things they do, their interests, their expertise, and anything else that can connect two people together who otherwise might not even know to look for each other.

Similarly, you can link that metadata with metadata associated with pieces of content, again helping people discover relevant information they might not even know to look for. Connecting people to relevant knowledge based on their individual profiles, this is the essence of social computing.

▓ **Note**   To learn more about research into the relationship between information technology and society, please see the Intel Science and Technology Center for Social Computing at `http://socialcomputing.uci.edu`.

As you can see (I hope), there is nothing to be scared of with social computing. If you face a lot of resistance, try to debunk the myths by defining the goals and business value of a social computing initiative. If all else fails, simply adopt new terms, or focus on the individual applications in your social strategy, which should include the following:

- **People Search:** A rich experience moving beyond simple lookups by name, focusing as well on finding people using other criteria and attributes, such as responsibilities, skills, or expertise.

- **People Profiles:** The source data powering a rich people search—some data fields imported from a human resources system, other data fields stored locally and editable by the user him or herself.

- **Communication Options:** Features to engage users with each other to share knowledge and ideas, such as comment fields, blog posts, wiki pages, forums, and microblogs—all content sources that help feed a rich people search.

- **Tagging and Content Classification:** Pointers to content based on labels and organization indexes using language that users are familiar with, without applying strict classification processes and formalized taxonomies.

Social computing is not bad and it does not mean your network will be flooded with useless posts. It provides a means to connect knowledge and expertise in your organization. You do, however, have to expose aspects of that expertise to provide a hook for the link. This hook can be a person's profile information or it might be how he or she tags content or his or her site membership. There are several ways to expose one's knowledge for others to discover. Similarly, there are several ways to capture their expertise in an archival format for other users to discover.

CAPTURING EXPERTISE

Connecting existing employees to senior employees helps to facilitate knowledge sharing and discovery of expertise among the current team, but as I mentioned earlier, many organizations have a worry about the day when these experienced employees retire and leave a knowledge gap, an expertise void in the organization.

When the knowledge is in someone's head, then the person's retirement means that knowledge also retires and leaves the organization. The solution is to capture that knowledge *before* people retire. One option is to have them document everything they know and archive that on a network share or team site; that option is usually not overly practical and may feel like a chore for the retirees.

My preference is to have them make a series of videos and place these in an asset library for future generations of workers to reference. These can include a range of types of videos, everything from a podcast discussing a topic to an interviewer asking leading questions. You can even use video to shadow them on their jobs as they walk through and explain the different things they do and why (this is especially valuable content for tradespeople performing certain tasks and discussing the safety aspects of their steps).

Overview of Social Computing Capabilities

Practically every feature in SharePoint is loosely collaborative in nature and related in some way to social computing concepts. Nevertheless, I selected a handful of key social features to study closer in this section. Any features I omit are not necessarily less social in nature; I just wanted to highlight a few key features.

My Sites provide the hub for different social aspects in SharePoint. Most notably, users can manage their profile information and store personal content. These are two key sources of data for the search engine to crawl and return in search results for other users to discover people and their knowledge in the organization.

Within the My Site host, users can view and post to a microblog and activity feed known in SharePoint 2013 as a *newsfeed*. This allows for interactions with other users, alerting a crowd to things such as projects a user is working on, documents a user found interesting, and even notices alerting a user's title change, among others. This can help a community of users to stay connected and informed of each other's activity.

■ **Note**   Microsoft acquired Yammer, which provides a private social network for enterprise microblogging with some similarities to the newsfeed. You can find out more about this service at `https://about.yammer.com`.

People can populate their newsfeeds by following the activities of other people, sites, documents, or tags. When someone posts a note to his or her newsfeed or takes an action on one of the related items, an activity will appear in the newsfeed aggregation.

Those aspects that feed into the newsfeed are also social—the activities on sites or documents, for example, that a user follows. Activities can notify when an item changes, making it easy and convenient for a user to stay updated on any changes or developments of items he or she is interested in following.

Activity updates in a newsfeed are an unobtrusive way to notify users of changes without overloading their inbox; however, at times a piece of content may be of particular interest and of such importance that a user needs a more prominent notification so that he or she does not have to risk missing a change if his or her newsfeed becomes busy with other activities streaming in. In these cases, the user can subscribe to a SharePoint alert to notify him or her of any changes meeting specific criteria.

SharePoint sends alerts by e-mail to the user, and the user can choose whether to receive an immediate alert after each change, or he or she can opt for a daily or weekly summary on a specified schedule. Alerts and activities are such a simple, yet powerful, tool to help users stay informed of changes to content they are interested in.

Other types of activities posted to the newsfeed are particularly social in nature: social tagging and rating content. Social tagging involves a user tagging a piece of content with a term—a word or string of words describing the content in plain English (or whatever language and locale is in use). Users will see these activities in their newsfeeds when they follow either the content being tagged, the user doing the tagging, or the tag itself. Similar to social tagging, users apply ratings to a piece of content as a social means contributing to the content's relevance for other users. Ratings can take a numerical value or a binary selection indicating that the content was liked or it was not.

Users take explicit social actions on a piece of content through tagging and rating it. They also take implicit social actions by opening and interacting with the most valuable content to them. When users click links to content, SharePoint tracks their activities and calculates the most popular locations. You can expose these trending popular locations through one of the relevant built-in web parts designed to report on the trending popularity.

SharePoint enables users to be social directly with other users in a variety of ways. One is (again) via the newsfeed where they can mention and reply to each other's posts and activities. Another option is through discussion boards or forums. SharePoint 2013 includes a site template for Community Sites, which is essentially a forum with threaded discussions where users can ask and answer questions, or simply discuss ideas with each other. Any site can also add a Discussion Board app to include similar functionality for a specific team or project.

■ **Note** On my blog post at `http://stevegoodyear.wordpress.com/2012/08/02`, I discuss the Community Site template and provide an example of how you could use this as part of an employee onboarding community.

Other social site templates include the wiki and blog sites. A wiki provides a flexible way for multiple users to collaborate and post web pages with content to the wiki. A blog provides functionality for users to post articles of content to an audience. The key difference between the two is how they are organized: blogs are typically organized in a sequence from newest to oldest, whereas wikis typically adopt some other organizing method, such as grouping content by topic.

SharePoint also includes the ability to personalize and target content on a page. You can plan for and design tailored experiences for different types of users, depending on what holds the most relevancy for them. You can use these features to design additional social experiences, such as allowing users to opt in and out of communities based on their profile settings.

Social computing can help bring users together to discover information through each other, ultimately facilitating knowledge transfer and expertise sharing. However, simply enabling features will not provide you with an adequate social solution; instead, you need to analyze your requirements and plan for the social experience you wish to provide to your users.

■ **Note** For more information on the features in SharePoint 2013, including the social computing features, please see the TechNet article at `http://technet.microsoft.com/fp142374`.

Analyzing Your Social Computing Requirements

I have often heard about concerns for the number of workers an organization anticipates will retire in the coming years—an exodus of an older, more experienced generation. This concern has come up with my consulting clients in a range of industries, from trades such as line workers in utility corporations to government workers in the public sector, and even to senior employees in corporations.

People retire and have been retiring all along. This is not anything new, but there appears to be a greater proportion of people set to retire (at least in my region)—people with experience and expertise contained in their heads who will take that knowledge with them when they leave. My mission is often to offer advice on a way to capture as much of that knowledge before they retire and leave, making it available to newer workers and, ideally, preserving it for future workers.

Capturing the expertise of your knowledge workers may be the driver for your social computing initiative and this could make up your primary requirements. Closely associated to capturing expertise, your other requirements may relate to connecting people to knowledge by discovering relevant expertise in the organization. These are often the main reasons my clients become interested in a social computing initiative, at least initially. However, these are still high-level and vague requirements, but they can give you a place to start and they can identify the overarching goal for a social computing solution.

For me, the requirements tend to revolve around the desired user experience I want to provide and the primary objectives I want the overall solution to achieve. I like to write use cases to capture the details of a scenario and its sequencing. This helps me visualize how users interact with the system and the processes they take to produce or discover knowledge.

■ **Note**   For more information on use cases, I recommend Alistair Cockburn's book, *Writing Effective Use Cases* (Addison-Wesley, 2001). You can find a preview of this book at `http://alistair.cockburn.us/get/2465`.

When I work on identifying the primary objectives, I ask myself questions about the goals of a social computing solution, such as the following list. These can help to clarify the underlying driver and objectives the solution ought to achieve.

- Do I want to capture expertise?

- Do I want to identify relevant and popular content?

- Do I want to enable people to discover one another?

- Do I want to facilitate interactions and collaboration among people?

One of the first places you can start is facilitating ways people can discover and connect with each other. The primary tool you can build around is an effective people search, a search engine where people can search based on another's experience and expertise. A tuned and functional people search connects people with knowledge in an organization, establishing a fundamental centerpiece, one I usually start with to build any social computing solution around.

Deploying a People Search

You might already have some form of a people search, likely a directory to lookup someone by name. What if you spell the name wrong or use the wrong form—is it Steve or Steven or Stephen? (Or Zach or Zack or Zachary, as my technical reviewer pointed out.) This is a model I equate to corporate white pages, and it works as long as you know who you are looking for and how his or her name is spelled in the directory.

The kind of rich people search experience I want to focus on here moves beyond a white-pages style, lending itself more as a corporate yellow pages using phonetic search results. Figure 10-1 shows a typical people search for *steve*, which happens to match the name I used for my profile.

Figure 10-1. *People search*

In the results, you can see a preview pop up on the right because I hovered the mouse over this item. This shows recent documents I authored, as well as a link to my profile. Within the search results, notice how SharePoint is aware that I have searched for myself, and as a result it has included some statistics along with my search result to show the number of times that searches have led to my profile in the last month and in the last week. (Although in this example, my profile is not yet a popular destination for people searching on my demo server because both show zero searches that led to my profile.)

The nuances with the different spellings of a name highlights a practical example of the richness in a SharePoint people search. Figure 10-2 shows the same search result, even though in this example I searched for *stephen*—an alternate spelling of *steve*.

Figure 10-2. *People search with an alternate spelling*

I could have searched using any other profile property, which is handy when you need to find someone and you do not know his or her name. When users discover someone in the search results, they can click through to the person's profile page to learn more details, such as profile pictures, interests, skills, and other organizational information. Figure 10-3 provides an example of a profile page.

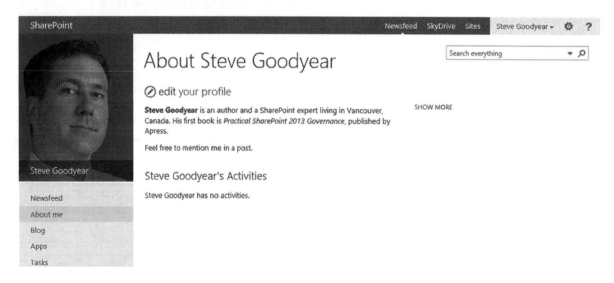

Figure 10-3. *Example of a profile page*

Employee onboarding is one example I use to describe the potential value of a rich people search such as this. You might remember that when you joined your current organization or when you took a new class, there were several people to meet—and that meant several names to learn. One way you can ease the stress and challenge with learning everyone's name is to point your new hires toward the people search and show them how they can search for different colleagues to learn names. For example, you can show a new hire to search by his or her new department or team, and he or she can use the search results to learn everyone's name.

SharePoint indexes profiles and My Site content using two different protocols. When you configure the search content source for people, use the regular `http://` protocol for the My Site content's start address and the `sps3://` protocol for people profiles. If you are using SSL, you can use `https://` and `sps3s://` for the URL as well. Figure 10-4 provides an example of a content source using these two protocols as start addresses to index people information for the enterprise search.

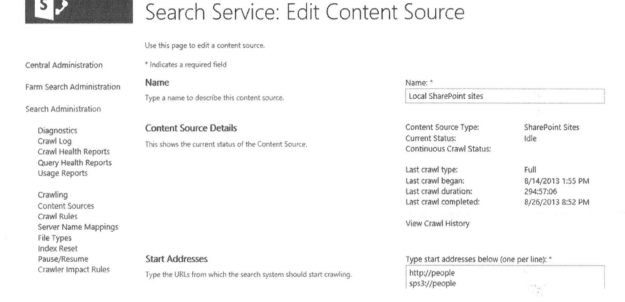

Figure 10-4. *Edit content source*

■ **Note**   Please see Chapter 9, where I discussed search and configuring content sources in more detail.

For a people search to be effective, you need to configure user profiles and other My Site features. If nothing else, managing these features defines the profile fields that users can use for advanced searches.

Managing My Site Features

There are several My Site configuration options available to you to manage a variety of settings. I want to highlight a few key settings that are the most important for you to be aware of, starting with how to set the permissions to grant permissions for users to manage the User Profile Service.

Figure 10-5 shows the permissions you can grant or limit on the User Profile Service. You can set these permissions by navigating to the Manage Service Applications page in SharePoint Central Administration, selecting the User Profile Service, and clicking the Administrators button in the ribbon.

Administrators for User Profile Service

Specify the users who have rights to manage this service application. These users will be given access to the Central Administration site and will be able to manage settings related to this service application. Members of the Farm Administrators group always have rights to manage all service applications.

To add an account, or group, type or select it below and click 'Add'.

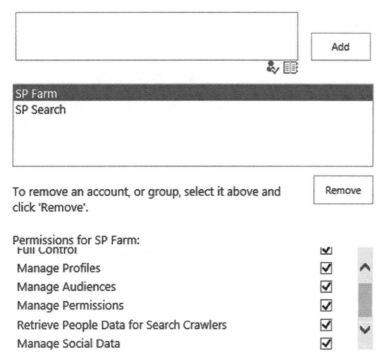

To remove an account, or group, select it above and click 'Remove'.

Permissions for SP Farm:

Full Control	☑
Manage Profiles	☑
Manage Audiences	☑
Manage Permissions	☑
Retrieve People Data for Search Crawlers	☑
Manage Social Data	☑

Figure 10-5. *User Profile Service permission settings*

You manage most settings related to My Sites and the User Profile Service on the Manage Profile Service page, accessed by selecting the User Profile Service and clicking the Manage button in the ribbon on the Manage Service Applications page. Click the Setup My Sites link in the My Site Settings section on the Manage Profile Service page to navigate to the My Site Settings page shown in Figure 10-6.

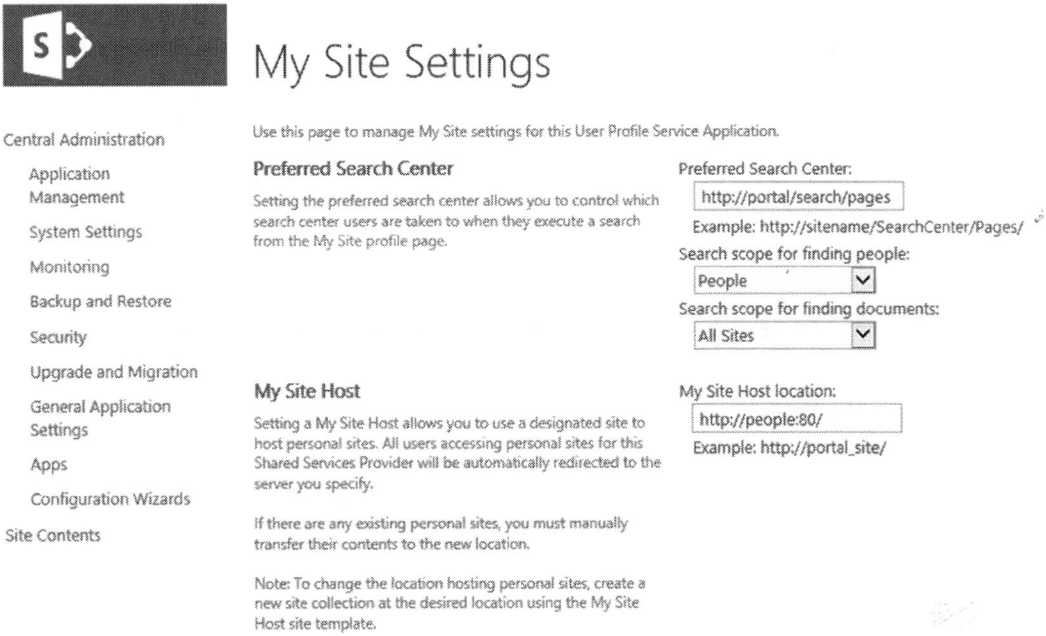

My Site Settings

Use this page to manage My Site settings for this User Profile Service Application.

Central Administration

Application Management

System Settings

Monitoring

Backup and Restore

Security

Upgrade and Migration

General Application Settings

Apps

Configuration Wizards

Site Contents

Preferred Search Center

Setting the preferred search center allows you to control which search center users are taken to when they execute a search from the My Site profile page.

Preferred Search Center:

http://portal/search/pages

Example: http://sitename/SearchCenter/Pages/

Search scope for finding people:

People

Search scope for finding documents:

All Sites

My Site Host

Setting a My Site Host allows you to use a designated site to host personal sites. All users accessing personal sites for this Shared Services Provider will be automatically redirected to the server you specify.

If there are any existing personal sites, you must manually transfer their contents to the new location.

Note: To change the location hosting personal sites, create a new site collection at the desired location using the My Site Host site template.

My Site Host location:

http://people:80/

Example: http://portal_site/

Figure 10-6. *The My Site Settings page*

On the My Site Settings page, you can configure the following options:

- **Preferred Search Center:** Allows you to control which search center to direct users to when they submit a search query from the My Site profile pages.

- **My Site Host:** Specifies the site to host personal sites and the My Site host to redirect users to the selected User Profile Service.

- **Personal Site Location:** Specifies the managed path location to create personal sites under, which should be an existing wildcard managed path configured for the web application hosting My Sites.

- **Site Naming Format:** Specifies the format to use to name new personal sites and how to resolve naming conflicts.

- **Language Options:** Selects whether users are permitted to choose the language of their personal sites when they first access it and queue its provisioning.

- **Read Permission Level:** Specifies the accounts or groups to grant the Read permission level at the time of site provisioning, granting read access for shared areas of a user's personal site.

- **Security Trimming Options:** Selects the security trimming options for links in activity feeds, ratings, social tags, and notes, configuring whether feed items should be hidden from users who lack permissions to see them, which is the default settings.

- **Newsfeed:** Selects whether you want to enable activities on My Site newsfeeds.

- **E-Mail Notifications:** Specifies the e-mail address to use for sending certain e-mail notifications, such as replies to conversations in which a user has participated.

- **My Site Cleanup:** Specifies whether a user's manager or a secondary My Site Owner should be granted access when a user's My Site is flagged for deletion after the user's profile has been deleted.

- **Privacy Settings:** Selects whether to make all users' My Sites public by default to allow other users to see a list of a user's followers and other activities, such as social tagging, content rating, birthdays, job title changes, and new blog posts.

Users might find that their newsfeed contains a lot of activities as they follow more and more things. There may be some activities they would prefer to exclude from their newsfeed to prevent other activity items from being lost in the noise. You can configure some options globally while managing the User Profile Service, but in many cases, it is probably easier to have the users set their own preferences. When a user edits their profile, they can click the Newsfeed Settings option to set their preferences. Figure 10-7 shows the options for the newsfeed settings.

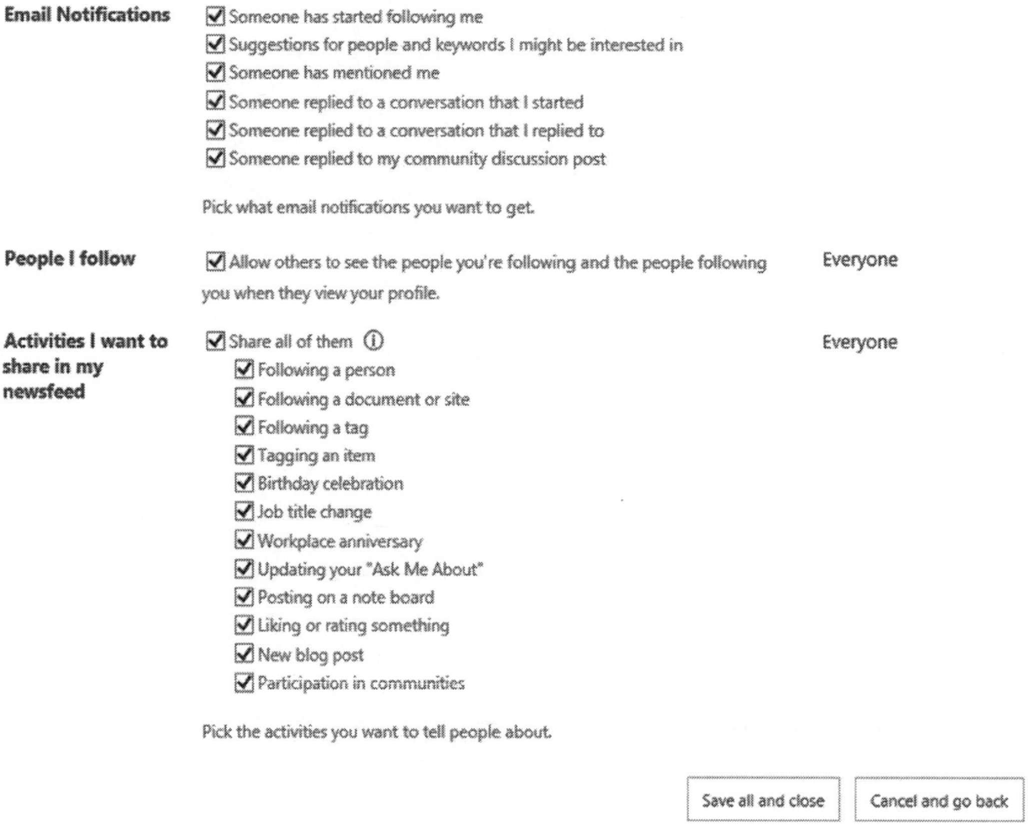

Email Notifications
- ☑ Someone has started following me
- ☑ Suggestions for people and keywords I might be interested in
- ☑ Someone has mentioned me
- ☑ Someone replied to a conversation that I started
- ☑ Someone replied to a conversation that I replied to
- ☑ Someone replied to my community discussion post

Pick what email notifications you want to get.

People I follow
- ☑ Allow others to see the people you're following and the people following you when they view your profile.   Everyone

Activities I want to share in my newsfeed
- ☑ Share all of them ⓘ   Everyone
  - ☑ Following a person
  - ☑ Following a document or site
  - ☑ Following a tag
  - ☑ Tagging an item
  - ☑ Birthday celebration
  - ☑ Job title change
  - ☑ Workplace anniversary
  - ☑ Updating your "Ask Me About"
  - ☑ Posting on a note board
  - ☑ Liking or rating something
  - ☑ New blog post
  - ☑ Participation in communities

Pick the activities you want to tell people about.

[Save all and close]   [Cancel and go back]

Figure 10-7. *The Newsfeed setting options*

After you create and configure a User Profile Service with its My Site settings, you are ready to populate it with profiles and properties. You can populate profile data by configuring the profile synchronization connections.

Managing Profile Properties and Synchronization

A user profile includes a place to store profile pictures. If you use Active Directory and have Exchange and Lync deployed for your users, you can configure SharePoint to share this picture across all three applications, effectively making a user's My Site in SharePoint the form for managing their enterprise picture. To achieve this, you need to configure the Picture profile property to export its value back to Active Directory. In addition, you can map the SIP Address and Work E-mail profile properties to their respective Active Directory fields.

To configure the profile properties and map them with their respective Active Directory field, follow these steps:

1. Open SharePoint Central Administration and click the Manage Service Applications link in the Application Management section.

2. Select the User Profile Service and click the Manage button in the ribbon to navigate to the Manage Profile Service page.

3. Click the Manage Profile Properties in the People section.

4. On the Manage Profile Properties page, edit the Mapped Attributes for each of these properties to verify their synchronization mapping settings:

    *   **Picture:** The My Site profile picture's thumbnail image to share with Exchange and Lync. The export direction populates this property in Active Directory.

        *   **Direction:** Export

        *   **Attribute:** thumbnailPhoto

    *   **SIP Address:** The SIP Address property maps the profile value to enable the presence indicator at different locations in SharePoint sites. The import direction pulls the value from the identity source.

        *   **Direction:** Import

        *   **Attribute:** msRTCSIP-PrimaryUserAddress

    *   **Work E-mail:** The work e-mail maps the default e-mail display field in the user profile with the default e-mail field's imported value from an identity source system such as Active Directory.

        *   **Direction:** Import

        *   **Attribute:** mail

With the profile fields properly mapped, you are ready to configure the profile synchronization settings and begin importing profile values from the identity management system. The following steps walk you through how to configure the profile synchronization settings.

1. Return to the Manage Profile Service administration page.

2. Click the Configure Synchronization Connections link under the Synchronization category.

3. On the Synchronization Connections page, click the Create New Connection button to navigate to the Add New Synchronization Connection page shown in Figure 10-8.

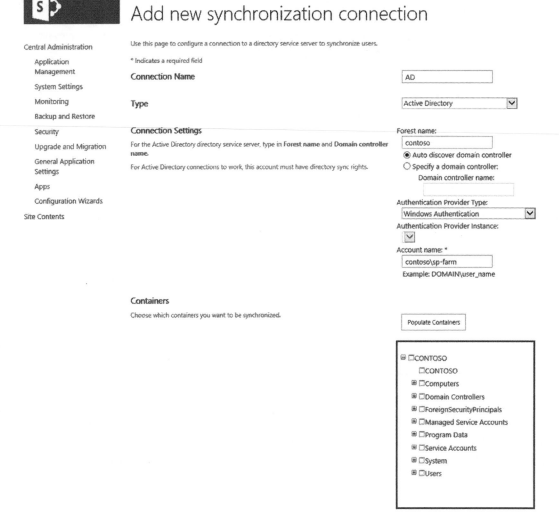

Figure 10-8. *The Add New Synchronization Connection page*

4. Enter a Connection Name and select a Connection Type from the drop-down box. You can select from the following Connection Types:

    - Active Directory

    - Active Directory Logon Data

    - Active Directory Resource

    - Business Data Connectivity

    - IBM Tivoli Directory Server (ITDS)

    - Novell eDirectory

    - Sun Java System Directory Server

5. Enter the authentication information and the remaining connection information. Click the OK button at the bottom of the page.

6. Return to the Manage Profile Service administration page and click the Start Profile Synchronization link under the Synchronization category.

7. On the Start Profile Synchronization page, select between an incremental and a full synchronization.

8. Click the OK button to begin importing and synchronizing profiles.

In addition to configuring the synchronization connection, you can also set synchronization options. To set these options, follow these steps:

1. Click the Configure Synchronization Settings link in the Synchronization section on the Manage Profile Service page.

2. Select whether to include users and groups or just users for the Synchronization Entities.

3. Select whether to include BCS connections for synchronization.

4. Select the Synchronization Option for the connection from the following options:

- Select Use SharePoint Profile Synchronization for the full-featured SharePoint profile synchronization.

- Select Use SharePoint Active Directory Import for the lightweight import option.

- Select Enable Identity Manager to use an external identity manager for the profile synchronization.

You should schedule regular profile synchronizations to capture changes and keep your profile data fresh. This will help ensure a fresh and relevant people search. The frequency of your synchronization schedule depends on how often data changes in the source system. Typically, I set the synchronization schedule as nightly. You can configure the schedule by clicking the Configure Synchronization Timer Job in the Synchronization section on the Manage Profile Service page.

PREPOPULATING PROFILE PICTURES

Often my clients will use a user's picture for his or her security access badge, and usually they store these pictures on a network share somewhere. These pictures can be a nice place to start for user profiles, and you can programmatically prepopulate a user's picture in his or her profile using his or her badge picture. This helps give your social computing launch more of a *wow* factor since users will see profile pictures right from the start.

You can use PowerShell or you can create a .NET utility to import the pictures. If the pictures are already online and available, you only need to update the Picture URL property value with the URL of the existing picture. The following C# code illustrates how to set the profile picture URL for a specific user.

```
string accountName = @"contoso\steve";
UserProfile userProfile = userProfileManager.GetUserProfile(accountName));
userProfile["PictureUrl"].Value = pictureUrl;
userProfile.Commit();
```

If you want to mimic the SharePoint functionality for situations when a regular user uploads his or her picture, you can also upload three thumbnails to the Profile Pictures folder in the User Photos library on the host My Site. Once you upload the thumbnails, you can set the Picture URL property value to the uploaded thumbnail. The following code illustrates the folder to upload the profile picture thumbnails to.

```
SPFolder folder = = web.Folders["User Photos"].SubFolders["Profile Pictures"];
```

Prepopulating default profile pictures, along with any other profile properties you wish, can help to get users started and it helps you provide a rich people search as soon as you launch, rather than waiting for users to upload their profile pictures and edit their profiles.

Promoting a Site

Promoted sites in SharePoint 2013 provide a way for you to list important sites for users to discover on the Sites page. This offers an alternative to linking everything from a global navigation on an intranet or maintaining a global site directory. Instead, users can discover promoted sites prominently displayed on the Sites page, along with a list of sites they are following and any recommended sites.

To promote a site, follow these steps:

1. Navigate to the Manage Profile Service page and click the Manage Promoted Sites link in the My Site Settings section.

2. On the Promoted Sites page, click New Link to navigate to the Promote A Site page, as shown in Figure 10-9.

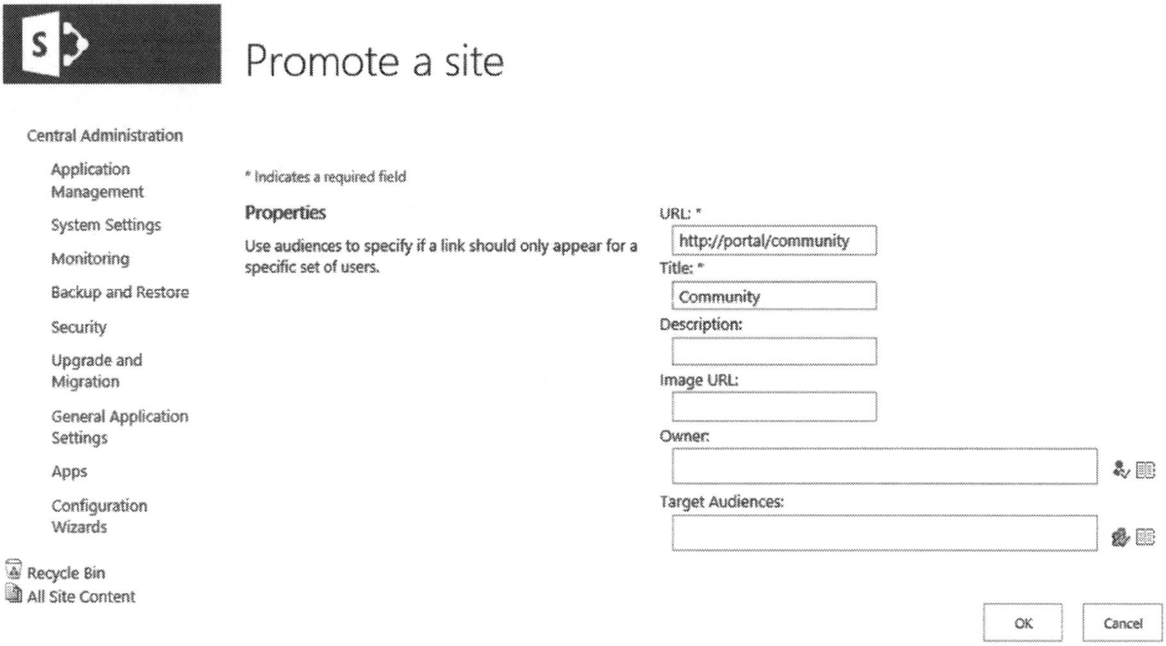

Figure 10-9. The Promote A Site page

3. Enter the URL, Title, and, optionally, a description and an image URL for the promoted site tile background. You can also specify an owner and target the promoted site to specific audiences. Click OK.

You can test the promoted site by navigating to the Sites page. Figure 10-10 shows an example of the Community promoted site I created.

Figure 10-10. *Example of a promoted site*

One way to organize your promoted sites is to only show them to people who would find the site relevant. In SharePoint, you can target promoted sites, links, web parts, and other user interface elements to specific users through a feature known as *audience targeting*.

Configuring Audience Targeting

Audiences are groups of related users you can identify through common memberships or property values. You define the membership of an audience by specifying the rule criteria to use for evaluating each user. For performance reasons, SharePoint compiles the membership of an audience on a recurring schedule rather than conducting a real-time dynamic membership evaluation for each request.

To create a new audience, follow these steps:

1. Navigate to the Manage Profile Service page and click Manage Audiences.

2. On the View Audiences page, click New Audience to navigate to the Create Audience page.

3. Specify an audience Name.

4. Specify if the audience includes users based on whether they match *all* or *any* of the rules you will define for the audience. Click OK.

5. On the Add Audience Rule page, you can select between User and Property for the rule Operand.

   • If you select *User*, you can set the rule criteria for users who report to a specified manager or for users who belong to a specified membership group.

   • If you select *Property*, you can set the rule criteria for users who share a specified property value. For example, in Figure 10-11, I selected the *Skills* property and set the value as *SharePoint* to create an audience of SharePoint Experts.

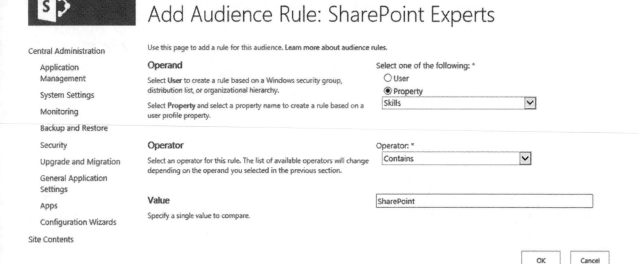

Figure 10-11 content:

Add Audience Rule: SharePoint Experts

Central Administration
- Application Management
- System Settings
- Monitoring
- Backup and Restore
- Security
- Upgrade and Migration
- General Application Settings
- Apps
- Configuration Wizards

Site Contents

Use this page to add a rule for this audience. Learn more about audience rules.

Operand

Select **User** to create a rule based on a Windows security group, distribution list, or organizational hierarchy.

Select **Property** and select a property name to create a rule based on a user profile property.

Select one of the following: *
- ○ User
- ● Property
  - Skills ▼

Operator

Select an operator for this rule. The list of available operators will change depending on the operand you selected in the previous section.

Operator: *
- Contains ▼

Value

Specify a single value to compare.

SharePoint

[OK] [Cancel]

Figure 10-11. The Add Audience Rule page

6.   Click OK to create the rule, and then navigate to the View Audience Properties page, as shown in Figure 10-12.

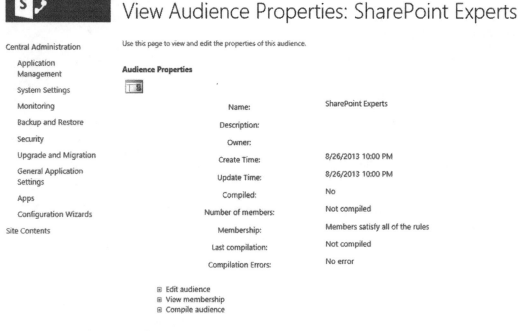

View Audience Properties: SharePoint Experts

Central Administration
- Application Management
- System Settings
- Monitoring
- Backup and Restore
- Security
- Upgrade and Migration
- General Application Settings
- Apps
- Configuration Wizards

Site Contents

Use this page to view and edit the properties of this audience.

Audience Properties

Name:	SharePoint Experts
Description:	
Owner:	
Create Time:	8/26/2013 10:00 PM
Update Time:	8/26/2013 10:00 PM
Compiled:	No
Number of members:	Not compiled
Membership:	Members satisfy all of the rules
Last compilation:	Not compiled
Compilation Errors:	No error

- ⊞ Edit audience
- ⊞ View membership
- ⊞ Compile audience

Figure 10-12. The View Audience Properties page

7. Click Compile Audience to compile the audience and populate its membership of users who meet the rule criteria you specified.

■ **Note** Remember that SharePoint compiles the audience's membership on a schedule, so if a user changes a profile property value that matches an audience rule, he or she will not actually be included in the audience until the next scheduled audience member compilation.

With your new audience created and compiled, you can use it to target user interface elements anywhere SharePoint provides the option to specify an audience for targeting, such as with web parts and links. This can help you design a page with the highest content relevancy for users by omitting any irrelevant items.

■ **Important** Audiences do not provide, nor do they enforce, security; they selectively render an element based on targeting rules, but this is not the same as security trimming because the underlying content is still accessible to the users.

Creating a Personal Blog

Blogs are a handy way to publish articles and communicate with an audience. You can quickly create your personal blog by navigating to the My Site personal profile and clicking the Blog link. The first time you click this link, SharePoint will provision a new blog site for you, similar to the one shown in Figure 10-13.

Figure 10-13. *The default blog welcome page*

Notice on the right, the Blog Tools web part lists several administrative links in a convenient location. The most useful for any blog is the Create A Post link, which navigates to the New Blog Post page shown in Figure 10-14, where you can enter the content and publish a new blog post.

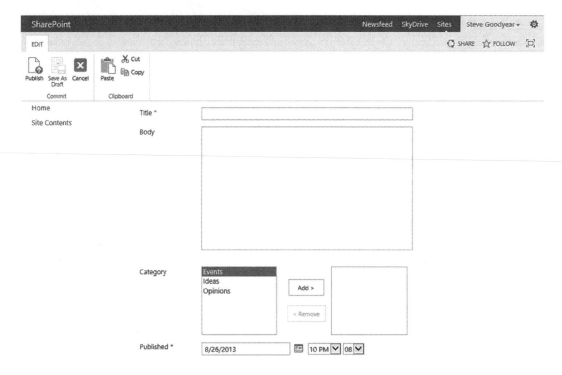

Figure 10-14. *The New Blog Post page*

Wrapping Up

People can discover knowledge and expertise in an organization through other people: colleagues, peers in other departments, subject-matter experts, and the like. Finding these people and discovering related information might be easier when you already know the people or what you are looking for, but without a social computing strategy, much of what you do not know to look for can be missed. Social computing does not equate to social networking; instead, I noted how it is about people discovering and accessing information through other people. I described some key social features in SharePoint 2013 to aid in this sort of content discovery, including people search, people profiles, social tagging, and blogs.

Social computing helps regular users discover relevant information in the context of their job functions. Between search and the social aspects that SharePoint provides, knowledge workers have the tools they need to find and research information. The organization's compliance officers can also use these tools to locate content relating to any compliance or legal requirement. They can use either the search tools for ad hoc discovery or the more sophisticated tools to manage eDiscovery—tools that leverage the search index with an emphasis on compliance. In the next chapter, I discuss eDiscovery and discovery case management in more depth, stepping through the product features and providing guidance on how to plan for and manage discovery cases.

CHAPTER 11

Managing eDiscovery and Discovery Cases

However beautiful the strategy, you should occasionally look at the results.

—Winston Churchill

How can you prepare your organization for legal or regulatory cases? Your strategy might demand a quick and comprehensive disclosure response, and you can achieve this using the eDiscovery feature in SharePoint 2013. In this chapter, I provide an overview of eDiscovery in general and its capability within SharePoint 2013. I also walk you through how to configure the feature and add content sources to make organizational content available for eDiscovery. Finally, I share the steps and techniques to manage and configure individual discovery cases.

After reading this chapter, you will know how to

- Describe the eDiscovery capability in SharePoint.

- Configure eDiscovery in SharePoint.

- Manage and configure discovery cases.

- Perform a content audit.

Overview of eDiscovery

What is eDiscovery? The term *eDiscovery* stands for *electronic discovery*, and quite simply, it is a means of discovering electronic or digital assets and artifacts existing within an organization. It is more formal and inclusive than an end user's search seeking to discover content on a particular subject. Instead, it involves locating every instance related to a specific case, usually a case of a legal or regulatory compliance nature. An organization uses eDiscovery to identify each unit of information, packaged together for discovery and even disclosure.

Before I get too far into the theory and features, let's consider the problem eDiscovery tries to solve. Imagine, if you will, an organization filled with structured and unstructured data, most pertaining to some aspect of the organization's operations. Now imagine one of several things happening that would require that organization to comb through its data and account for every instance of information relating to a particular topic. Some things that can happen include:

- A lawsuit against the organization requiring full disclosure

- An internal incident a team wants to investigate and determine its root cause

- A regulatory compliance audit against the organization

- An antitrust case related to a Competition Act

All of these incidents typically include a subpoena or court order legally requiring the organization to provide full disclosure of information to the other party. Without an effective system in place, the organization may face contempt of court charges for burdening the other party with too much irrelevant information or for unknowingly withholding information.

For example, what if a maker of one product felt that another firm was acting in an anticompetitive manner? The first firm might bring about an antitrust investigation through its local government. The government would require copies of any information related to the antitrust investigation in a timely manner, including formal records and transitory content such as collaborative documents and any e-mail messages that still exist.

An organization with a good eDiscovery strategy and system in place can respond quickly, feeling confident that it has disclosed all the required information. The organization can also efficiently determine what its risk exposure is and how motivated it should be to settle or fight the case, all by having a global view of any relevant enterprise content.

Electronic discovery involves two aspects for an effective case management system: a business process and the underlying technology to support the case management implementation details. The technical side consists of the implementation and configuration of system features (in this case, SharePoint product features). Your business processes include any policies and procedures you have related to legal or regulatory discovery, as well as the roles and responsibilities related to each. This can include a variety of processes, such as:

- Who has the authority to manage an eDiscovery case?

- What triggers an eDiscovery case?

- How is disclosure packaged and transmitted?

- What repositories does an eDiscovery system access?

These are not easy questions, although they might sound reasonably straightforward. In my experience, it is best to work through the different scenarios and potential exceptions ahead of time, defining the different business processes with the case management policies and procedures before you need them. That way when an incident occurs or a case otherwise arises, you will have the systems and processes in place to respond quickly and efficiently. The alternative could catch you unprepared, potentially interrupting your regular operations and possibly even putting the organization at risk.

Another characteristic of eDiscovery involves working alongside the ongoing operations of the organization— rarely does a case completely shut down an organization before allegations are proven and due diligence exhausted. This means that an eDiscovery process needs to work without impairing the day-to-day operations of an organization, and without an effective system in place, the discovery process and case management could consume too much manual effort and interfere with conducting business.

By setting up an effective system, you mitigate your organization's risk exposure. Legal and regulatory compliance issues will usually catch you by surprise, and an eDiscovery system will not make you immune to that, but an effective system with predefined processes will leave you prepared and enable you to respond with the best available information and in a timely manner.

The manual eDiscovery option is overly cumbersome mostly because a typical organization has too many repositories of content. Figure 11-1 illustrates some of the different repositories of information in an organization that an eDiscovery case will involve. As you can see, for a case manager to check each repository individually would be time consuming, and exponentially more so in repositories without a search capability available. What a case manager needs is an enterprise solution, one that spans and indexes all enterprise systems and content repositories so that when an eDiscovery case occurs, he or she can efficiently identify any related content.

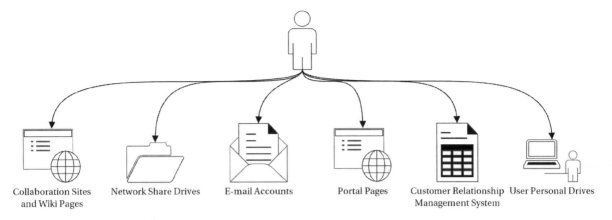

| Collaboration Sites and Wiki Pages | Network Share Drives | E-mail Accounts | Portal Pages | Customer Relationship Management System | User Personal Drives |

Figure 11-1. *Potential repositories included in an eDiscovery case*

When an incident occurs or something else initiates the need for electronic discovery in your organization, you can conceptually group the discovery requirements and needed actions together as an *eDiscovery case.* Each case can relate to a regulatory or legal case. It provides a case manager with a useful way to map and track cases with external discovery requests. A case manager role can include legal counsel, information or records managers, or auditors.

Case management includes the tools as well as the processes for effectively managing and processing discovery cases. This can include things such as specifying the discovery criteria, identifying the content sources, and packaging the content for disclosure. SharePoint 2013 introduces the eDiscovery feature, which it implements through a combination of sites and its search engine. In the next section, I provide an overview of the different characteristics and features of eDiscovery in SharePoint.

SharePoint 2013 eDiscovery Features

The new eDiscovery feature is one of those key features I find moves organizations to upgrade to SharePoint 2013. In the past, an organization might consider delaying an upgrade or skipping a version for a variety of reasons, such as those relating to costs or standardization. Often in these cases, one could justify deferring an upgrade because other workaround solutions existed. A solution may involve a compromise on the available functionality or user experience vs. a newer version, or it may involve higher development costs to fill a gap, but usually a reasonable alternative was available. With eDiscovery, the alternative (typically manual) solutions are much less desirable, so the need for eDiscovery continues to increase.

SharePoint 2013 introduces the eDiscovery Center site template, a specialized site with features to support discovery case management. Figure 11-2 shows the default welcome page of a site created using the eDiscovery site template.

Home

eDiscovery

Cases

Site Contents

 Welcome to the eDiscovery Center

Use this site to create, manage and work on eDiscovery Cases. With eDiscovery Cases you can manage the identification and in-place hold of Exchange mailboxes, SharePoint sites, and other sources of content. You can also create and manage search queries to identify relevant content and then export the search results.

 Create new case

Get Started

1. Grant your legal users permissions to access content across your SharePoint deployment. We recommend creating a security group that contains your legal team members.
2. To discover Exchange mailboxes, ensure your administrator has installed the Exchange Web Services Managed Client on all SharePoint servers and have your administrator configure authentication between Exchange and SharePoint.
3. Give your legal team security group user policy

In-Place Hold, Search, & Export

- With in-place holds you can specify SharePoint sites and mailboxes to place on hold. When content is modified or deleted it will be stored in-place until you need to export it.
- In-place eDiscovery search allows you to search across SharePoint sites, file shares, and Exchange mailboxes. Use proximity, wildcards, Boolean logic, and refiners to scope the results to the content you

Figure 11-2. *The SharePoint 2013 eDiscovery site*

The eDiscovery site template contains features to create and manage a discovery case itself, such as the discovery query and any content holds. These site features provide the user experience for case management. The site does not contain features to crawl the actual content; eDiscovery utilizes the SharePoint search index to query and discover content.

■ **Note**   Please see Chapter 9, where I discuss the SharePoint search engine in more detail.

By using SharePoint search, an eDiscovery case can take advantage of the powerful enterprise search engine for querying content. It also standardizes and simplifies how SharePoint accesses, crawls, and indexes content. Figure 11-3 illustrates the logical architecture of an eDiscovery site utilizing the SharePoint search service, which in turn crawls and indexes the content.

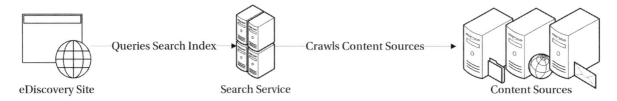

eDiscovery Site   Queries Search Index   Search Service   Crawls Content Sources   Content Sources

Figure 11-3. *Logical architecture of eDiscovery components in SharePoint 2013*

As you are planning your eDiscovery solution, keep in mind that with this search component in the eDiscovery architecture, you can include practically any unit of information on your organization's network as part of your eDiscovery solution's scope. The content sources that your SharePoint search engine can crawl also serve as an eDiscovery content source. This is significant because it allows you to include much more than documents.

■ **Important**   The scope of your eDiscovery solution can include SharePoint farms, Exchange, and Lync, enabling you to implement a thorough enterprise-wide electronic discovery solution.

The following lists some ideas about the different content sources you can include by taking advantage of the search service:

- SharePoint sites

- Exchange mailboxes and public folders

- Network file shares

- Web sites and wiki pages

- Third-party content repositories and records centers using SharePoint connectors

If the search engine can reach the content source on the network and you have configured it to access and crawl the content, then your eDiscovery solution will include that content source as well. I am excited by the possibilities this brings because it enables a case manager to have a global view of all electronic content, anywhere on the organization's network.

Another important feature of SharePoint eDiscovery is the concept of *in-place holds* for SharePoint and Exchange content. This allows a case manager to discover content without interfering with the ongoing operations of teams working with the content. When a case manager applies an in-place hold to content, the content remains in its original location and users can continue to work with it in context. If a user edits content with a hold applied, SharePoint captures a copy of the content at the time the hold was placed and stores the copy in the *Preservation Hold* library.

The Information Management Retention timer job runs periodically and cleans up the Preservation Hold library by comparing the library's contents with eDiscovery filters. Unless content matches at least one of the filters, the timer job deletes the content from the preservation hold library.

■ **Note**   For more information on eDiscovery in SharePoint 2013, please see the TechNet article at
`http://technet.microsoft.com/fp161516`.

Creating and Configuring an eDiscovery Portal

You can create an eDiscovery portal the same way as any other site collection. On the Create Site Collection page, select the eDiscovery Center template in the Template Selection section, as shown in Figure 11-4.

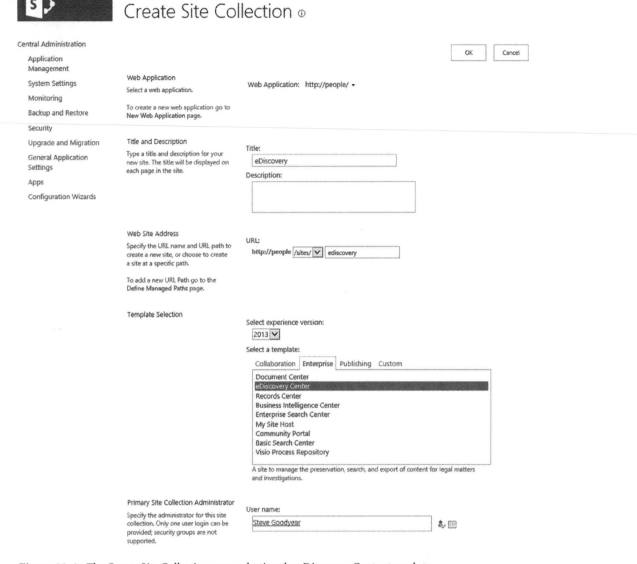

Figure 11-4. *The Create Site Collection page selecting the eDiscovery Center template*

The eDiscovery Center hosts all the discovery cases, with each case contained in a sub site. When you create a new eDiscovery Center, SharePoint provisions the default site groups—Owners, Members, and Visitors. I like to create an additional group to manage the case manager membership and permissions.

1. To add a new group, navigate to the Site Settings page and click the People and Groups link.

2. Click the Groups link in the left navigation menu to navigate to the People and Groups page, as shown in Figure 11-5.

Figure 11-5. *The People and Groups page*

3. Click the New button to create a new group.

4. Enter a Name for the group, such as *Case Managers*, and check to grant the group Full Control, as shown in Figure 11-6. Specify any other settings you wish, and then click Create.

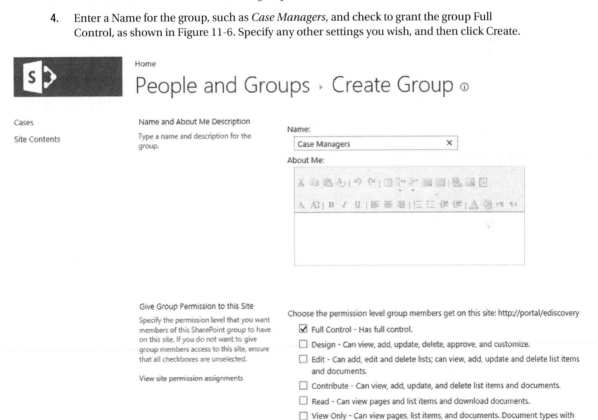

Figure 11-6. *The Create Group page*

I recommend that you use an Active Directory security group to centrally manage the group membership from a single location. You can create a new group using the Active Directory Users and Computers tool. Figure 11-7 provides an example of creating such a security group.

Figure 11-7. *Creating a new security group in Active Directory*

Once you have a domain security group, you can add it to the *Case Managers* SharePoint site group, as shown in Figure 11-8.

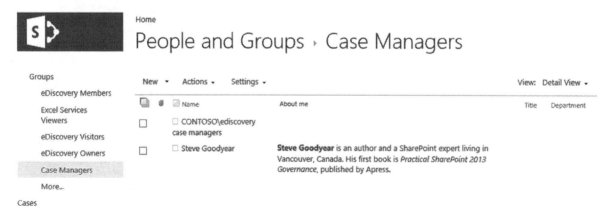

Figure 11-8. *The Case Managers group membership*

You can reuse this group to grant full read access permissions to all site content by granting a User Policy to any of the source web applications. To grant a User Policy on a web application, follow these steps:

1. Navigate to the Application Management page in SharePoint Central Administration and click Manage Web Applications.

2. Select the desired web application and click the User Policy button in the ribbon.

3. Click Add Users and add the eDiscovery Case Managers security group you created previously in Active Directory, as shown in Figure 11-9.

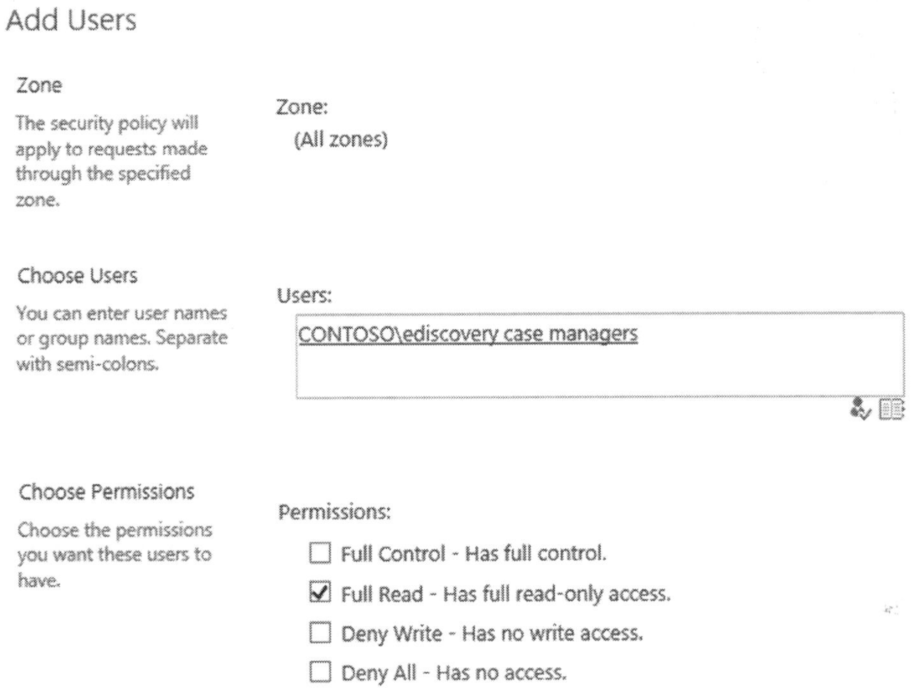

Add Users

Zone

The security policy will apply to requests made through the specified zone.

Zone:

(All zones)

Choose Users

You can enter user names or group names. Separate with semi-colons.

Users:

CONTOSO\ediscovery case managers

Choose Permissions

Choose the permissions you want these users to have.

Permissions:

☐ Full Control - Has full control.

☑ Full Read - Has full read-only access.

☐ Deny Write - Has no write access.

☐ Deny All - Has no access.

Figure 11-9. *Adding users to a User Policy on a web application*

> ■ **Note**   You will also have to grant read permissions to the eDiscovery Case Managers security group for any Exchange mailboxes you wish to include as a discovery source, as well as any network file shares and any other content repository to include as a source location in the eDiscovery solution.

Because this security group has such wide and elevated access to content, it is best to plan your security using a principle of least privilege. One option is to create an administrative account for your case managers to use when they create a discovery case, and you can add this account to the eDiscovery Case Managers security group. Alternatively, you can grant membership to the security group only when a case manager has an active discovery case to manage. This will help to prevent accidental disclosure of information by minimizing the amount of time a case manager's account has elevated read permissions.

Once you have your eDiscovery Center configured, you can begin to create discovery cases. In the next section, I step through how to create a discovery case and the different settings you can use to query and filter content.

Creating and Managing Discovery Cases

You can create a discovery case by clicking the Create New Case button on the eDiscovery Center welcome page. This creates a new SharePoint site within the eDiscovery Center site collection and it uses the eDiscovery Case site template, as shown in Figure 11-10.

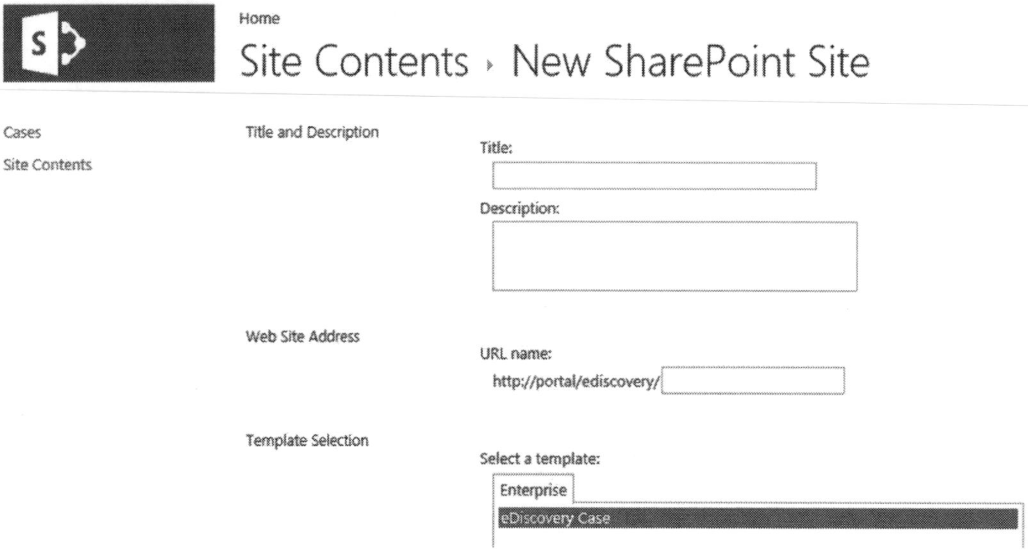

Home

Site Contents › New SharePoint Site

Cases

Site Contents

Title and Description

Title:

Description:

Web Site Address

URL name:

http://portal/ediscovery/

Template Selection

Select a template:

Enterprise

eDiscovery Case

Figure 11-10. *Creating a new Case site using the eDiscovery Case site template*

■ **Tip**   Consider using a descriptive naming convention for your eDiscovery case sites. You can use the site Title or Description fields to reference a case number or some other identifying characteristic to map back to an external case or compliance order.

Figure 11-11 shows the welcome page for a new discovery case site. You have two main options to discover content: you can create an eDiscovery Set or a Query.

Figure 11-11. *The welcome page for a new discovery case site*

- **eDiscovery Sets** find and preserve content located in Exchange mailboxes, SharePoint sites, and file shares. You can optionally apply an in-place hold to the SharePoint and Exchange sources.

- **Queries** find and export content based on a filter defining your search criteria from sources that include Exchange mailboxes, SharePoint sites, file shares, and eDiscovery Sets. You can use a query to export and download a copy of the matching content.

To create a new eDiscovery Set, click the New Item button in the Identify and Hold section on the discovery case site welcome page.

1. Specify a descriptive Name for the eDiscovery Set.

2. Click the Add & Manage Sources link to add any applicable sources, as shown in Figure 11-12. Add the applicable sources and click OK.

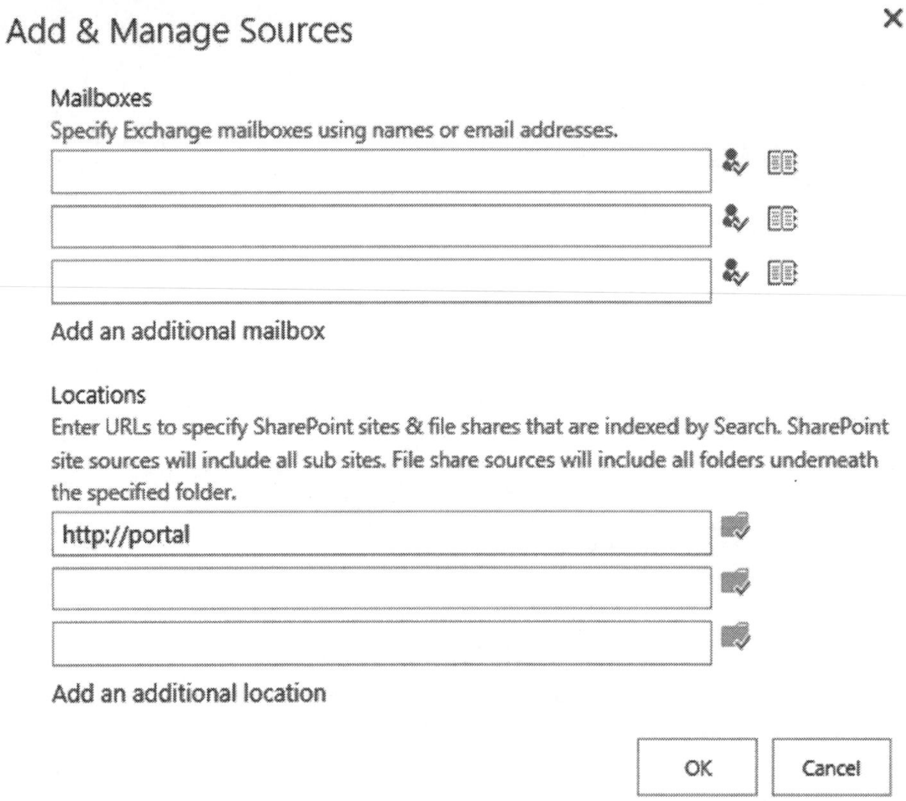

Add & Manage Sources ✕

Mailboxes

Specify Exchange mailboxes using names or email addresses.

Add an additional mailbox

Locations

Enter URLs to specify SharePoint sites & file shares that are indexed by Search. SharePoint site sources will include all sub sites. File share sources will include all folders underneath the specified folder.

http://portal

Add an additional location

OK   Cancel

Figure 11-12. *The Add & Manage Sources modal window*

■ **Note** For eDiscovery integration with Exchange, you first need to install the Microsoft Exchange Web Services Managed API 2.0 on the SharePoint servers. Please see the TechNet site at www.microsoft.com/download/details. aspx?id=35371 for information on these components.

---

3. If desired, enter a search query in the Filter field.

4. Enter the other filter parameters, such as the Start and End Date, Author, or Sender.

5. Click Apply Filter.

6. Select to Enable or Disable In-Place Hold.

7. Click Save.

Figure 11-13 shows an example creating a new eDiscovery Set. In this example, I set the filter parameters to find content authored by *Steve Goodyear* during the month of July. For simplicity, I also entered an advanced Filter query to search for content titled *Sample*.

Home

New: eDiscovery Set

Search this site

eDiscovery Sets
Queries
Sources
Exports
Documents
Site Contents

eDiscovery Set Name *   Steve Goodyear July Content

Sources (Add & Manage Sources)

Name	Source Type	In-Place Hold Status	Items	Size
Portal	SharePoint	On hold with filter	...	
			Total: 1	20.90 KB

Filter

title:sample

Start Date: 7/1/2013

End Date: 7/31/2013

Author/Sender:
Steve Goodyear x

Domain (Exchange only):

Search syntax and tips   Apply Filter

In-Place Hold

Certain sources such as SharePoint and Exchange can be held in place. This will protect content in its original location so if it is modified or deleted it will be retained in a secure location. If a source does not support in-place hold, you can export the content and place it in a secure location to protect it.

◉ Enable In-Place Hold
○ Disable In-Place Hold

Figure 11-13. *An example creating a new eDiscovery Set*

After you create an eDiscovery Set, the In-Place Hold Status dashboard on the case site welcome page will display the number of affected content items and their respective hold statuses, similar to the example in Figure 11-14.

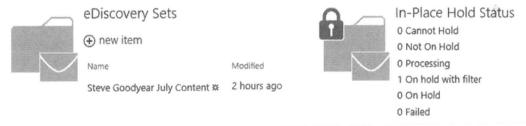

Identify and Hold

eDiscovery Sets

⊕ new item

Name	Modified
Steve Goodyear July Content ✳	2 hours ago

In-Place Hold Status

0 Cannot Hold
0 Not On Hold
0 Processing
1 On hold with filter
0 On Hold
0 Failed

Figure 11-14. *The In-Place Hold Status dashboard*

Using eDiscovery Sets provides a means to discover content and place it on hold. However, compliance or legal requirements may require you to provide disclosure of the content involved in the discovery case. Lucky for you, SharePoint 2013 eDiscovery also enables you to export content.

Exporting and Packaging Content

As part of the eDiscovery Case site template, you can export a copy of content matching a query. You cannot directly export an eDiscovery Set; instead, you need to create a Query, and the query can optionally use the eDiscovery Set as a source location.

■ **Tip** If your eDiscovery Set includes a source that does not support in-place holds, you can use a query to export the content included in your eDiscovery Set to store and hold in a safe location.

The first thing to do if you do not have an existing source location or eDiscovery Set configured is to create a source to use for the discovery and export query. To create an eDiscovery source location, click Sources in the left navigation menu, and then click New Item. On the New Source page, you can select between a Mailbox and a Location content type, as shown in Figure 11-15. Use Mailbox for Exchange mailboxes and Location for SharePoint or file share locations.

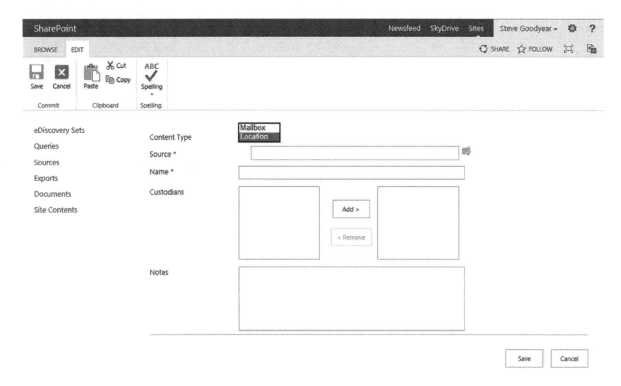

Figure 11-15. *The Create Source page*

Alternatively, you can use an eDiscovery Set as a source, if one exists matching your source criteria. You can choose either a source location or an eDiscovery Set as you create a query. To create a new query, click Queries on the left navigation menu and click New Item. Enter the following Query information:

- **Name:** Provide a descriptive name for the query.
- **Query:** Enter a search query to filter the results based on relevance.

- **Start Date:** Enter the start date range to query.

- **End Date:** Enter the end date range to query.

- **Author or Sender:** Enter the author or sender to filter the results based on either.

Click the Modify Query Scope link in the Sources section to select between source locations and eDiscovery Sets, as the example in Figure 11-16 shows.

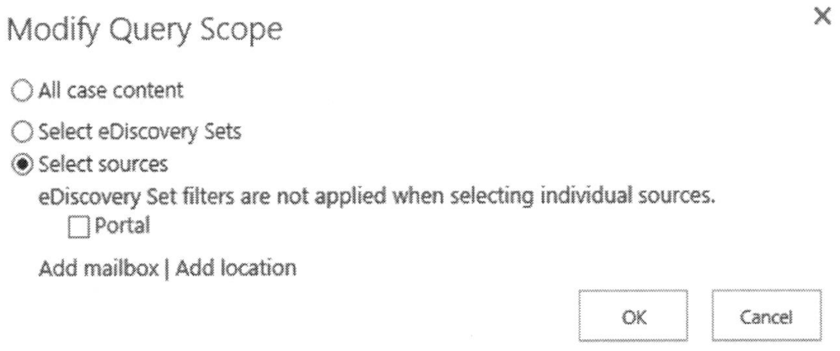

Figure 11-16. *The Modify Query Scope page*

Toggle between the Exchange and SharePoint tabs to configure the options as appropriate. For example, in Figure 11-17, I specified a query to search for content authored by *Steve Goodyear* between a date range of July to September. I then further filtered the results by specifying a filter based on Word documents (the *.docx* file extension).

Figure 11-17. *Example of a query to discover content by a specific author in a date range*

After you configure your query options, click Save to save the query. You can then use the query to export content. To export content, click the Exports link in the left navigation menu on the case site welcome page.

1. Click New Item.

2. Select the query you want to use to select the content for export, and then click Next.

3. Check any desired options and click OK.

■ **Note**   Content exports include a load file based on the Electronic Discovery Reference Model standard.

SharePoint exports the content into a folder structure mimicking the structure from the source locations. To simplify disclosure, you can compress this folder structure into a zip file and transmit that file to the other party, or you can copy the directory as it is.

PERFORMING A CONTENT AUDIT

Part of an exported package from a Query includes a report inventorying all the files in the export. Alternatively, you can also generate this report without exporting all the content using the same eDiscovery Download Manager component. SharePoint generates an Excel spreadsheet for this report, which you can use to audit and analyze the content for a given query.

Wrapping Up

You can prepare your organization for legal and regulatory cases by planning your search index and creating an eDiscovery Center to manage discovery cases. This involves creating a site collection based on the eDiscovery Center site template, and then granting the required permissions to case managers to discover content. In this chapter, I described eDiscovery and how to configure it in SharePoint 2013. I also walked you through how to create and configure discovery cases, including the options for querying and filtering content. Finally, I explained how to export content for disclosure.

Setting up an effective eDiscovery solution will help you save time and respond quickly to any legal or regulatory discovery and disclosure requirements. Content discovery is useful in a variety of ways, as I have shown in the past few chapters, including connecting users with information and helping them to be productive. There are times, however, when you want to prevent discovery of content to protect its information. In the next chapter, I provide an overview of the different security aspects available in SharePoint and I share some guidance on how to protect secrets as part of your enterprise content management solution.

CHAPTER 12

■ ■ ■

Securing Your Content

The trouble is, you think you have time.

—Gautama Buddha

How much information should your users discover and have access to, and how do you prevent unintentional disclosure of all the other information? This involves security decisions identifying which content to expose and which to keep secret. In this chapter, I provide guidance on analyzing and identifying your security requirements to prevent unauthorized discovery of content and breaches of information, particularly as it relates to your organization's intellectual property. I also describe how SharePoint implements security to protect and control access to content. Finally, I provide an overview of the Active Directory Rights Management Service (AD RMS) and how it uses encryption to protect content beyond access control.

After reading this chapter, you will know how to

- Describe security concepts and the need to protect information.

- Create a threat model.

- Analyze and identify security requirements.

- Describe and configure SharePoint groups and permissions.

- Configure web application policies and permission levels.

- Understand Active Directory Rights Management Service (AD RMS).

Overview of Security

Not everything should be discoverable by everyone. Some information is sensitive for a variety of reasons, and the disclosure of that information can be damaging. I included this chapter on security in the part of the book that covers discovering content because it completes the picture of content discovery. Part of planning for how your content should be discovered involves planning who should discover the content—and for whom should the content not be exposed.

Connecting users to the information they need is important, a goal to strive toward as you design your search and social computing solutions. But that is only part of the picture, because not every user needs access to every piece of information in an organization.

Even in a highly transparent organization, it is best to hold back or filter some information from a general audience rather than making it directly accessible to every user. Not every member of an organization shares the same context or the same perspective, and so the different users might not interpret the information in the same manner. There are practically a limitless number of reasons and scenarios to secure content, many of which directly relate to the type of content. The following lists examples of several types of content requiring some degree of security to limit its audience from discovering and accessing its information:

- Employment information and other personal employee information

- Intellectual property and proprietary competitive information

- Financial information and other data considered within the insider trading domain

- Business strategy and marketing plans

Another reason is that people might simply feel more comfortable securing their content. Regardless of the reason, you implement security at the content level by managing permissions. Two important concepts for you to understand when planning permissions to secure content are *authentication* and *authorization*.

- *Authentication* concerns the process of confirming the requestor's identity, such as logging in with an account.

- *Authorization* concerns the process of confirming a requestor has permission or the rights to take some action, such as permission to access a document.

The two work hand-in-hand, since authorization can only be effective when you are certain you are authorizing the correct account. Figure 12-1 illustrates the difference between authentication and authorization.

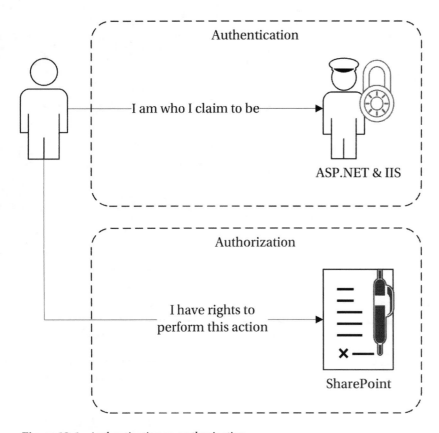

Figure 12-1. *Authentication vs. authorization*

SharePoint does not perform any authentication. You specify an authentication provider to validate a user's identity, such as the Windows authentication provider that Internet Information Services (IIS) will use to authenticate a user, or a custom ASP.NET forms authentication provider. Once a user is authenticated, the user's credentials are passed to SharePoint. SharePoint handles any authorization within the application, and you manage this by restricting permissions to content and granting permissions to users.

■ **Tip** As you plan your security solution, design it with a defense-in-depth strategy. This strategy uses layered defenses so that if any one layer is breached and compromised, another layer will limit the exposure and prevent a wider attack. For example, instead of relying on a single firewall, consider using multiple firewalls, and then add other defensive layers with hardened servers and complex service account passwords.

One challenge with security is that it can sometimes feel chaotic. An attacker can come from practically anywhere and only needs to find a vulnerability in one of the access points. You might feel pulled in every direction, running wild, chasing all sorts of potential threats. What you need is a systematic process to prioritize and focus your security efforts. One such process is to create and use a threat model.

Threat Modeling

A threat model helps you to focus and prioritize your security efforts by modeling possible threats against the risk, cost, and probability of a security breach. Once you design how you want to rank and model potential threats, you will have a systematic process to prioritize your security efforts.

Not all content holds the same value for an organization. As I noted earlier in this book, some content is transitory and will only provide value for a short time, while other content serves as official records, preserving evidence for a transaction or decision.

- Determine the value of an asset to protect.

- Consider the risk and probability of unintentional information disclosure.

- Calculate the costs associated with unintentional information disclosure.

- Evaluate the exposure and attractiveness of the asset to an adversary.

- Estimate the discoverability of an exploit or the asset's existence.

When I perform a threat model assessment, I usually use an Excel spreadsheet where I list all of the potential threats down the rows. I then list the ranking factors I noted in the previous list across the columns and apply a weight for each factor. Finally, I specify a relative value for each threat and have Excel calculate the overall rating for each threat. You can either sort or highlight the highest priority threats (those most valuable assets with the highest risk for attack).

■ **Note** Microsoft provides a threat modeling tool to help you analyze the security of a system. You can download the tool at www.microsoft.com/download/details.aspx?id=2955.

It is important for you to consider all the possible threats and vulnerabilities in your system, not just the obvious. Your threat model will be incomplete otherwise. Part of your threat model should consider the different users of the system and how they access the system. A large portion of your threat model for a SharePoint farm should consider the intended content you will be storing within the farm, content such as official records, financial information, and intellectual property.

IDENTIFYING YOUR INTELLECTUAL PROPERTY

Intellectual property (IP) is a work or invention resulting from creativity, often produced through research and development. A unit of information containing intellectual property is often valuable to an organization and something to protect because it will be damaging to an organization if the information is disclosed to the wrong party. Usually, intellectual property provides a competitive advantage to an organization.

This valuable and sensitive content warrants special attention in your threat model. Identify and list any intellectual property assets within your organization, and then ensure your users apply the appropriate security policies to protect this content.

Analyzing Your Information Security Requirements

First and foremost, you need to decide what information consists of a secret and what you can make available for general knowledge. Too much security, where everyone locks down their content to a limited audience, only leads to information silos. The risk here, of course, is that other knowledge workers will not be able to discover and benefit from the knowledge contained in a limited workgroup.

If you created a content inventory, as I discussed in Chapter 3, you will have a sense of what kinds of content the different sites store. This can help you determine how secure or how open the content should be. You can also use content classifications to guide decisions about the appropriate level of security based on an organization-wide classification scheme such as *Sensitivity* or *Security Level*.

___

■ **Note**   Please see Chapter 6, where I discuss content classifications in more detail.

___

As you analyze your information security requirements, you also need to consider the security of the SharePoint farm itself. If an attacker is able to compromise a farm, he or she will be able to thwart the security you apply within the farm. You can secure your farm using a defense-in-depth strategy and limiting the available attack surface. Some farm security strategies I consider include:

- Disabling unnecessary services

- Not installing extraneous software or components

- Blocking unused ports

- Deploying firewalls and proxy servers to segregate the SharePoint and database servers

___

■ **Note**   For more information and guidance on planning security hardening for SharePoint 2013 servers and farms, please see the TechNet article at `http://technet.microsoft.com/cc262849`.

___

You can also limit the surface available for attack by disposing any unused or no longer needed content. I discuss and provide guidance on content retention and disposition in Chapter 15, but I wanted to point it out here because once you dispose of content, it is no longer at risk for a security attack. There are plenty of reasons to dispose of content in a timely manner, and avoiding security breaches is one.

A good portion of your security requirements will relate to who may access particular content and what rights a user will possess to take actions against the content. In SharePoint, these access controls are managed through SharePoint permissions and SharePoint site groups.

Configuring SharePoint Groups and Permissions

You can grant permissions to a SharePoint group and add the user to that group, or you can grant the permissions directly to the user in a site. I prefer to add users to SharePoint groups and only assign permissions to the group because this makes it easier to update and manage any permissions in the future.

By default, a SharePoint site is created with three SharePoint groups: site owners, site members, and site visitors. You can add user accounts directly to these groups and the accounts will be granted the permissions applied to the group. Alternatively, you can add an Active Directory security group to the SharePoint group membership if you prefer to manage group membership through Active Directory. The default SharePoint site groups hold the following permissions:

- **Site Owners**: Group members are granted full control over the site, including granting permissions to other users.

- **Site Members**: Group members are granted contributor access to the site, where they can add, edit, and delete items in lists and libraries.

- **Site Visitors**: Group members are granted read access to the site.

Navigate to the Site Settings page, and then click People and Groups to manage the group membership. Select a group from the left navigation menu and click the New tab for the group to display the drop-down menu shown in Figure 12-2. In the Share modal window, add the name or e-mail address for each user you want to add to the group's membership. You can also add "Everyone" to the group to grant the group's permissions to all authenticated users. Click the Share button to complete adding the users to the SharePoint site group.

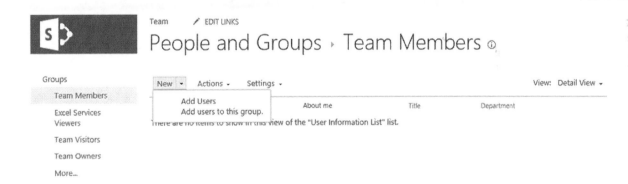

Figure 12-2. *The SharePoint site group's Add Users button*

> ■ **Note** For an example walking through the steps of creating a custom SharePoint site group, please see Chapter 11, where I explain how to create a custom group for eDiscovery Case Managers.

You can view the permissions assigned to a site group by clicking the View Group Permissions menu option on the group's Settings drop-down menu, as shown in Figure 12-3. This allows you to view the group's permission level assignments for the site and any subsite in the site collection.

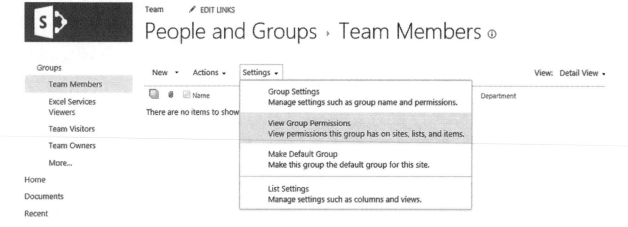

Figure 12-3. *The People And Groups settings page*

When you create a new SharePoint site group, you assign the permission level to the group. If you need to assign a different permission level to the site group, you can modify the permission level settings on the Site Permissions page. To modify a group's permission level, follow these steps:

1. Navigate to the Site Settings page.

2. In the Users and Permissions section, click Site Permissions to navigate to the Permissions page shown in Figure 12-4.

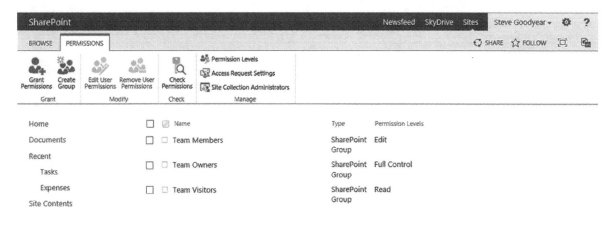

Figure 12-4. *The Permissions page*

3. Click the check box for the group you wish to edit the permissions for and click the Edit User Permissions button in the ribbon.

4. On the Edit Permissions page, select the desired permissions you want to grant to the group and click OK.

By default, SharePoint offers the following permissions levels to choose from:

- **Full Control**: Can manage permissions and administer the entire site and its content

- **Design**: Can view, add, update, delete, approve, and customize

- **Edit**: Can add, edit, and delete lists; can view, add, update, and delete items

- **Contribute**: Can view, add, update, and delete items

- **Read**: Can view pages and list items and download documents

- **View Only**: Can view pages, list items, and documents

These six sets of permissions are referred to as *permission levels*. Permission levels group individual permission rights for a user or group. In most cases, these defaults will suffice. However, at times you may have a requirement to grant a different combination of permission rights for a user, such as a subset of the permission rights in an existing permission level. In those cases, you can create a custom permission level.

▨ **Tip** It is always better to create a custom permission level rather than edit an existing permission level. Users will expect the default permission levels to behave a certain way. As such, users will not anticipate you changing the individual permission rights for one of those default permission levels, an unexpected change that could then cause a security or usability issue.

To create a custom permission level, follow these steps:

1. Navigate to the Site Permissions page shown in Figure 12-4.

2. Click the Permission Levels button in the ribbon.

3. On the Permission Levels page, click the Add A Permission Level button.

4. On the Add A Permission Level page shown in Figure 12-5, specify a name and description for the custom permission level and select the desired permissions to include. Finally, click Create.

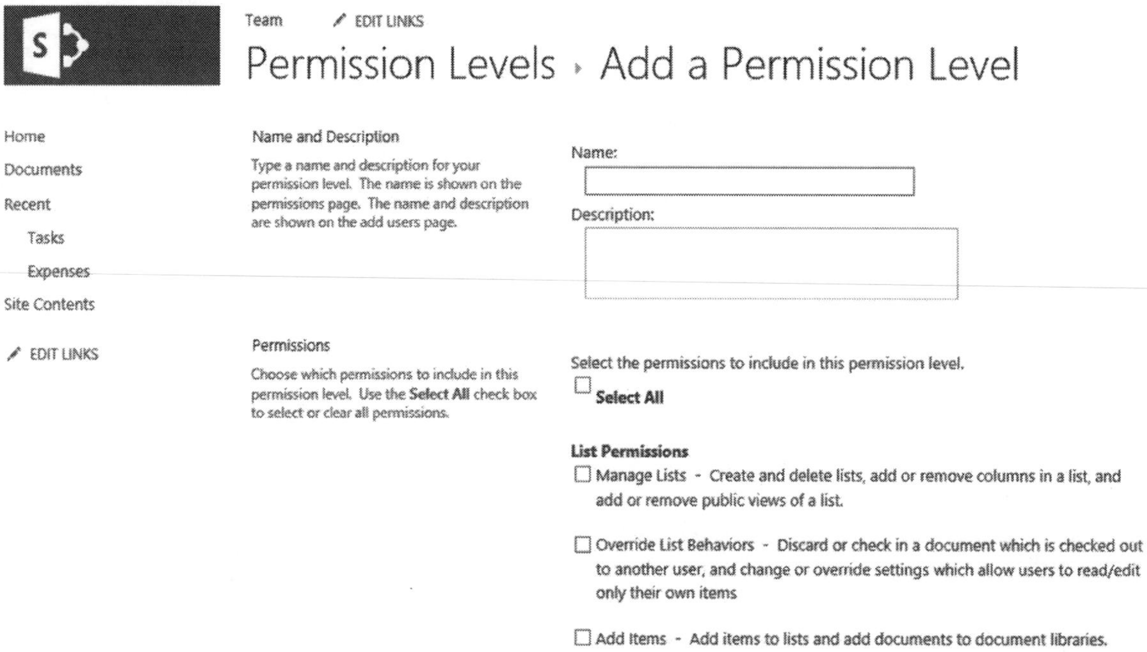

Team　　✎ EDIT LINKS

Permission Levels › Add a Permission Level

Home

Documents

Recent

  Tasks

  Expenses

Site Contents

✎ EDIT LINKS

Name and Description

Type a name and description for your permission level. The name is shown on the permissions page. The name and description are shown on the add users page.

Name:

Description:

Permissions

Choose which permissions to include in this permission level. Use the **Select All** check box to select or clear all permissions.

Select the permissions to include in this permission level.

☐ **Select All**

List Permissions

☐ Manage Lists - Create and delete lists, add or remove columns in a list, and add or remove public views of a list.

☐ Override List Behaviors - Discard or check in a document which is checked out to another user, and change or override settings which allow users to read/edit only their own items.

☐ Add Items - Add items to lists and add documents to document libraries.

Figure 12-5. *The Add A Permission Level page*

    SharePoint offers the following individual permission rights that you can include in a custom permission level. This list shows how granular you can configure and set permissions for a SharePoint site group to grant users and fulfill a variety of permission requirements.

- **List Permissions**
  - Manage Lists
  - Override List Behaviors
  - Add Items
  - Edit Items
  - Delete Items
  - View Items
  - Approve Items
  - Open Items
  - View Versions
  - Delete Versions
  - Create Alerts
  - View Application Pages
- **Site Permissions**
  - Manage Permissions
  - View Web Analytics Data

- Create Sub-sites
- Manage Web Site
- Add and Customize Pages
- Apply Themes and Borders
- Apply Style Sheets
- Create Groups
- Browse Directories
- Use Self-Service Site Creation
- View Pages
- Enumerate Permissions
- Browse User Information
- Manage Alerts
- Use Remote Interfaces
- Use Client Integration Features
- Open
- Edit Personal User Information
- **Personal Permissions**
  - Manage Personal Views
  - Add/Remove Personal Web Parts
  - Update Personal Web Parts

Some requirements involve granting users permission to every site collection in a web application. One option is to grant these permissions on each individual site collection, which can quickly become a management headache. For this reason, the SharePoint team added the ability to set a user policy to grant permissions for an entire web application.

Configuring Web Application User Policies

You may also wish to deny certain permission rights for users or groups and apply this restriction globally on a web application. You can set this using a user policy as well. To apply a user policy to a web application, follow these steps:

1. Navigate to the SharePoint Central Administration and click Manage Web Applications.

2. On the Manage Web Applications, select the web application for which you wish to apply a user policy.

3. Click the User Policy button in the ribbon.

4. On the Policy for Web Application page, click the Add Users button.

5. If desired, specify a zone for the user policy. Click Next.

6. On the Add Users page shown in Figure 12-6, specify the users and choose the permissions to grant or deny. Click Finish.

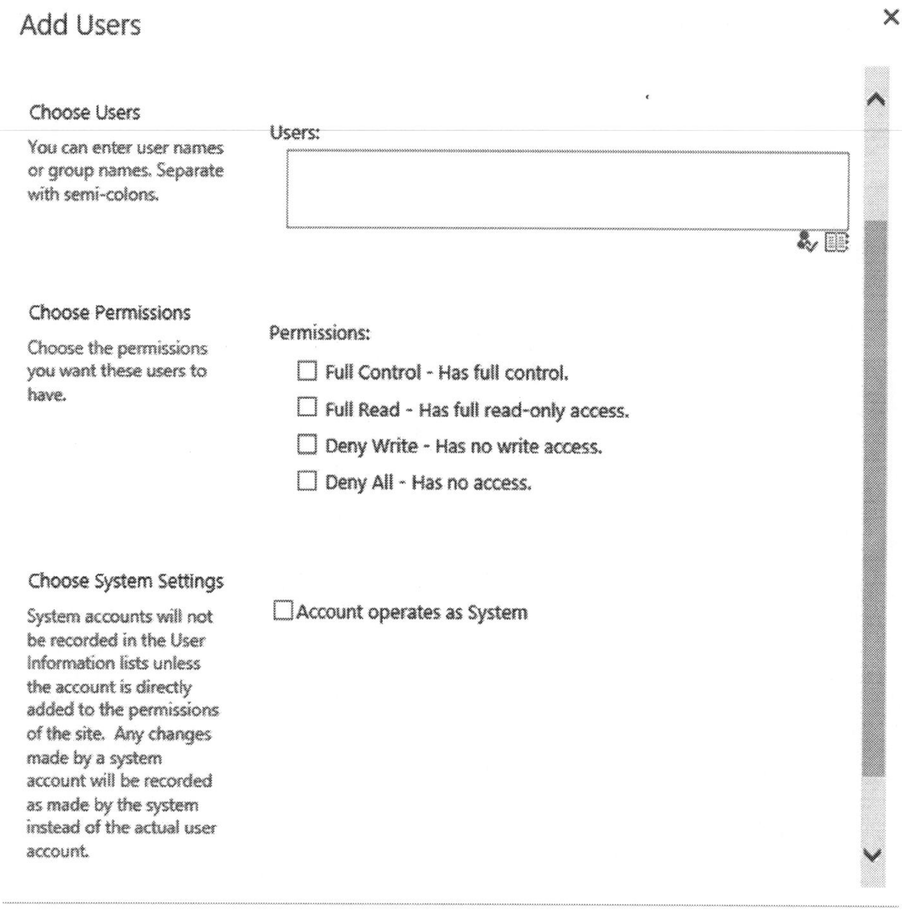

Add Users ✕

Choose Users

You can enter user names or group names. Separate with semi-colons.

Users:

Choose Permissions

Choose the permissions you want these users to have.

Permissions:

☐ Full Control - Has full control.

☐ Full Read - Has full read-only access.

☐ Deny Write - Has no write access.

☐ Deny All - Has no access.

Choose System Settings

System accounts will not be recorded in the User Information lists unless the account is directly added to the permissions of the site. Any changes made by a system account will be recorded as made by the system instead of the actual user account.

☐ Account operates as System

Figure 12-6. *The Add Users page for a web application User Policy*

By default, SharePoint offers four Permission Policy Levels:

- **Full Control**: Has full control

- **Full Read**: Has full read-only access

- **Deny Write**: Has no write access

- **Deny All**: Has no access

You may have requirements that need a special combination of permission rights to grant or deny to users on an entire web application. To create a custom permission policy, follow these steps:

1. Navigate to the Manage Web Applications page in SharePoint Central Administration.

2. Select the desired web application and click the Permission Policy button in the ribbon.

3. Click the Add Permission Policy Level button on the Manage Permission Policy levels page.

4. Specify the desired settings on the Add Permission Policy Level page shown in Figure 12-7. Click Save.

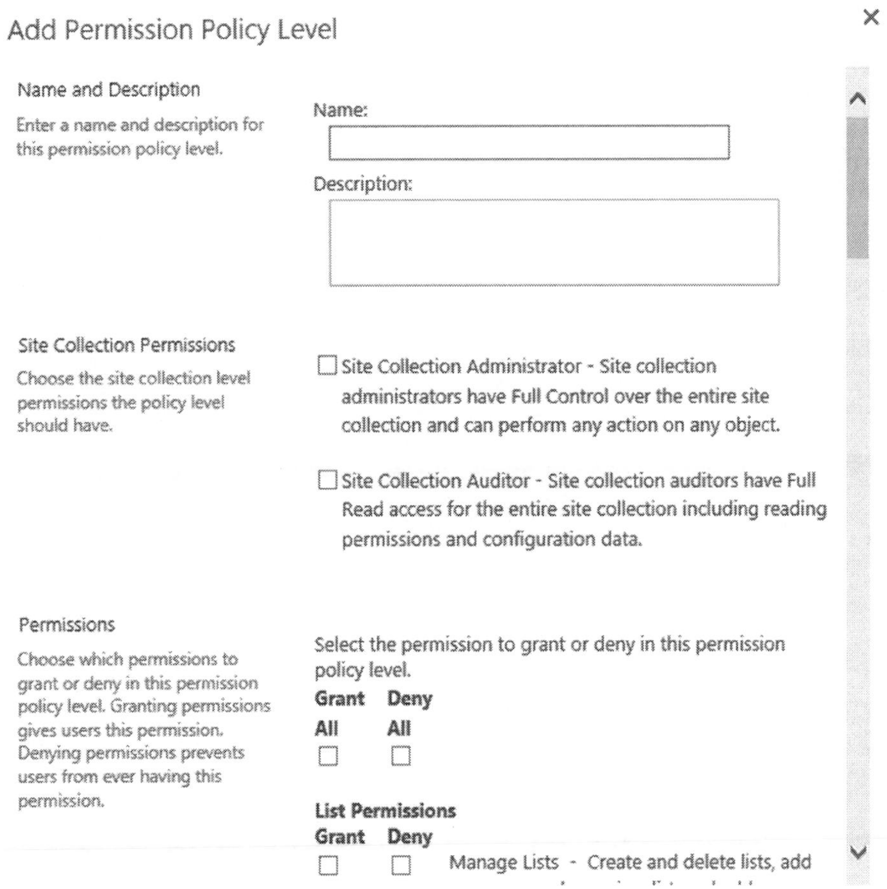

Figure 12-7. *The Add Permission Policy Level page*

Notice that you can create a permission policy level to grant Site Collection Administrator or Site Collection Auditor permissions. The administrator is the same as the Full Control default permission policy level. The auditor option allows you to grant full read access to the entire site collection for every site collection in the web application. This can be a useful option for managing eDiscovery or auditing permissions.

Each permission right offers the ability to grant or deny the permission. Creating a custom permission policy level and denying the desired permission level offers an effective solution to remove functionality from an entire web application for specified users whenever you want to prevent certain functionality.

Understanding Rights Management Service (RMS)

An Access Control List (ACL) stores the permission entries that determine which users can access a resource and what actions they can take on the shared copy. However, once a user executes his or her permission to access and download a piece of content, the access controls no longer enforce any restrictions on the content. One security risk with this security model is when a user downloads a file and then forwards it to another user who may not have permission granted to the original location.

The risk for this type of accidental or intentional disclosure of sensitive information drives the need for security that can protect a secret contained in a document beyond the initial access. Rights Management Service (RMS) mitigates this risk by providing an extra layer of security for a document using encryption technology. RMS encrypts a document, leaving it in an unreadable state.

When a user accesses a rights managed document, the Rights Management Service's client component contacts the Rights Management Service to identify what rights to grant the user. Figure 12-8 illustrates how RMS adds an additional layer of security in the content request process.

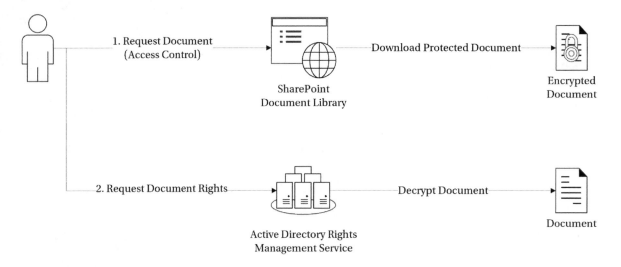

Figure 12-8. *Added layer of Rights Management Service in the content access process*

There are several reasons you might want to protect content with the added layer of Rights Management Service, including:

- Enforce a limited audience for a piece of content.
- Expire a piece of content after a specific duration.
- Prevent printing, copying, and taking screenshots of a piece of content.

The different scenarios you can implement using the Rights Management Service stem from different combinations of permission rights settings. You can grant or restrict the following permission rights for a piece of content:

- **Full Control**: Grants users every right listed, plus the right to change permission rights for the protected content.

- **View**: Allows users to open and read the protected content.

- **Edit**: Allows users to edit and change the protected content.

- **Save**: Allows users to save a protected file.

- **Extract**: Allows users to make a copy of any part of the protected content and paste it into another application.

- **Export**: Allows users to save the protected content in another file format using the Save As command.

- **Print**: Allows users to print the protected content.

- **Allow Macros**: Allows users to run macros against the protected content.

- **Forward**: Allows e-mail recipients to forward a protected message and to add or remove recipients.

- **Reply**: Allows e-mail recipients to reply to the sender of a protected message.

- **Reply All**: Allows e-mail recipients to reply to all recipients of a protected message.

- **View Rights**: Allows users to view the permission rights associated with the protected content.

▨ **Note**   For more information about the Active Directory Rights Management Service (AD RMS), please see the TechNet article at http://technet.microsoft.com/hh831364.

Configuring RMS in SharePoint

SharePoint is aware of the Rights Management Service and detects protected content when a user saves it to a library. Before saving a protected document, SharePoint will access the Rights Management Service and decrypt the document; it will then encrypt the content again before streaming any downloads to users. The reason it stores content without the Rights Management encryption applied is to optimize the search indexing process, otherwise the index crawler would have to decrypt each document every time it crawled content in a SharePoint farm.

To enable SharePoint to work with the Rights Management Service, navigate to SharePoint Central Administration and configure the settings in the following steps.

1. Click the Security link in the left navigation menu to navigate to the Security page.

2. Click the Configure Information Rights Management link in the Information Policy section to navigate to the Information Rights Management page.

3. On Information Rights Management page, select to use the default RMS server, as shown in Figure 12-9. Alternatively, you can specify a RMS server. Click OK.

Figure 12-9. *The Information Rights Management settings page*

■ **Note**   For more information about Rights Management Service in SharePoint 2013, please see the TechNet article at http://technet.microsoft.com/cc179103.

Inside Story: Notes from the Field

Securing a piece of content prevents others who lack permission from discovering it or its contents. In most cases, this is the desired behavior for the application. Users who have rights to access and read content are able to discover and consume the available information, and users who lack the necessary rights will most likely be oblivious to the content's existence since SharePoint security trims the item from search and site pages based on what a user has permission to view. But what about a user who needs to conduct research across the organization but who does not warrant holding permissions to every piece of content?

Usually, having SharePoint filter out search results a user does not have permission to access (also known as *security trimming*) improves the user experience, because users do not want to click on a result that interests them, only to discover they do not have permission to view it. Just from the very nature of showing a search result can expose a security hole, even without providing access to the content itself. SharePoint search results include the title, a summary, and often even a preview of the content, which can disclose sensitive information if the result is not security trimmed. For example, if I conduct a search for "layoffs 2013" and see an Excel spreadsheet in the search results, I could learn some details about an upcoming event that the organization did not yet want to disclose.

Nevertheless, if SharePoint filters out the results users do not yet have permission to view, then a researcher cannot discover the content until he or she becomes aware of its existence and then requests permissions to access it. This can affect productivity and even lead an organization to make incorrect decisions based on limited information.

■ **Note**   For more information about SharePoint search, please see Chapter 9.

I had this requirement come up once when I was consulting with a mining company. This firm has a large corpus of information about its different mining operations, as well as any potential mining sites it researched or conducted feasibility studies for. Sites can be attractive for a variety of reasons, but there are times when the market prices for a particular mineral or resource does not warrant the costs with establishing a mine at the time. When the market shifts and the prices rise, then a particular site may become more attractive. Therefore, the mining company collects and saves all its research for future feasibility studies, whether it purchases rights to a site or not.

The challenge is that people may turnover or transfer to new divisions, or the firm may acquire new information by acquiring a new firm. All of this information represents a significant portion of the firm's intellectual property and competitive advantage; thus, they need to secure the content and limit its audience to provide access strictly on a need-to-know basis.

Geologists and other researchers for a site needed a reliable way to discover the content and knowledge the firm already has about a site to avoid duplicating efforts or overlooking an opportunity. Here I identified the security-related discovery requirement: a researcher's access level cannot prevent them from discovering that the organization possesses some knowledge (a piece of content or some other unit of information) relating to a topic (the search query).

I implemented the solution for this requirement by customizing the security trimming behavior in the search results. Rather than trim the result, I displayed a custom result informing the user that the submitted query matched a search result in some way, but that the user did not have permission to view the result. I suppressed any information about the content, including its title or description, and simply listed a contact who could grant permission to the piece of content.

Although this exposes some security information because it reveals that a result does exist for a particular query, it does not disclose any details about the content, offering a compromise where researchers can discover content otherwise hidden from them while following *the principle of least privilege*.

THE PRINCIPLE OF LEAST PRIVILEGE

Jerry Saltzer and Mike Schroeder first defined the principle of least privilege in a co-authored 1974 IEEE paper on computer security titled "The Protection of Information in Computer Systems." They define the principle as, "Every program and every user of the system should operate using the least set of privileges necessary to complete the job."

Operating using the absolute least privileges required for a task reduces the available surface for attack. If an attacker compromises a user's account, the attack will at least be contained as much as possible because, ideally, the user account will not have wide and unlimited access to network resources.

Wrapping Up

Information you make available to your organization's users typically consists of knowledge beneficial to everyone, contributing to everyone's productivity, and the disclosure of which to a wider audience will not be damaging. This availability of information allows others to collaborate and build on each other's ideas, extending the organization's knowledge and wisdom. For other more sensitive information, you can prevent its discovery and disclosure to a wider audience by securing it. In this chapter, I provided guidance on how to determine the security needs for a piece of content by building a threat model and analyzing security requirements. I also discussed how to configure security settings in SharePoint and how to utilize Rights Management Service.

Securing content specifies which users can discover a piece of content and which users cannot. The security requirements might change over time as the content itself progresses through its life cycle, particularly as you archive the content or declare it as an official record. The chapters in the next part of this book focus on those topics related to capturing and archiving records, including their retention and disposition. I begin in the next chapter by first looking at how to design the organization hierarchy or content classification index for your records repository, a taxonomy known as a *file plan*.

PART 4

Designating and Managing Your Records

Records management often seems to be a driver behind an enterprise content management initiative, usually one driven by an organization that requires a formal records repository for archival or regulatory purposes, or both. The challenge then is that records management occurs late in the content's life cycle, requiring the larger scope of enterprise content management to plan the earlier aspects of the content life cycle and lead into an effective records management solution. I saved this part of the book until last so that you can leverage the analysis and design work you did in the earlier stages of your enterprise content management solution, building on that knowledge and filling in the details for how to preserve your records.

The chapters in this part look at how to manage official records as I guide you through how to design and implement a records management solution. I start with an overview of file plans and then I look at how to design one for your organization, which designs the content classification index for content within a records management repository. From there, I discuss how you can implement a records repository in Microsoft SharePoint 2013, and how you can manage content retention and disposition through policies and workflows in your records repository. Finally, I provide some considerations for how to integrate with other records repositories as part of your records management solution.

As you consider your records management needs, remember that records preserve an evidentiary account of a transaction, decision, or historical reference, maintaining which should provide some future value or meet some future retention requirement. This perspective will help guide your design decisions, from what type of retention policies to apply, to how to store the content. You organize and associate your retention policies and storage design through a content classification scheme, the most notable of which is your file plan, which is where I start.

■ ■ ■

CHAPTER 13

Designing Your File Plan

Finally, if you are lucky and if the right reader comes along, the stone will speak. It alone will remain in the world to tell the story.

—Margaret Atwood

Eventually, some transitory content will progress through the life cycle and become official records. Records involve a complexity of management requirements, starting with their storage. But what is the best way to store records? In this chapter, I provide an overview of file plans for records management and I offer guidance on how to design a file plan. I also discuss how to create a content classification index. Finally, I discuss considerations for different archive file formats you can consider for your file archival to store in the file plan.

After reading this chapter, you will know how to

- Describe the concepts of file plans.

- Create a content classification index.

- Design your file plan.

- Consider physical disk storage options.

- Identify different archive formats.

Overview of File Plans

Records managers refer to the scheme to physically organize content storage as a *file plan*. A file plan serves as a blueprint for the records repository and it consists of a taxonomy of terms in a relevant hierarchy for the organization and its goals for managing records.

During my research for this book, I perused other books on the topic to see how those authors organized their ideas and what topics they focused on. I noticed that records management books from 20 years ago were only just beginning to introduce the concept of electronic records, and yet here we are today with this book focusing almost exclusively on electronic content. The environment has changed rapidly, but the concepts and design approaches continue to hold relevancy.

All the books I referenced dedicated some focus to classification systems, even some books I skimmed dating back to the 1960s. For those earlier books, classification was based on the physical world, such as where the piece of content was physically located. Then, as now, classifications took two forms: *direct* or *indirect*. You specify a direct classification by locating a file in a physical location to classify it, such as a location in a filing cabinet for physical content or a network folder for electronic content. Conversely, you specify an indirect classification using an index.

Those 1960s-era books that I skimmed each devoted almost half the book to planning and designing the physical layout of a file plan and storage system, providing tips to the reader on how to maximize floor space utilization and how to design for efficient physical handling. In this book, the portion devoted to physical layout is dramatically less than half the book (it is closer to a fifth, actually), and this is because the system takes care of the physical handling of the content, saving me from including those sections on ergonomic filing tips and the like.

For me, my primary goal in designing a file plan is to design one with an ability to accommodate future system maintenance and changes. You cannot anticipate everything in the future, but you can design with flexibility to adapt as needed. One strategy is to design a granular file plan to help avoid dividing nodes into more granular parts later.

As you design your file plan, aim for an inclusive design across your enterprise, not just the content SharePoint currently manages for you. This will help you design a more complete file plan. It will also help maintain a broad focus where you can think through and standardize the different processes and content classification systems across your organization.

Ultimately, you should strive to design a file plan to encourage user adoption and provide a positive user experience. If your file plan can help your users to work productively while implementing compliance transparently or naturally with how your users work with the system, your likelihood of success increases as the system steers users toward optimum behaviors.

■ **Tip**   Do not rely on users to make compliance decisions. The records system should guide users toward a compliant state, including auto classifying content wherever possible and enforcing compliance rules.

As I mentioned, a file plan provides the underlying storage structure for the content in your archival or records repository. Therefore, the overarching driver in its design considers an optimum storage scheme. Nevertheless, this does not have to be a brand-new analysis exercise. If your organization has defined an enterprise taxonomy or a portion of metadata terms as part of its information architecture, you can use this as the basis of your file plan design. It can also provide a user-friendly way to query and access relevant records.

■ **Note**   Please see Chapter 4, where I discuss designing an information architecture.

You can use several different metadata categories to classify and organize content. Figure 13-1 illustrates an example of a document associated with multifaceted metadata. This enables users to search and filter using a variety of metadata terms.

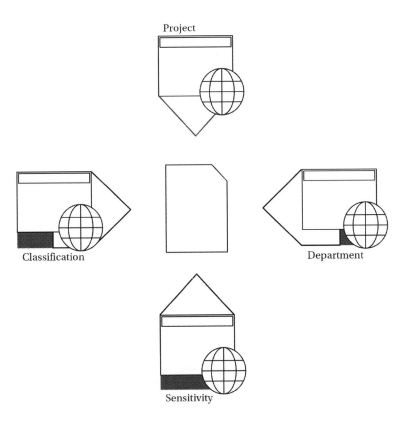

Figure 13-1. *A document associated with multifaceted metadata information*

While the metadata associated with a piece of content is simply a pointer reference and unrelated to the actual storage implementation, you still need to organize the storage for the files. Although much can be done with metadata and virtual taxonomy structures, under the covers you will need to address where to physically store the data, what security you want to apply, and how you want to organize it.

Your enterprise taxonomy or a portion of it can guide your physical storage scheme. This design typically groups similar types of content together and applies the same security and retention policies to the content. Figure 13-2 illustrates an example of a physical storage hierarchy scheme that separates areas of the file plan by business unit, and then divides the business unit by department. Within a department, it further divides the accounts. This is a simple example to contrast the multifaceted metadata scheme with the physical hierarchy of a file plan.

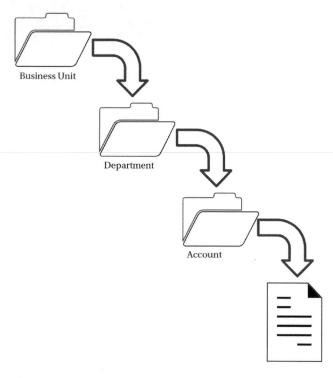

Figure 13-2. *Example of a physical storage hierarchy in a file plan*

If you have not created an information architecture to draw an organizing structure from, or if you want to adapt your enterprise taxonomy, you can analyze your content and create a hierarchical content organizing scheme referred to as a *content classification index*.

Creating a Content Classification Index

A content classification index is a classification scheme an organization uses to organize its content. It involves a single classification index, encompassing all of the organization's types of content. An organization's classification index is similar to a biology classification system, such as the *International Code of Zoological Nomenclature* for animals, or the *International Code of Phylogenetic Nomenclature,* known as the *PhyloCode*. The PhyloCode builds a taxonomy based on the following levels:

- Family
- Class
- Order
- Subclass
- Superclass

You might have noticed another classification system if you have ever searched for books in a library: the *Dewey Decimal System*. Melvil Dewey first conceived of the system in 1873 and it uses a numbering system to categorize and organize knowledge using standard categories and hierarchies. It uses three summary levels to group and arrange knowledge, starting with the following ten main classes at the first summary level:

- 000: Computer Science, Information, and General Works

- 100: Philosophy and Psychology

- 200: Religion

- 300: Social Sciences

- 400: Language

- 500: Science

- 600: Technology

- 700: Arts and Recreation

- 800: Literature

- 900: History and Geography

▓ **Note**   To learn more about the Dewey Decimal System, please see the Online Computer Library Center (OCLC) article at `www.oclc.org/dewey/resources/summaries.en.html`.

You can use these and other classification systems as a model for how you design your content classification index. The general pattern is to move from broad categories to more specific categories as you move down the levels of a taxonomy. A common approach is to start at the broadest organizing categories for your organization, which are often the business units or departments.

Another aspect to your content classification index involves the naming of nodes in the taxonomy. Biology classification systems use common root Latin words while the Dewey Decimal System uses common numbering ranges. Users can classify content in several ways. The following lists the most popular classification schemes:

- By index reference

- By subject term

- By geographic tag

- By numeric sequence

- By alphabetic identifier

- By alphanumeric scheme

For physical storage, a numbering or alphanumeric scheme made it easier for a human to scan and locate a file location. This system eased the physical filing and retrieval process because there is a consistent order to numbers and letters, one that helps a human to efficiently access a file location without having to scan every folder. Figure 13-3 illustrates an example of a folder using an alphanumeric classification scheme.

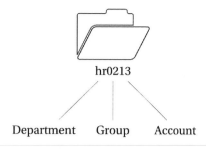

Department   Group   Account

Figure 13-3. Example of an alphanumeric classification scheme

Although a numbering or alphanumeric classification scheme was immensely helpful and productive in a human-managed filing system, it provides little value in a computer-managed repository. Computers perform particularly well at parsing and ordering strings of text. A computer system does not require you to number your files for efficient storage and retrieval; it uses reference pointers to order and locate a file.

Your users, on the other hand, are more efficient at reading self-descriptive text labels rather than alphanumeric schemes. As such, I recommend you use descriptive labels for each node in your content classification index to increase your users' productivity in classifying, storing, and retrieving content. A self-descriptive naming system will help your users to identify relevant categories quickly by avoiding any translations between numbering schemes and the category itself.

The single most important thing to do is to ask how users will ask for the material. You do not want to design a taxonomy with such complexity that users would need extensive training to understand the different classification nodes (unless, of course, that level of complexity is required for your situation and your users possess specialized knowledge to work with such a classification system).

■ **Important** How will users query for records? Consider the user experience you want to provide and use this to guide your content classification index, and ultimately, your file plan design.

Designing a content classification index can be a lengthy process involving a lot of analysis work. I find the best approach is to start with defining the first level, those broad categories to first classify content. Next, I work my way through each category, and then each category's levels as I define all the relevant nodes to classify content. This process is iterative and can involve many revisions, but a systematic approach such as this can help focus the taxonomy design into individual discrete areas.

■ **Tip** In the marketplace, you can find organizations designing and selling existing taxonomies. Purchasing one of these can save you the analysis and design time involved with building your own taxonomy. If you purchase an industry-specific taxonomy, you can adopt it to standardize with other firms in your industry.

If you do not procure an existing taxonomy, the best place to start building your content classification index is by looking at examples and samples. You can start with the popular taxonomies from biology or library sciences, or you can look at how other firms organize their information. In the meantime, I included a sample content classification index to help get you started.

Sample Content Classification Index

I find it overly abstract to discuss a content classification index in theory without considering an actual example. At the risk of consuming a lot of precious space in this book, I wanted to provide you with a detailed sample from a content classification index I frequently use. Although the sample spans a few pages, I felt that providing you with a tangible sample would leave you with something real.

The following is a sample snippet from a standard content classification index I use. I selected the parts I felt would be most relevant to the widest audience, while also providing enough of the index to give you something to work with. You are welcome to use this list as a starting place or a template to create your own content classification index. Please expand or contract on items as they fit your situation and reword terms to fit your terminology.

- **Accounting Department** (typically retained for seven years or as required)

    - Accounts Payable

    - Accounts Receivable

    - Annual Reports

    - Assets and Property Records

    - Audit Reports

    - Bank Statements and Reconciliation

    - Bond and Bondholders' Records

    - Building Plans and Specifications

    - Contracts and Agreements

    - Consolidated Balance Sheets

    - Control Ledgers

    - Corporate Records

    - Correspondence

    - Cost Sheets

    - Credit Tickets

    - Departmental Reports

    - Financial Statements

    - Insurance Policies

    - Inventory Records

    - Leases

    - Licenses

    - Minutes of Meetings

    - Mortgages

    - Petty Cash Records

    - Property Records (typically retained for the life of a property)

    - Research Data

- Stock and Stockholder Records
- Tax Records
- Trial Balances
- **Advertising Department** (typically retained for three years or as required)
    - Contracts
    - Correspondence
    - Illustrations
    - Inventory of Advertising Material
    - Market Research
    - Manuscripts
    - Mock-Ups, Sketches, and Layouts
    - Newspaper Clippings
    - Orders
    - Photographs
    - Publication Production Files and Proofs
    - Testimonial Letters
- **Engineering and Production Department** (typically retained for seven or more years)
    - Blueprints, Drawings, Sketches, and Charts
    - Experiment and Test Records
    - Flow of Work and Material Charts
    - Formulas
    - Laboratory Production Records
    - Maps
    - Operating Reports
    - Other Procedures
    - Planning Records
    - Plant Inventory and Machine Location Records
    - Plant Layout Charts
    - Production, Progress, and Job Records
    - Research Data Files and Records
    - Specification Sheets
    - Templates
    - Work or Shop Orders

- **Human Resources Department** (typically retained for seven or more years as required)

  - Accident Records

  - Employee Records

  - Employment Insurance Records

  - Group Insurance Records

  - Payroll Records

  - Pension Plan Records

  - Personnel Records

  - Retirement Records

  - Salary and Wage Records

  - Time and Motion Studies

  - Time Records

  - Workers' Compensation Reports

- **Information Technology Department** (typically retained for three years or as required)

  - Asset Inventory

  - Licenses

  - Policies and Procedures

  - Vendor Enterprise Agreements

- **Legal Department** (typically retained for seven or more years as required)

  - Applications for Tax Files, Returns, and Appeals

  - Applications for Titles and Deeds (typically retained for the lifetime of the asset)

  - Copy Files, Affidavits, Testimony, and Dispositions

  - Claims, Evidences, and Proofs

  - Copyrights and Applications for Dockets

  - Information Files

  - Patents (typically retained for the lifetime of the patent)

  - Trademarks (typically retained for the lifetime of the trademark)

- **Order Department** (typically retained for three years or as required)

  - Inspection Reports

  - Orders

  - Returned Goods

  - Shipping Notices and Reports

- **Purchasing Department** (typically retained for three years or as required)

    - Contracts with Suppliers

    - Correspondence

    - Invoices

    - Price List Files

    - Purchase Orders

    - Quotations

    - Specifications

    - Vendor Records

- **Sales Department** (typically retained for three years or as required)

    - Closed Accounts

    - Correspondence

    - Confidential Contracts

    - Contracts

    - Expense Accounts

    - Mailing Lists

    - Prospect Records

    - Sales Records and Summaries

    - Sales Territory Maps

    - Salesperson Reports

- **Service Department** (typically retained for three years or as required)

    - Complaints and Service Records

    - Correspondence

Next to some classifications, I indicated the typical retention times for each. Although your retention times may vary from my example, I hope this will give you something to start with.

■ **Note**   Please see Chapter 15, where I discuss content retention and disposition in more depth.

Designing Your File Plan

When designing a file plan, I generally build on the content classification index. One question I usually have to decide on is how granular to make each node in my file plan. If it is too granular, it might add unnecessary complexity; if it is not granular enough, then it might make it difficult to manage groups of files as a unit.

Deciding on the level of granularity is a balancing act, and it involves considering different aspects of the content that a particular node will contain. I generally like to group similar content together, as similar content usually fit together in a category. Similar content also usually shares other attributes, such as security settings, retention policies, and disaster recovery requirements.

In analyzing a category, I usually consider the following topics to define the attributes of the classification category or to identify any relevant subcategories:

- Description of the types of content

- Taxonomy for categorizing a record

- Retention policies defining how long to retain a record and how to handle its disposition

- Information about who owns a record throughout its life cycle

- Information about who should have access to a record

As I consider the different aspects of a potential classification category, I focus on the common attributes that the content it contains will share. The information structure of your organization will define a lot of the taxonomy, but the content itself can help you identify additional branches in the classification hierarchy. I also use this information to ensure I am designing the file plan with the right balance of granularity.

One important driver for me is the security question: Who needs to access the content? I like to group content together in a container with the same security requirements. That way I can grant permissions to the container rather than to grant item-level permissions on each document (something I try to avoid whenever possible, whether in a records repository or a regular document library, to increase the manageability of the permission management).

▓ **Tip** Professionals in archival and library sciences have specialized skills and expertise in analyzing information to design an effective content classification system. This chapter can help get you started, but it is no substitute for a professional with expertise in information design.

Part of your file plan design has to consider the actual content storage. An archival and records repository can encompass a vast corpus of content, and as such, can require a significant amount of storage resources. Depending on your storage requirements, you may find that the storage options can affect your file plan design by highlighting areas where you need additional granularity with subcategories.

Understanding Disk Storage Options

Because a key consideration of a file plan is the underlying storage scheme, I find that it is important to consider how you want to physically store the content on disk as you design the file plan blueprint for your records repository. Some of the decisions you make in the file plan will directly affect the storage implementation when you configure your records repository.

Remember, a site collection in SharePoint can exist in one (and only one) content database—it cannot span content databases. You can store several site collections in a single content database, and you can even move a site collection to a new content database using a simple PowerShell command. But you cannot split a site collection's data *across* multiple content databases without creating multiple site collections and migrating the content to different site collections.

When designing your file plan, you can start to consider how you want to store the different nodes on a disk and which categories you want to segregate on dedicated disks. This can help you design the right level of granularity that you will need to achieve your storage requirements.

Figure 13-4 illustrates how you can conceptually partition your records repository into different content databases, and then distribute those databases across different disks. This might be a desirable design for storing and managing a large number of items in your records repository. Even if you store multiple site collections in the same content database, you can reallocate the site collections into different content databases later, with little impact on the records repository.

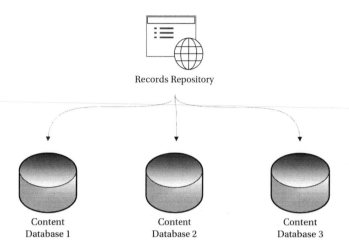

Records Repository

Content
Database 1

Content
Database 2

Content
Database 3

Figure 13-4. *Distributing content across databases and disks*

Another occasion to partition the repository content into separate content databases is when you want to physically store the content in different ways. For example, you can configure a content database to use SQL Server Remote BLOB Storage (RBS), which stores the files in a directory rather than in the database page files. For larger files, this storage option can often perform better. Yet for other areas in your records repository, you may prefer to store the file content in the regular database file.

A records repository partitioned across multiple content databases will give you these storage options. Considering them early in your file plan design phase can help guide your design decisions as you identify the nodes you require. For instance, you might need to make a general classification category more granular by using subcategories to accommodate the different storage options within the classification.

■ **Note**   For more information on Remote BLOB Storage (RBS), please see the TechNet article at
http://technet.microsoft.com/ee748649.

Identifying Different Archive Formats

How you store the content can serve as another factor in your storage requirements. I have had clients who wanted to transform a piece of content into an image rather than maintain the original format. In some cases, this can reduce file sizes, but more likely, the requirement stems from the need to ensure that the system captures a record of a unit of information's state.

An example of this is a web page or a Microsoft Word document with an embedded reference link to an external object, such as an image. If the system only captures the page or document, and the image changes, then the record would not be accurate. A solution to this problem is to capture an image of all the pieces making up a unit of information at its current state.

You can develop a workflow to process items as users declare them as records. A step in the workflow could then transform the content into the desired format. Alternatively, you could use the SharePoint 2013 Word Automation Service or other document conversion services to transform the content. Figure 13-5 illustrates an example of the Word Automation Service taking a copy of a Word document to generate a PDF image of the content.

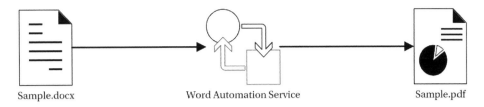

Figure 13-5. *Document conversion process*

▓ **Note**   For more information about the Word Automation Service in SharePoint 2013, please see the MSDN article at http://msdn.microsoft.com/jj163073.

As you plan your file plan, you do not have to decide on all the implementation details for the records repository. However, this is a good time to consider what format you want to use to archive content because you are closely analyzing the different content and content classifications. Reflecting on these considerations can also help you to identify additional nodes that you may need in your file plan, particularly if you want some content in a classification to retain its original format while transforming other content into an archival format.

Inside Story: Notes from the Field

Several years ago, I was engaged with an insurance company client on a records management architecture and design project. They wanted to scan the claim forms their customers submitted as part of their employee benefits, using these digital copies to transition away from physical document management. The organization decided to use SharePoint as a repository for these scanned benefit claims and any contracts.

A key consideration was the file sizing: they decided to capture the scans as PDF documents, but the system could scan at different quality levels, each involving a different file size. Higher quality meant significantly more disk space—even a slight file size change adds up to a lot over millions of files. This affected the number and size of content databases.

For a scenario such as this, the file plan should be based on client groups rather than departments, and then on months and years for a convenient way to segregate the content into different content databases. This gave us content areas where we could scope and estimate the size to determine whether the system would meet acceptable performance levels. It would also highlight how partitioned the content is for system processes such as backup and restore jobs.

By thinking through your file plan while it is still a blueprint for your records repository, you can consider different alternatives and scenarios for implementing the storage architecture. Your file plan can give you a global view of your records repository *before* you implement it, guiding your analysis and design while making changes easy.

Wrapping Up

Storing records begins with designing a comprehensive taxonomy structure to organize content, a scheme commonly referred to as a *file plan*. Your file plan serves as a blueprint for your records repository. In this chapter, I described a file plan as the physical storage structure to group and organize related records. From there, I provided guidance on how to design a file plan and I shared a sample file plan to help get you started with designing a file plan for your organization.

With a file plan designed, the next step is to implement it in a records repository, such as the Records Center site template in SharePoint 2013. In the next chapter, I provide guidance on how to create and configure a records repository, including configuration tasks to support inspecting records submitted to the repository and automatically routing them to the correct file plan location.

■ ■ ■

CHAPTER 14

Implementing Your Records Repository

The future depends on what you do today.

—Mahatma Gandhi

How do you archive and manage records you need to retain? The first of the key criteria requires a destination, typically a records repository, to archive and manage records within. In this chapter, I provide guidance on how to plan and create a Records Center in SharePoint 2013. I also discuss how to design workflows to process your records, how to audit and report on records, and how to manage in-place records. Finally, I share techniques to optimize your disk storage design for archival content.

After reading this chapter, you will know how to

- Plan and create a records repository.

- Manage in-place records.

- Configure document Send To connections.

- Configure document routing.

- Design workflows to manage and process records.

- Audit and report on records.

Overview of Records Repositories

In the past, managing records was a laborious process of collecting, conditioning, inspecting, indexing, and filing pieces of content for archiving. For example, indexing involved manually using index cards with a written pointer reference to the physical file's actual location. Records managers created and filed index cards in helpful orders, depending on how they expected users to search for and request information.

Electronic records repositories share many of the concepts of the former paper-based system. Indexes still maintain pointers to records, with organization based on the different ways to query the content. Rather than requiring a records manager to create index cards, the system crawls the content to build the index. Instead, the records manager focuses on managing and optimizing the record's life cycle, including these tasks:

- Applying retention and auditing policies to content

- Organizing the file plan and designing content routing

- Configuring eDiscovery cases and applying holds

- Managing the records repository and monitoring compliance

■ **Note**   Records repositories may have changed, and in the process this changed the records manager's role; yet a records manager is still a vital role on your team.

Like their paper-based equivalent of paper records filed in cardboard records boxes (such as the Bankers Box), your records repository stores digital records in folders and online libraries at each node of your file plan. When you store records in a records box, such as the example shown in Figure 14-1, you can add additional metadata to the container by writing additional details on the box's face with a marker.

Figure 14-1. *A records box for paper records*

Records boxes served as the containers for records, and a records manager organized the boxes using the file plan. The SharePoint folders and libraries that you provision for different nodes in your file plan act as a container in a similar way to the records box. Rather than writing on the box with a marker, you can capture metadata by specifying property attributes for the container. Otherwise, it contains documents and other pieces of content related to a particular topic area in the file plan.

■ **Note**   Please see Chapter 13, where I discuss file plans in more detail.

There are several needs you may find requiring your organization to capture and preserve records. Some may be driven internally for content that you expect will provide some future value. Others can come from an external organization or regulatory body mandating the records retention. The following are some of the external record areas that may apply to your organization:

- Government compliance

- Tax-related

- Securities and security commissions

- Environmental

- Health and safety

- Product and consumer protection

- Legal compliance

Ultimately, your organization has an obligation to protect and preserve certain data to avoid litigation and protect the company. Without the ability to produce required evidence to prove the organization is in compliance for a regulatory requirement, the organization, and possibly even its officers, could face fines or stricter penalties.

Records serve as the memory of an organization, preserving evidence about a decision or a transaction in the organization's operations. They provide historical reference information to support future organizational use or to meet regulatory compliance requirements. They are important, but not every record holds the same degree of importance, as some are more important than others are.

To identify the relative importance of a record to your organization, I recommend you create categories to group different importance levels. You can create as many categories as you need to meet your requirements, but typically most organizations will only need a few. The following are common categories that records managers use to specify importance levels, along with examples of the types of records each include.

- **Nonessential Records:** Information with no ongoing value; typically not worth retaining, or retained for temporary storage of 60 days to one year. These types of records include:

  - E-mail messages with no ongoing value

  - Working documents no longer in use

- **Useful Records:** Helpful references to support ongoing operations; typically retained for short-term storage of up to three years. These types of records include:

  - Reports

  - Executive communications

- **Important Records:** Contain pertinent information that needs to be re-created or replaced if lost; typically retained for long-term storage of seven to ten years. These types of records include:

  - Financial data

  - Credit histories

  - Sales data

- **Vital Records:** Necessary for defining an organization's legal and financial status, and essential for business continuity; typically retained permanently. These types of records include:

  - Shareholder statements and ownership records

  - Contracts and agreements

You can apply these categories to each node in your file plan, as well as to each type of content. This information can help you design appropriate operations and maintenance tasks, such as the backup strategy and the retention policy. Just knowing the relative importance of a record can define how long you need to retain it and the process for disposition.

■ **Note**   Please see Chapter 15, where I discuss content retention and disposition in more detail.

Digital records repositories often share common characteristics, such as associating metadata and a retention policy with a record. And as I mentioned, they also share characteristics with a paper-based records repository. Planning a SharePoint records repository is consistent with planning any archival document repository; even still, I look next at some SharePoint features and implementation details you can consider in your planning.

Planning Your SharePoint Records Repository

Much of your planning should happen during the design phase, when you would focus primarily on designing a blueprint for your records repository in the form of a file plan. A file plan defines the structure and hierarchy of a records repository, and you can use this to guide your repository implementation, but there are still SharePoint-specific configuration decisions you need to make.

■ **Note**   Please see Chapter 13, where I discuss designing a file plan in more depth.

You implement your records repository in SharePoint 2013 using the *Records Center* site template. This creates a SharePoint site that is, in essence, like any other site, but it also has activated features for records management. This template includes the feature to route and organize content, which provides some of the key functionality for an efficient Records Center, as I describe later in this chapter.

Before you get too far along with planning your records repository, you have to decide whether you want a centralized or decentralized repository. In SharePoint terms, this is a question of whether or not you want to capture and preserve *in-place* records. The following lists some benefits for centralized and decentralized records management.

- **Centralization:** Standardizes in a well-known single archival repository and manages records in a consistent manner; responsibility for records management is held with a records manager who possesses specialized archival and information management skills.

- **Decentralization:** Keeps record in context at its content creation origin; responsibility for records management is delegated to knowledge workers who can adapt a process to fit their information needs.

My preference is usually to design for a centralized records repository managed by a records manager, unless there are compelling requirements for a decentralized design. I like a centralized design because I like the consistency in managing the records; I also like that the physical storage of record content would be separate from the transitory content where the record originates.

SharePoint provides an option to move the record to a Records Center while retaining a link in the original location. For me, this provides a good experience for accessing the record from its original context, while still managing the record centrally.

Centralizing your records places together similar records from across the enterprise. This allows you to view records in context with other similar records. I also find a centralized design easier to apply and manage security permissions for users who require access to a particular record type but who may not be members of the collaboration site where the record originated. In a centralized repository, you can grant permissions to those users for the different libraries they require.

For example, in Figure 14-2, you could grant permissions on the Records Center to an auditor who needs to access the records. You can avoid granting item-level permissions for the individual origin sites, thus avoiding complexity in permission management, and you can avoid granting access to the origin site collections, which could grant more content access than the auditors require.

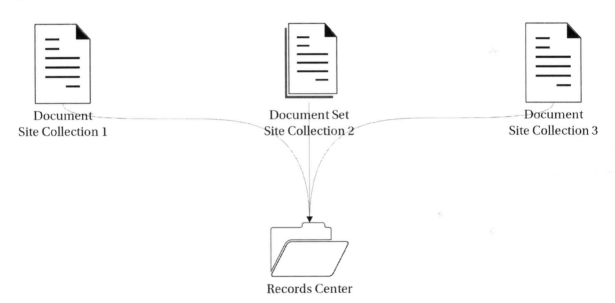

Figure 14-2. *Copies of records captured in a centralized records repository*

Vital records are another, very notable reason I prefer to design centralized records repository centers around the ability to group and store similar content together. As I noted earlier, a vital record contains valuable content and is typically crucial to business continuity. If you preserve your vital records in-place, distributing them across potentially multiple content databases, you have to restore all those databases to restore the vital records. Conversely, if you preserve your vital records in a centralized records repository, you can group them together in a content database, allowing you to target your disaster recovery response.

For example, if you span your Records Center across multiple site collections, you can allocate different site collections in different content databases, as shown in Figure 14-3. With this design, you can designate a site collection to preserve all of your vital records, grouping them together in a common content database.

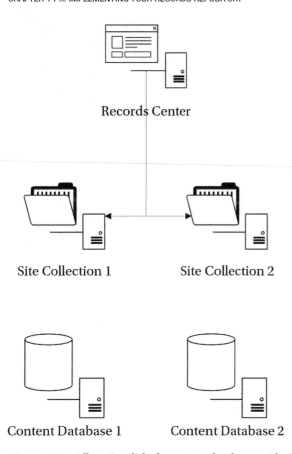

Records Center

Site Collection 1   Site Collection 2

Content Database 1   Content Database 2

Figure 14-3. *Allocating disks for content databases with vital records*

The choice between designing a records repository in a single site collection and spreading it across multiple site collections depends on the total content size. If you are archiving up to 100 GB or 200 GB of content, a single site collection will likely work well for your purposes. If, on the other hand, you are archiving several terabytes of content, then you will be better served with a multisite collection and a multicontent database design.

In both cases, you start by creating a Records Center. This provides the main entry point into the records repository, both where users submit new records and where users browse existing records. Next, I discuss some considerations for creating and configuring your Records Center in SharePoint.

Creating and Configuring Your Records Center

A Records Center is a specialized portal for a records repository in SharePoint. It includes several features related to records management, particularly with the routing and organizing of new records submitted to the repository.

To create a Records Center site, navigate to the Create Site Collection page in SharePoint Central Administration and enter the appropriate information in the Name, Description, and Site Owner fields. For the Template Selection option, select the Records Center site template located on the Enterprise tab. After you create a new Records Center site, you can navigate to the site's welcome page, similar to the one in Figure 14-4.

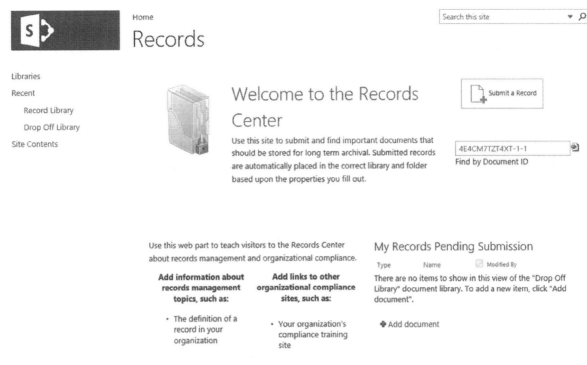

Figure 14-4. *The SharePoint 2013 Records Center*

SharePoint Record Centers rely on content types to process and manage content properly. The routing engine uses content types as the first means to identify content and route it to its proper location. If you have set up an enterprise content type hub to manage and synchronize content types across all site collections, then your Records Center will already have the necessary content types configured; otherwise, you will need to create any content types you require.

▓ **Note**   Please see Chapter 6, where I discuss the enterprise content type hub in more detail.

Next, you need to create a hierarchy of the different records libraries and folders you wish to implement based on your file plan and your records repository design plan. This is the place where you decide to either implement the file plan hierarchy within a single site or structure it across multiple sites. I prefer to structure across multiple sites, even if they all share the same content database initially, because this provides room to grow and scale the records repository easily in the future.

Create and configure each site you identify as needed for the repository structure, and then create the necessary records libraries within each site. Finally, create any folders, if needed, in each library. This establishes the shell structure of your records repository, where you will physically store the individual records.

▓ **Tip**   If you need to partition content across multiple databases, you will need multiple Records Center site collections to implement your records repository across. Each site collection can share a content database with another site collection or you can dedicate its own content database, as required.

The Records Center uses the content types to identify a submitted piece of content and route it to the appropriate records library you provisioned in your file plan implementation. Because the content types and records libraries are things you created and configured, SharePoint has no way of knowing how to route content until you tell it, which you do by configuring document routing rules.

Configuring Record Routing

At the heart of an effective Records Center is content routing. This feature processes new records submitted to the Records Center and routes each to its predefined container within the repository hierarchy, automatically organizing pieces of content based on routing rules.

If your records repository spans multiple sites and site collections, you need to enable an option in the Document Routing Settings. You need to enable the Content Organizer feature on any other site collection you wish to route content to and include it in your records repository.

To enable routing content to another site, navigate to the Site Settings page and click the Content Organizer Settings link in the Site Administration section. On the Content Organizer Settings page, check to allow rules to specify another site in the Sending To Another Site section, as showing in Figure 14-5.

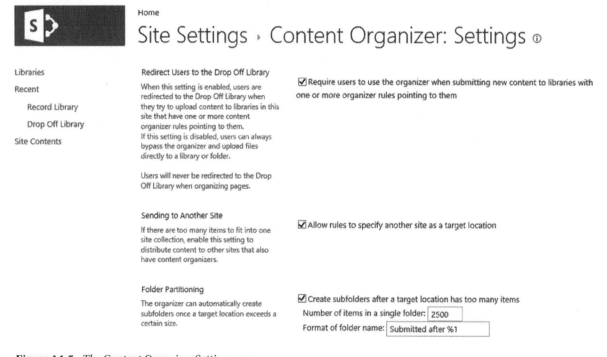

Figure 14-5. *The Content Organizer Settings page*

To create a content organizer rule to route content to records libraries, navigate to the Site Settings page for the Records Center and click the Content Organizer Rules link in the Site Administration section. On the Content Organizer Rules page, click the New Item button to create a new content organizer rule, as shown in Figure 14-6.

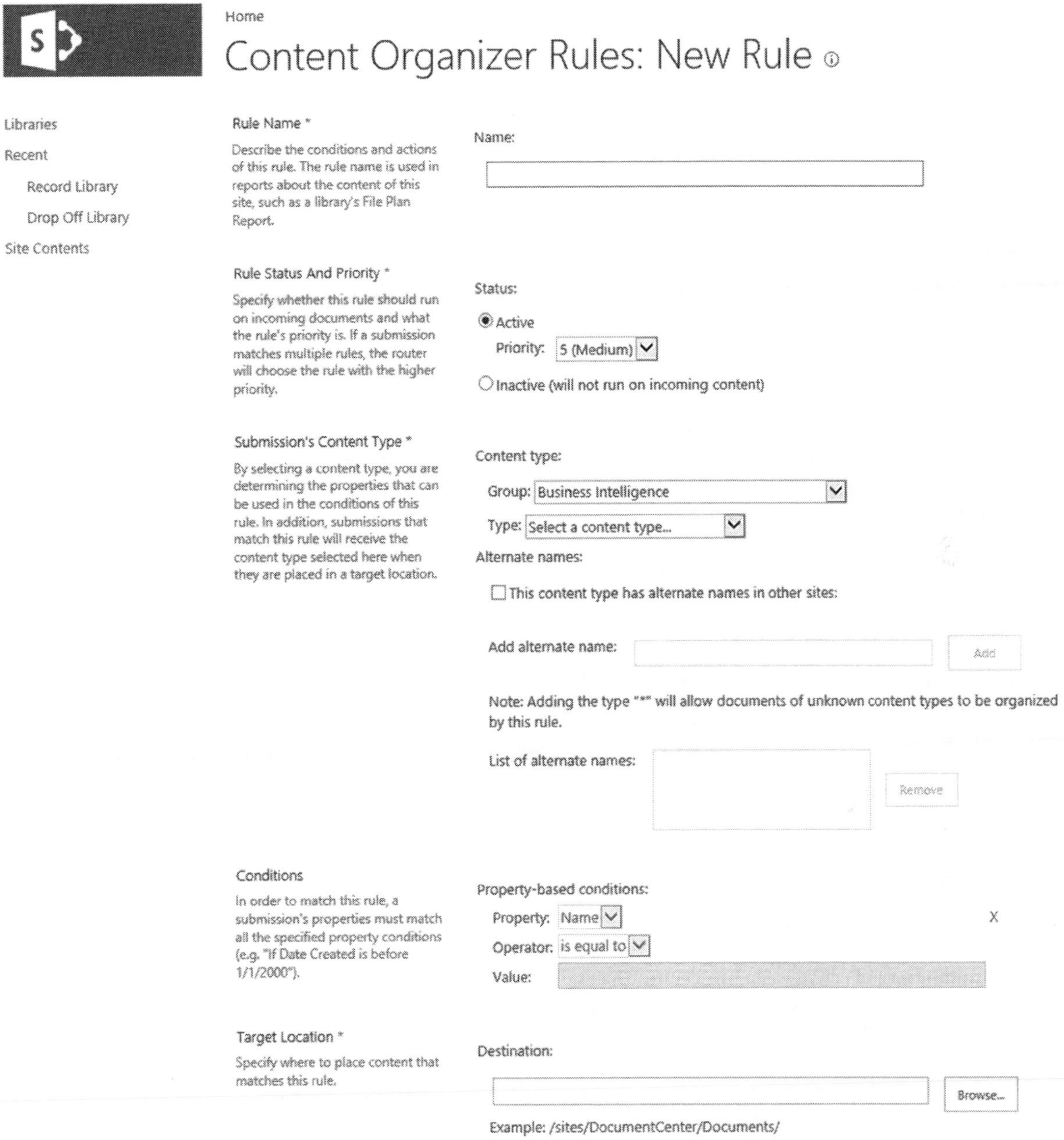

Home

Content Organizer Rules: New Rule ⊙

Libraries

Recent

    Record Library

    Drop Off Library

Site Contents

Rule Name *

Describe the conditions and actions of this rule. The rule name is used in reports about the content of this site, such as a library's File Plan Report.

Name:

[   ]

Rule Status And Priority *

Specify whether this rule should run on incoming documents and what the rule's priority is. If a submission matches multiple rules, the router will choose the rule with the higher priority.

Status:

⦿ Active

    Priority: 5 (Medium) ▾

◯ Inactive (will not run on incoming content)

Submission's Content Type *

By selecting a content type, you are determining the properties that can be used in the conditions of this rule. In addition, submissions that match this rule will receive the content type selected here when they are placed in a target location.

Content type:

    Group: Business Intelligence   ▾

    Type: Select a content type...   ▾

Alternate names:

    ☐ This content type has alternate names in other sites:

    Add alternate name: [   ] [Add]

Note: Adding the type "*" will allow documents of unknown content types to be organized by this rule.

    List of alternate names: [   ] [Remove]

Conditions

In order to match this rule, a submission's properties must match all the specified property conditions (e.g. "If Date Created is before 1/1/2000").

Property-based conditions:

    Property: Name ▾   X

    Operator: is equal to ▾

    Value: [   ]

Target Location *

Specify where to place content that matches this rule.

Destination:

[   ] [Browse...]

Example: /sites/DocumentCenter/Documents/

Figure 14-6. *The New Content Organizer Rule page*

On the New Content Organizer Rule page, enter the following information to create a new content routing rule:

1. Provide a Rule Name. SharePoint uses this name in reports about the records repository's content.

2. Specify the Rule Status And Priority. If a submission matches multiple rules, the content router will choose the rule with the highest priority.

3. Specify the Submission's Content Type by selecting the content type's Group and the Type from the drop-down lists. If other sites use a different name for the content type, select the Alternate Names option and add the alternate names.

4. Optionally, specify any further Conditions you wish to use to route content, such as a content type's property value, in addition to routing based on the content type itself.

5. Specify a Destination records library in the Target Location section.

6. Click the OK button (not visible in Figure 14-6).

When the Records Center receives a new piece of content in the Drop Off Library, the content organizer will evaluate it and select a matching rule with the highest priority to route the content to a records library. Content that does not match a rule will remain in the Drop Off Library until a records manager manually routes the content or creates a new rule to match and route the piece of content.

A Records Center with routing rules set up is ready to receive content. Your Records Center can receive a piece of content from users manually submitting it or from a workflow processing the content. Both of these methods for submitting content use a *Sent To Connection* to identify the drop-off library for the Records Center.

Configuring Send To Connections

In the top-right area of the Records Center welcome page there is a Submit A Record button. Users can click this button to submit a record to archive in the records repository. Although this is a useful button to receive records into the repository, your users will probably prefer to declare and submit in the context of the sites they are working in.

To enable the Send To capability, you first need to configure a *Send To Connection* for the web application by following these steps:

1. Navigate to SharePoint Central Administration and click the General Application Settings link in the left navigation menu. On the General Application Settings page, click the Configure Send To Connections link.

2. In the Send To Connections section, select New Connection.

3. In the Connections Settings section, enter the Display Name and the Send To URL, specify an Explanation to display to users and record in the audit log, and select a Send To Action. The following describes the different Send To Actions:

   - **Copy:** Creates a copy of the document and sends the copy to the repository.

   - **Move:** Deletes the document from its current location and moves it to the repository.

   - **Move and Leave A Link:** Moves the document to the repository and creates a link at the current location to direct users to the repository.

4. The Configure Send To Connections page should look similar to the one shown in Figure 14-7, depending on the options you selected and the URL to your Records Center.

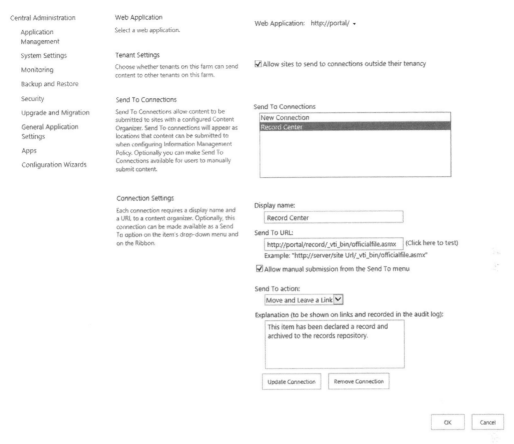

Figure 14-7. *The Configure Sent To Connections page*

5. Note that the Send To URL must point to a valid routing destination. To test, you can click the Click Here To Test link next to the Send To URL. You should receive an alert similar to the one shown in Figure 14-8, verifying the URL is a valid routing destination.

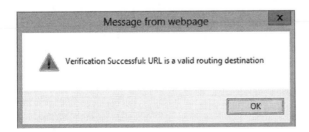

Figure 14-8. *Routing destination URL verification message*

6. Click the Add Connection button to add the new Send To connection. You can select a connection in the Send To Connections section to update a connection's property; otherwise, you can click OK at the bottom of the page.

Once you have the Send To Connection set up properly for a web application, users can manually send their documents to the Records Center. They can perform this function by selecting an item in a site library and clicking the Send To button on the Item tab of the ribbon, as shown in Figure 14-9.

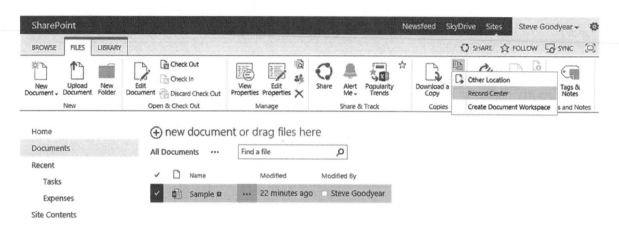

Figure 14-9. *The Send To drop-down menu in a document library*

You can also use a workflow or retention policy to submit a record to a record repository. To configure a policy on a document library, navigate to the library Settings page and follow these steps:

1. Click the Information Management Policy Settings link.

2. Check the Enable Retention option.

3. Click the Add A Retention Stage For Records link.

4. Specify the relevant options in the Retention Stage Properties dialog, as shown in Figure 14-10. Click OK.

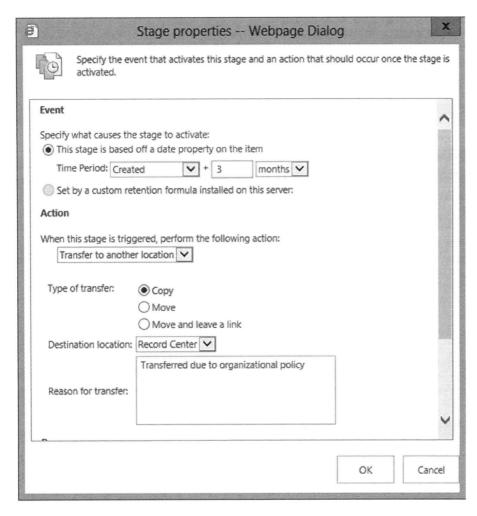

Figure 14-10. *Retention stage properties*

■ **Note**   Please see Chapter 15, where I discuss content retention policies in more depth.

Designing Workflows to Process Records

Records Centers that automate the processing of records tend to be the most successful. Manually processing and routing individual records was necessary in a physical records repository, but in a digital one, you can take advantage of the compute processing power to automate the common tasks. This level of automation enables a Records Center to scale without requiring a significant increase in records manager resources.

The routing and content organizer feature in a Records Center absorbs much of the management burden for records, as I noted earlier in the chapter. This feature organizes the content within the repository. You can use workflows to automate several of the remaining routine records management tasks. This can range from a workflow declaring a piece of content as a record during its publishing process and submitting it to a records repository.

Figure 14-11 illustrates the conceptual steps involved in a document approval workflow that ultimately submits an approved version to the Records Center. I like records management workflows that integrate in user processes for document creation and publishing, because this seamlessly ensures compliance without even having users think about records management—they simply go about their regular work and the system fits their process without having to burden them.

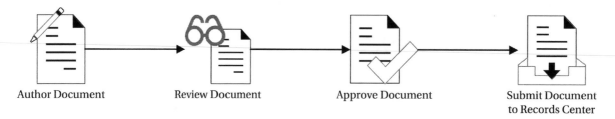

Author Document   Review Document   Approve Document   Submit Document
                                                                                   to Records Center

Figure 14-11. *A sample records workflow process*

I discussed options for workflows at several places throughout this book. You can create useful approval workflows on a document library though the browser; you can create more sophisticated workflows using Microsoft Visio 2013 or SharePoint Designer 2013. The functionality in these power-user tools can achieve a surprising range of workflow needs.

There are situations where these tools reach their limit with configuring workflow actions, instead requiring a developer develop custom actions. Requirements such as this often come up for system integration or any type of specialized processing logic. A developer can develop custom actions for SharePoint 2013 workflows using Microsoft Visual Studio 2012 with the SharePoint 2013 project templates installed.

■ **Note**   You need to install the Microsoft Office Developer Tools for Visual Studio 2012 to create projects using SharePoint 2013 project templates. Download and install the required components from the Microsoft download site at http://aka.ms/OfficeDevToolsForVS2012.

To create a SharePoint 2013 workflow in Visual Studio 2012, open Visual Studio and follow these steps:

1.   Create a SharePoint 2013 Empty Project.

2.   Open Solution Explorer in Visual Studio. Right-click on the new project, hover over Add, and click New Item on the submenu.

3.   In the Add New Item window, select Workflow, as shown in Figure 14-12. Click Add.

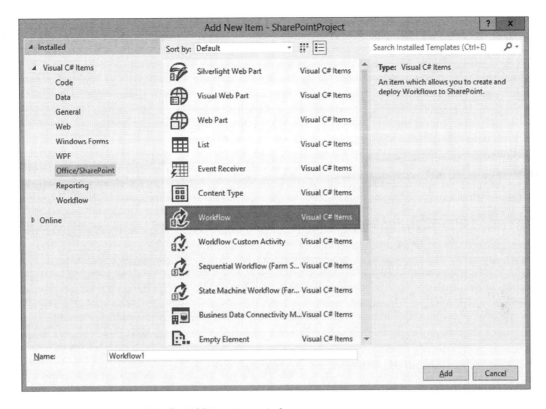

Figure 14-12. *The Visual Studio Add New Item window*

Visual Studio completes the range of workflows you can create for a SharePoint application. Its limits are practically your imagination and budget to write code. It is a productive development environment for all sorts of development, and this is especially true for SharePoint development, including SharePoint workflows. If you find yourself reaching the limits creating workflows within the SharePoint Designer 2013 tool, I encourage you to experiment with developing custom workflow actions within Visual Studio 2012.

■ **Note** For more information on SharePoint development using Visual Studio 2012, including code samples and technical references, please see the MSDN site at `http://msdn.microsoft.com/aa905690`.

Auditing and Reporting on Your Records

Capturing, preserving, and managing records cover the majority of a records manager's tasks, but also important is the ability to audit and report on the records within a repository. You might want to audit and report on a variety of things, such as compliance, content inventory, configuration setting review, and general usage. SharePoint supports these requirements through the site usage and audit reports, in addition to the Records Center file plan report.

You can view the reports in a Records Center from the Records Center Management page. On the Settings menu, click the Manage Records Center menu item to navigate to the Records Center Management page, as shown in Figure 14-13.

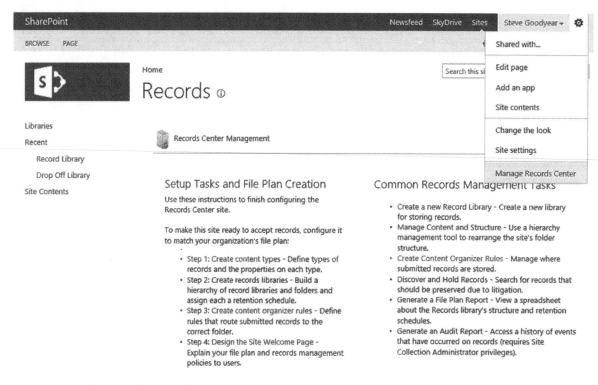

Figure 14-13. *The Records Center Management page*

In the lower-right area of the Records Center Management page under the Common Records Management Tasks section, the page presents the following two reporting options:

- **Generate A File Plan Report:** Generates a spreadsheet about the records libraries with details about the hierarchical structure and retention schedules.

- **Generate An Audit Report:** Navigates to the site collection auditing reports, including content viewing, policy modifications, expiration and disposition, and auditing settings reports.

Wrapping Up

You archive and manage your organization's official records in a records repository, referred to as a *Records Center* in SharePoint 2013. A Records Center includes the functionality to route and organize content by evaluating routing rules against the content that users submit to the repository. In this chapter, I walked you through how to create and manage a Records Center site, how to configure routing rules, and how to configure a Send To destination that users can use to submit content to the repository. Finally, I provided an overview of creating workflow using Visual Studio 2012 and generating auditing reports on the Records Center.

Capturing and preserving content protects the company's knowledge and evidence of transactions and decisions. However, at some point, the content may not provide your organization any further value and so it may no longer be necessary to retain the content. You can automate the retention and disposition of records using retention policies. In the next chapter, I walk you through how to create a retention policy with a disposition workflow and apply it to records in a records repository.

▨ ▨ ▨

CHAPTER 15

Managing Record Retention and Disposition

It is a very sad thing that nowadays there is so little useless information.

—Oscar Wilde

Preserving records leads to the need for a content disposition strategy. How do you get away from exponentially collecting more and more content over time? With properly designed retention policies, SharePoint can manage the time you need to retain a piece of content, and then orchestrate its disposal. In this chapter, I provide guidance on planning the life cycle of your official records and how to design archival strategies. I also discuss how to identify your retention requirements and how to model and configure your record disposition workflows.

After reading this chapter, you will know how to

- Identify record retention requirements.

- Plan the life cycle of records.

- Model and configure record disposition workflows.

- Configure a retention policy.

Identifying Your Record Retention Requirements

Retaining content costs money. There are storage costs involved, but I find those can be the smallest portion of the overall costs associated with retaining content. Every unit of information you keep crowds in with every other unit of information. If a document does not provide some value or meet some ongoing purpose, then storing it only creates noise.

The more content you retain, the bigger the pile that users have to sift through to find whatever relevant content they are looking for. But some may think this little inconvenience is a small price to pay to have a record of anything and everything that one might need someday—better safe than sorry, right? The trouble with this fallacy is that saving something on the *chance* that you might need it one day does not protect you, and instead, can put you and your organization at risk.

I recently had a customer who boasted that she had a copy of every e-mail she has sent or received over the previous decade or more. She spoke of this in a prideful way, as if she has achieved some near impossible feat that now protects her and her organization. Yet what she did not realize is that she is exposing her organization and herself to risk. If there is ever an incident compelling the organization to provide disclosure, her e-mails would be relevant and therefore need to be included in any disclosure. An e-mail from ten years ago can haunt an organization in surprising ways when legal teams comb through it and suggest possible interpretations.

The liability from an e-mail's contents is one cost, but the disclosure process itself can potentially come with higher costs, and thus higher risks for an organization. For example, imagine one company has horded a lot of content over the years, such as piles of e-mail. Now imagine a competing company suing this company and having a court order for information disclosure.

A company being sued has to locate all the relevant pieces of content for disclosure, likely using an eDiscovery solution such as the one I described in Chapter 11. Now, before a company discloses any information, it is most likely going to want its lawyers to review and assess the content first. This can be the most expensive step in the entire process because lawyers can be costly, especially if they have to go through an unnecessarily excessive amount of horded content. With the right blow, a competitor can cripple an organization with litigation that effectively causes a firm to self-destruct, all because people horded content.

You can mitigate against the costs and other risks associated with hording content by designing and implementing effective retention policies. Your record retention policies apply to the record, typically retaining the record for a given duration, and then disposing of the record. Figure 15-1 illustrates a content retention and disposition process.

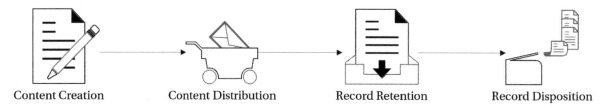

Content Creation   Content Distribution   Record Retention   Record Disposition

Figure 15-1. *Content creation to record retention to record disposition*

Retention and disposition requirements for physical paper-based records involve warehousing the record for the required period, and then shredding the paper files to dispose of them. This shredding adds an expense to the costs of records management; unless an organization is running out of space, it can be tempting to defer the shredding costs by allowing a record to persist.

Allowing records to pile up can be costly and risky, as I mentioned, but with a system-managed retention and disposition process, the disposition avoids extra costs such as shredding. This is because the records are digital files and you can dispose of a digital file by deleting it. If you configure SharePoint to automatically delete the file after a given retention period duration, then the system will delete the file without additional costs. Before you can achieve this, however, you have to determine your retention requirements.

To determine what your retention requirements are, consider the following questions:

- Do you need to retain the record?

- Are there any legal or regulatory requirements dictating how long you must retain the record?

- Are there any organizational policies dictating how long you must retain the record?

- Is there a known length of time when preserving the record is worthwhile, such as project durations or product iterations?

- Is the record vital to the organization's business continuity?

- What ongoing value will preserving the record provide the organization?

- How many copies of or references to the record exist?

- How active is the record and its contents?

- How long should your organization retain the record?

After you declare a record and archive it in a records repository, you may not want to retain it forever. You only want to retain a record for as long as its presence provides value to the organization. Knowing how long a record will be useful to an organization identifies its retention schedule, after which, you will want to dispose of the record.

This can be a scary proposition to someone who has pack-rat characteristics. But not all content is valuable, and not all content consistently maintains value to an organization. I find that by looking at the content itself, I am better able to design a rational and effective content retention policy. My process involves analyzing a content inventory, focusing primarily on the attributes for the different kinds of content. Some key attributes I try to identify in my content inventory as I am analyzing record retention and disposition include:

- Type of content or content category

- Content classification and sensitivity

- Owner or role with accountability for content

- Required preservation and retention duration

▨ **Note**   Please see Chapter 3, where I discuss building an inventory of content and identifying content attributes in more detail.

In Chapter 13, I listed a sample file plan snippet based on a department structure. I also noted typical retention requirements for the different departmental content. The following lists the main departments and their respective retention periods. Your retention periods may vary depending on your requirements, but this should give you something to start working with.

- Accounting Department (typically retained for seven years or as required)

- Advertising Department (typically retained for three years or as required)

- Engineering and Production Department (typically retained for seven or more years)

- Human Resources Department (typically retained for seven or more years, as required)

- Information Technology Department (typically retained for three years or as required)

- Legal Department (typically retained for seven or more years, as required)

- Order Department (typically retained for three years or as required)

- Purchasing Department (typically retained for three years or as required)

- Sales Department (typically retained for three years or as required)

- Service Department (typically retained for three years or as required)

Automated disposition efficiently shreds content on a given schedule, but you might not want to automatically purge certain records at the end of a duration of time. Instead, your retention and disposition requirements can include notifying a records manager of a proposed disposition and assigning a task to have him or her review the record and approve the final record destruction. You identify these types of requirements based on a records life cycle.

Planning the Life Cycle of Records

Capturing records protects an organization by maintaining its history of transactions and decisions, providing evidence to support a legal claim or to meet regulatory compliance requirements. A record's life cycle spans from the declaring of a piece of content as a record until the disposing of that record. The system must preserve a record in an immutable state, meaning it must prevent any changes or modifications to the record's contents.

Records retention defines the policies and procedures relating to what units of information the system retains and for how long. At the end of a records retention period, the process then disposes of the record, either destroying it automatically or initiating a workflow to involve a human to review and approve the disposition of a record.

Figure 15-2 illustrates the content life cycle model. The records life cycle is a subset within the content life cycle, located in the lower-right *Preserve* area in the model. Once the system declares a piece of content as an official record, it initiates the records life cycle by preserving it with a retention policy. At the end of that retention policy's schedule, the system then initiates a workflow to dispose the official record.

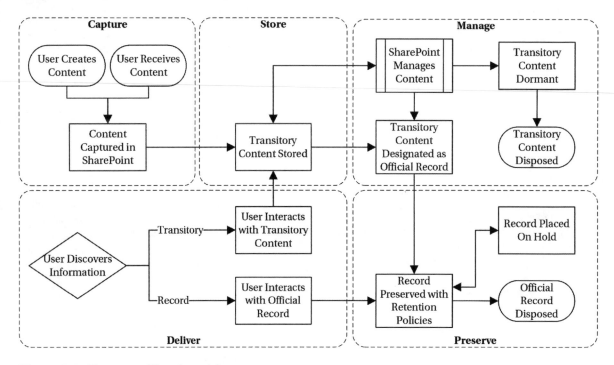

Figure 15-2. *The content life cycle model*

■ **Note**   For more information on the content life cycle model, please see Chapter 1.

The majority of the record's life cycle consists of its preservation. As I discussed in Chapter 14, this occurs as you archive the record in the records repository. Users can send a record to the records repository by selecting the option on the item's *Send-To* menu, where the records repository would then route the content to a location by matching a predefined routing rule with the content's metadata. The system then preserves the record in the repository location until a retention policy initiates a disposition process (or until a human manually disposes of the record).

You have the following options to automate the disposition of records at the end of a record's life cycle:

- Automatically delete the record

- Flag the record as deprecated and continue retaining for a short duration

- Initiate a disposition workflow to process the record's disposal

The most popular is often the workflow, although automatically deleting a record after a given duration works well for those records that do not require any additional logic or complexity in the disposal process. For those types of records where you do need to process logic, a workflow enables you to add extra steps and evaluate conditions in the disposition process. Ultimately, the workflow process extends the simple deletion, as an automated deletion is a single-step workflow. To identify the workflow steps you need, first model your record disposition process for each particular kind of content.

Modeling Record Disposition Workflows

Records retention requirements can change as the kinds of records change. Different content classifications, sensitivities, and criticalities affect the retention duration. These attributes can also affect the disposition process. For example, a record in a general classification with no sensitivity nor criticality might be fine to automatically delete in its disposition. A more critical or more sensitive record might require extra steps in the disposition process.

Before creating a workflow, I find it helpful to model it in a Microsoft Visio diagram first. This helps me see whether I covered all the steps and handled all the valid paths available in the disposition process. A diagram can also help you communicate the workflow to other business users and records managers, allowing them to provide feedback to ensure the workflow will meet their needs.

■ **Note**   Please see the Office site at `http://office.microsoft.com/visio` to learn more about Microsoft Visio 2013.

Figure 15-3 provides an example of a disposition approval workflow model. When the retention period expires, the workflow assigns a task to a records manager to review and approve the record's disposition. If the records manager approves the disposition, the workflow then disposes of the record; otherwise, the workflow assigns a new retention period to the record.

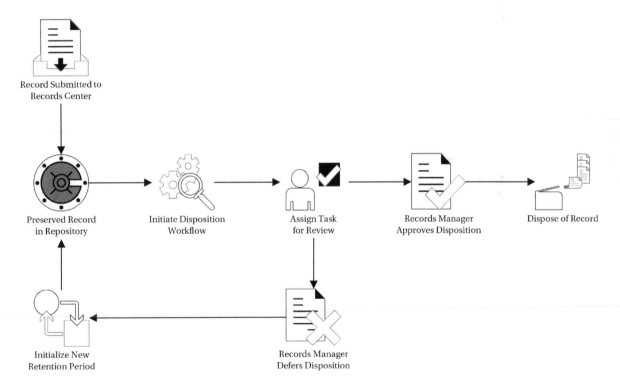

Figure 15-3. *A sample record disposition approval workflow*

You can add other steps in your model if required, particularly to process additional logic to add more automation to the workflow. Some examples of additional logic you might consider for your disposition workflow include:

- Escalate the disposition approval task to another records manager after a given duration.

- Analyze the record's metadata to match a predefined workflow rule to automatically determine whether to further retain the record or dispose of it.

- Determine whether other records reference the record under disposition and assign a new retention policy to match the other records.

In addition to the different approvals and artificial intelligence that you can include, your disposition workflow also might involve a multistaged disposition process. For example, after a given retention duration, a workflow stage could delete all previous versions of a record, retaining only the latest version for a new retention period.

Once you have the disposition workflow model finalized, use it to configure a disposition workflow and apply it to a SharePoint retention policy to automatically manage the records' retention and disposition. In the following sections, I provide the steps involved with configuring a disposition workflow and then configuring a content type's retention policy with multiple disposition stages.

■ **Tip** You can create SharePoint workflows directly in Visio 2013 using the Microsoft SharePoint 2013 Workflow template. Visio saves SharePoint workflows to your SharePoint site, where you can select it and apply it to a retention policy.

Configuring Record Disposition Workflows

The need for a disposition approval workflow is so common that SharePoint includes a disposition approval workflow template with the Records Center site template. You can achieve many of your simpler disposition approval requirements by associating this workflow with records libraries in your records repository.

To create a new workflow based on the disposition approval workflow template, navigate to the library settings page for a record library in your records repository and follow these steps:

1. Click the Workflow Settings link.

2. On the Workflow Settings page, select whether to associate the workflow to the entire library or to a specific content type.

3. Click the Add A Workflow link to navigate to the Add A Workflow page, as shown in Figure 15-4.

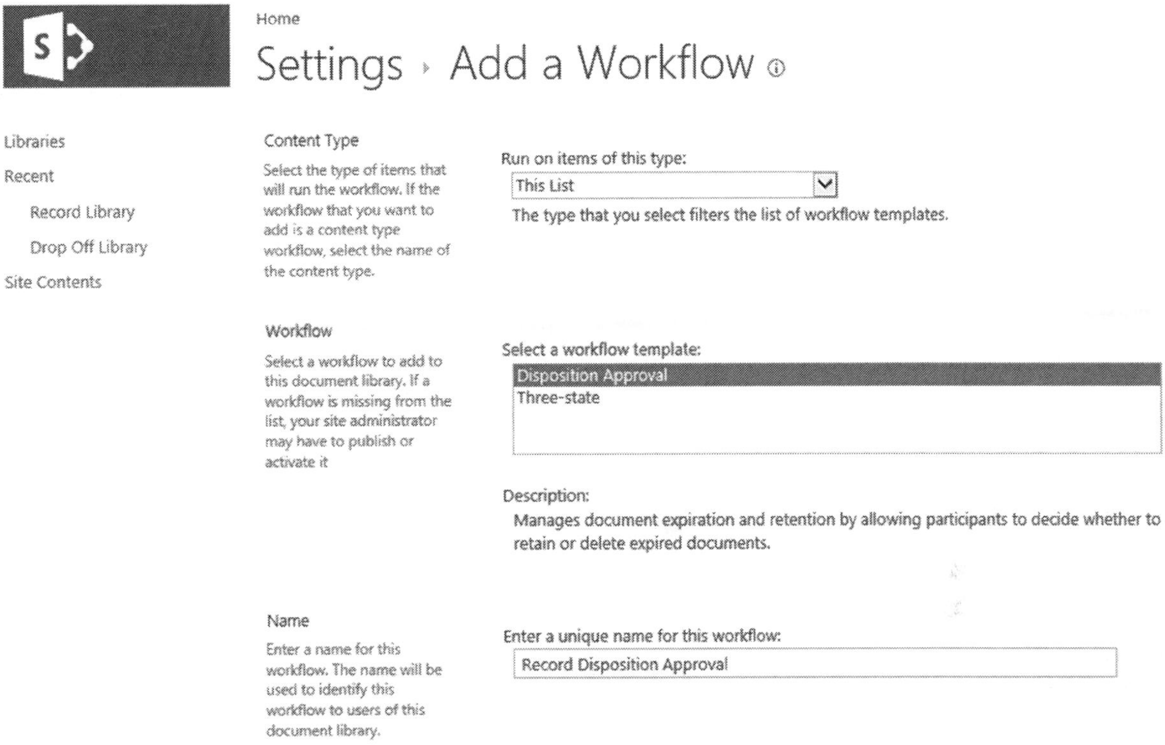

Home

Settings › Add a Workflow ⓘ

Libraries

Recent

    Record Library

    Drop Off Library

Site Contents

Content Type

Select the type of items that will run the workflow. If the workflow that you want to add is a content type workflow, select the name of the content type.

Run on items of this type:

| This List ▾ |

The type that you select filters the list of workflow templates.

Workflow

Select a workflow to add to this document library. If a workflow is missing from the list, your site administrator may have to publish or activate it

Select a workflow template:

| Disposition Approval |
| Three-state |

Description:

Manages document expiration and retention by allowing participants to decide whether to retain or delete expired documents.

Name

Enter a name for this workflow. The name will be used to identify this workflow to users of this document library.

Enter a unique name for this workflow:

| Record Disposition Approval |

Figure 15-4. *The Add A Workflow page*

4. On the Add A Workflow page, select the Disposition Approval workflow template.

5. Provide a unique name to identify the workflow with.

6. Configure your desired Start Options, as shown in Figure 15-5. The following are the available start options:

    •   *Allow this workflow to be manually started by an authenticated user with Edit Item permissions*: Allows a user to manually start the workflow.

    •   *Start this workflow to approve publishing a major version of an item*: Disabled by default because it requires the library to be configured with publishing and approvals. By their nature, records are already published and approved.

    •   *Creating a new item will start this workflow*: Enables the workflow to start automatically for each new item added to the library.

    •   *Changing an item will start this workflow*: Enables the workflow to start automatically anytime an item is edited.

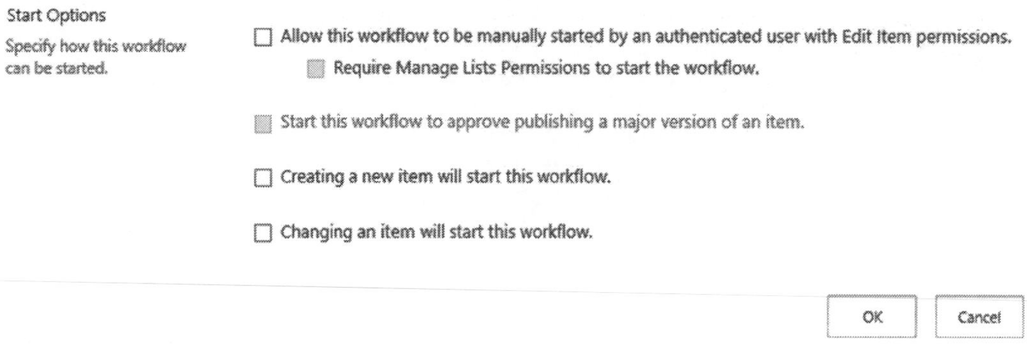

Start Options

Specify how this workflow can be started.

☐ Allow this workflow to be manually started by an authenticated user with Edit Item permissions.

    ☐ Require Manage Lists Permissions to start the workflow.

☐ Start this workflow to approve publishing a major version of an item.

☐ Creating a new item will start this workflow.

☐ Changing an item will start this workflow.

         OK   Cancel

Figure 15-5. *The Start Options on the Add A Workflow page*

    7.   Click OK.

You can change the workflow options at a later time by returning to the Workflow Settings page as shown in Figure 15-6. Simply click the desired link in the Workflow Name to change the settings for that workflow.

Figure 15-6. *The Workflow Settings page with the new disposition approval workflow*

The built-in disposition workflow template meets a lot of needs to add some logic beyond simply disposing of a record after a given duration of time. Its value comes with adding a step in the workflow to involve humans to first review and approve the disposition.

Of course, you may have disposition approval workflow requirements that go beyond what is available with the built-in workflow template. In that case, you can develop a custom workflow using Visual Studio. This allows you to programmatically control the processing logic of the disposition workflow, enabling you to process advanced tasks, such as:

- Coordinating a workflow with an external system or another process

- Performing sophisticated calculations based on different metadata attributes

- Analyzing any references or active links to the record

- Parsing the content to redact portions

■ **Note**   For more information on developing custom workflows using Visual Studio, please see the MSDN article at `http://msdn.microsoft.com/jj163199`.

Whether you use the built-in workflow template, configure a workflow using Visio, or develop a custom workflow using Visual Studio, you associate it with any relevant content types on the records site. SharePoint then activates and processes the workflow whenever content expires. To make content expire, you need to configure a retention policy.

Configuring a Retention Policy

A retention policy manages the life cycle for a record. You can apply a retention policy to an entire records library in a Records Center or to specific content types. I tend to apply retention policies to content types for the flexibility of having multiple retention durations in a given library. Nevertheless, if your records repository has granular records libraries where all contained content share the same retention duration, then you can apply the retention policy to the library rather than to individual content types.

To create a new retention policy, navigate to the record library Settings page and follow these steps:

1. Click the Information management Policy Settings link to navigate to the Information Management Policy Settings page, as shown in Figure 15-7.

Figure 15-7. *The Information Management Policy Settings page*

2. Notice that the Library Based Retention Schedule source of retention is set to Content Types by default. You can change the Source of Retention by clicking the Change Source link and selecting Library and Folders on the options page.

3. On the Information Management Policy Settings page, click the desired Content Type in the Content Type Policies section.

4. On the Edit Policy page, select the Enable Retention check box to access the link to add retention stages, as shown in Figure 15-8.

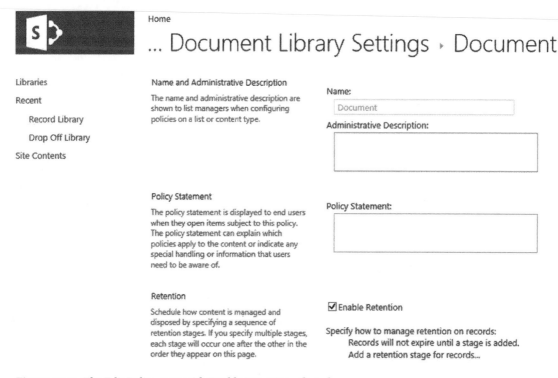

Figure 15-8. *The Edit Policy page with Enable Retention selected*

5. Click the Add A Retention Stage For Records link to open the Stage Properties dialog, as shown in Figure 15-9.

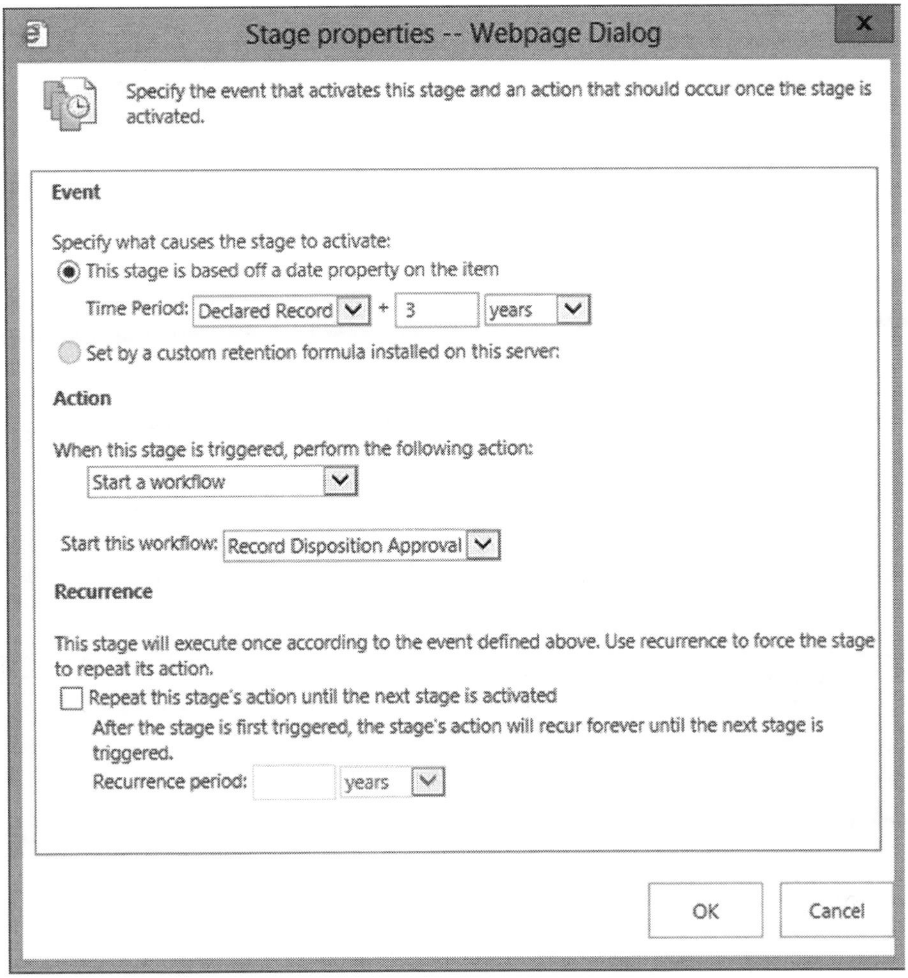

Figure 15-9. The retention policy Stage Properties dialog window

6. In the Event section, select the Time Period to specify what causes the stage to activate. For example, you can activate the stage by selecting Declared Record plus 3 Years, which will activate the retention stage three years after a piece of content is declared a record.

7. In the Action section, select the action to perform when the stage is triggered. For example, you can select Start A Workflow from the action drop-down menu, and then select a disposition approval workflow to start.

8. Click OK on the Stage Properties dialog to save the stage. Click OK on the Edit Policy page to save the retention policy.

Once you add a stage to a retention policy, you will see it in the Retention section on the Edit Policy page. You can add multiple stages to take different actions at different times. Figure 15-10 shows the Retention section for a sample retention policy with multiple stages.

Retention

Schedule how content is managed and disposed by specifying a sequence of retention stages. If you specify multiple stages, each stage will occur one after the other in the order they appear on this page.

Note: If the Library and Folder Based Retention feature is active, list administrators can override content type policies with their own retention schedules. To prevent this, deactivate the feature on the site collection.

☑ Enable Retention

Specify how to manage retention on records:

Event	Action	Recurrence
Declared Record + 1 years	Delete all previous versions	No
Declared Record + 3 years	Start the Record Disposition Approval workflow	No
Add a retention stage for records...		

Figure 15-10. *A sample retention policy with multiple stages*

A retention policy effectively allows you to delegate the retention and disposition details to SharePoint. This frees your records manager from having to track and dispose of content manually, allowing them to focus his or her efforts on more valuable activities.

You can configure a workflow to dispose of records after a given duration, but there may be copies in different SharePoint sites or in e-mail, and as I discuss in the sidebar, a copy of the record may exist in a backup file. If a copy exists, your organization still possesses that record and would need to disclose it in the event of litigation. If you need to handle this requirement, you would need to add an additional stage and workflow to your record retention policy and use custom code to locate and dispose of the additional copies.

RECORD DISPOSITION REQUIREMENTS AND BACKUPS

Beware of record copies existing in backups. If your database administrators back up the SharePoint databases regularly, as they most likely do, a copy of your records exist in those backups. This means that when you dispose of a record using a retention policy and workflow to expire and delete the record, a copy of the record will still exist in the backup files unless you program a workflow to take special action.

Often times, having a copy in your backup files is not a problem. If you only retain backups for the previous week on site and copies of backups for the previous month off site, then your records retention schedule will at most be out of sync in the backups by a month. Short durations expose short risk windows and may be acceptable to your organization rather than incur the expense to manage individual record retention all the way through to backup files.

If your organization has a habit of retaining backups for longer periods of time, such as those occurring during lengthy cycles of the offsite backup tape, then you may be at risk. Part of your risk might include the lack of awareness that your organization possesses a particular record after the records repository disposes of it but before the backup media is overwrote.

You can mitigate against risks associated with retaining records in backup files past a record's retention period by minimizing the length of time you retain backup files. You have to balance this with your organization's service level agreements and disaster recovery policy.

Wrapping Up

You use SharePoint retention policies to define how long to preserve a piece of content and how SharePoint should dispose of it once the content reaches the end of its life cycle. In this chapter, I discussed the need to plan and design record retention and disposition policies to determine the length of time to preserve a record. Although you can apply the retention and disposition concepts to any content in SharePoint, I focused specifically on managing the life cycle of official records, and in particular, on associating a disposition workflow with a SharePoint content type's retention policy to automate record disposition.

Capturing, preserving, managing, and disposing of records forms the essence of the activities involved with records management. SharePoint provides a feature-rich and highly capable records repository; but what if your organization uses another repository to capture and preserve records? Some organizations use SharePoint to create content, but they have a different system for records, either a more specialized records management system or a legacy records repository. In the next chapter, I discuss how to achieve these requirements and I provide guidance on how to plan for and design an integration solution with other records repositories.

■ ■ ■

CHAPTER 16

Integrating with Other Records Repositories

The scariest moment is always just before you start.

—Stephen King

Managing content and records within the SharePoint platform works well because Microsoft designed all the different capability areas to integrate with each other. But what happens when you have to integrate SharePoint with external records repositories? In this chapter, I discuss options for non-SharePoint records systems and how to integrate those systems with your SharePoint records management solution, particularly for physical records, document-imaging solutions, and other digital records repository systems. I also provide you with an overview of the extension capabilities available for SharePoint records management.

After reading this chapter, you will know how to

- Describe options for external records systems.

- Plan a document imaging solution.

- Integrate with external records repositories.

- Understand extensions for SharePoint records management.

Understanding Requirements for Integration

SharePoint is a broad product. It does a lot of things really well, but this breadth comes at the cost of it being less specialized in certain areas. Although the gap is narrowing with each release of SharePoint, competing products that specialize in a narrow functional area may make a stronger match to specific functional requirements. As a result, your organization might select SharePoint for a range of its capabilities, and yet select another product that is more specialized in a particular area, even though it may overlap some of the functionality SharePoint provides.

Alternatively, your organization might have an old system already in place before you ever deployed SharePoint, a system that many other applications, departments, and processes all depend on. The legacy system might have so many dependencies that migrating the records and consolidating on a single platform with SharePoint is not practical to achieve given your budget, timeline, or the politics involved.

Whatever the situation and motivating drivers behind maintaining a legacy system, you can integrate SharePoint with these external systems (at least to some degree, depending on the system and the level of integration the system's vendor exposes). Typically, the integration depends on a *SharePoint connector*, a component the vendor supplies to integrate SharePoint with the third-party repository, as shown in Figure 16-1.

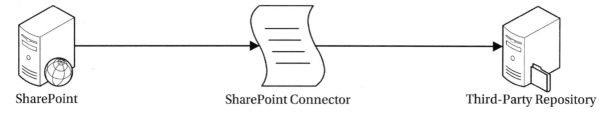

SharePoint   **SharePoint Connector**   **Third-Party Repository**

***Figure 16-1.** Example of an external records repository*

Integrating multiple enterprise applications introduces complexity and dependencies. I find that establishing the roles and responsibilities between the systems offers the best way to manage the complexities and ensure coverage. This documents what is expected and from whom, making it clear what tasks or decisions need to occur and by what role.

■ **Tip**   I discuss establishing roles and responsibilities, among other governance topics, in my first book, *Practical SharePoint 2013 Governance* (Apress, 2013). You can find out more about this book and access an online preview of it on the Apress web site at www.apress.com/9781430248873.

You might need to integrate with a variety of types of external systems, but the two popular types are document imaging solutions and external repositories. Document imaging systems input records into SharePoint by scanning a physical document. External repositories receive and preserve records from SharePoint and other systems. First, I discuss document imaging, and then in a later section, I return to discuss integrating with external repositories.

Planning a Document Imaging Solution

As far as technology has come in recent years, many organizations still retain large amounts of physical records. If your organization needs to work with physical paper documents as part of its process, then you might consider digitizing the document as part of its record declaration process. You might not always want to maintain a copy of a physical record. This is solved by scanning and capturing an image of those documents.

SharePoint itself does not have document-scanning features built in; instead, Microsoft relies on partners and independent software vendors to extend SharePoint and provide document imaging solutions. The implementation of each solution depends on the particular vendor, but in a general sense, they all perform the key task of scanning a physical document and then saving a digital image of it in a SharePoint library. Figure 16-2 illustrates the primary document imaging process.

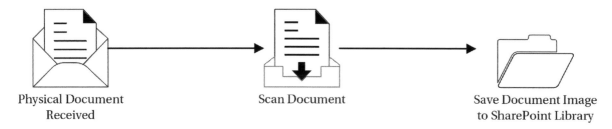

Physical Document   **Scan Document**   **Save Document Image**
Received   **to SharePoint Library**

***Figure 16-2.** Capturing scanned images of documents in a SharePoint library*

As SharePoint does not have a document-imaging component, you must implement a document scanning solution as a third-party product that works with SharePoint. There are several on the market from a number of different vendors. Some are specialized to work with a vendor's scanning hardware, while software products are more hardware independent.

To plan your document imaging solution, start with your scanning hardware. If you do not have scanning hardware, you should investigate the different products on the market to determine which best fits your organization's requirements and available budget. You should also consider whether it has a component to work with SharePoint by interfacing with the SharePoint Application Programming Interface (API).

Once you have the scanning hardware and software to capture the image to a SharePoint library, follow the configuration instructions provided by the vendor you choose.

■ **Note**   The implementation and configuration of the imaging solution is vendor-specific.

Document imaging follows a consistent process, and it mostly revolves around handling and then destroying the physical document. The following steps summarize the key points involved with a document imaging solution.

1.   Receive the physical document.

2.   Scan the physical document, capturing a document image and any relevant metadata.

3.   Save the document image and metadata to the SharePoint document library.

4.   Shred the physical document.

The physical document consumes the most effort in the entire process, from handling to scanning to shredding the document. In many cases, this is simply required. However, where possible, you might be able to optimize this process by having users scan and shred their own documents. This would simplify the document imaging process, or at least delegate its burden to the user, which can be beneficial in several applications, such as the expense report I discuss in the sidebar.

USERS SCANNING THEIR OWN DOCUMENTS

I have seen a number of different expense reporting processes, both from the different companies I have worked for and from the different customers I have advised. Two common elements are the itemized expense report and the expense receipt. Where they differ is how the expense workflow processes the receipt through the process.

At some point during the workflow, the receipts need to be digitized. During the first years of digital expense reporting, I noticed the receipts were often sent to a central scanning facility, which is one document imaging solution. Recently, however, I have been noticing more and more expense processes begin with the user photographing his or her expense receipt and submitting the expense through a smartphone app.

With users submitting documents already in a digital format, the entire workflow processes a digital file. This process speeds up the entire workflow because all the information is contained together as a package as soon as a user enters it into a system and initiates the process; it does not have to wait on an imaging step.

Interfacing with External Records Repositories

SharePoint cannot operate effectively as an island of information. Its value and the richness of its experience depend on connecting with your organization's records repository. This benefit is realized by surfacing the relevant information from the records repository in context in SharePoint, such as within the search results, and archiving SharePoint content to preserve as a record in the official records management system.

One important integration requirement is to include an external records repository's content in the SharePoint search results. As I mentioned in Chapter 9, a strong user experience involves providing users with an enterprise search portal where they can search across all content repositories, SharePoint and otherwise. Including archival content and preserved records in the search results gives users a single known location to find information in your organization.

You can interface your SharePoint search implementation with an external records repository by configuring a search connector. Some application vendors provide a SharePoint search connector you can install and configure to enable SharePoint to crawl the content. Alternatively, you can use a generic search connector in some cases or develop your own connector.

■ **Note** To learn more about the search connector framework in SharePoint 2013, please see the MSDN article at http://msdn.microsoft.com/ee556429.

There are several ways to input data into SharePoint, from users uploading files to workflows submitting files or data. But one technology still persists as a handy and functional way to transfer data: e-mail. Sending a document over e-mail is an easy way to share a copy with a colleague, and the same is true for interfacing with SharePoint.

You can configure a library to receive e-mail messages at a designated e-mail address. This enables users to send a document to a SharePoint library from Outlook. However, you do not have to limit this capability to users; any process that can send an SMTP e-mail message can forward and submit a document to a SharePoint document library.

■ **Note** To learn more about configuring incoming e-mail for a SharePoint 2013 farm, please see the TechNet article at http://technet.microsoft.com/cc262947.

Another type of system integration includes providing a connection that SharePoint can use to submit content to the external system. The vendors of enterprise applications often provide these integration connections. However, if your records repository does not provide a component to bridge a connection with SharePoint, then you can extend SharePoint by developing your own connection.

Extending SharePoint 2013 Records Management

Records management in SharePoint continues to evolve and mature. The product has included records management features for a few versions now, and the product team has made strong investments with enhancing the features with each iteration. Nevertheless, there may be things you want to do or ways you want SharePoint to manage records that the product does not do. In these cases, you can either develop your own solution or license one from an independent software vendor.

Microsoft provides an extensible application programming interface (API) with SharePoint 2013, enabling you to extend functionality in SharePoint. Although this is not a book on development or customizations, I did want to point out that the product team made an API available for developers to extend and customize functionality on top of the SharePoint platform.

■ **Note**   Please see the MSDN article at `http://msdn.microsoft.com/jj193038` to learn more about the
SharePoint 2013 API reference libraries.

Rather than develop your own components to extend SharePoint functionality, you can purchase third-party
products. Companies have developed packaged solutions for a number of different aspects of SharePoint, including
records management. You can find products that specialize in a variety of solutions, including the following areas:

- Workflows and electronic forms

- Metadata management

- Document imaging

- Auditing and reporting

- Content replication

- Retention and disposition

- Records reporting and dashboards

- Policy management

I have worked with a number of different products, each product with its own benefits. In the sidebar, I provide
an example of one product extending SharePoint specifically to add records management functionality. There are
several other firms that license apps or components to extend the default functionality in SharePoint, depending on
your needs.

EXTENDING SHAREPOINT WITH COLLABWARE

I am most familiar with the records management product from Collabware because the company is from my
hometown of Vancouver. My friend Graham Sibley started the company and its product with the belief that
SharePoint is a capable records management platform, but that there were some gaps that a third-party product
could fill to improve the overall records management experience.

A few of the key features of the Collabware CLM product and the gaps it fills include:

- Rule-based autocategorization and metadata autopopulation

- Automatic record declaration

- Records management dashboard

- Centralized compliance policy management

- Content surfacing and querying

To learn more about Collabware and to get some ideas about how you can extend SharePoint records
management, please see the company web site at `www.collabware.com`.

My point is that although SharePoint provides a rich environment for your organization's entire content life cycle,
including records management, it also exposes an extensible application programming interface (API) for vendors
or internal developers to develop products that extend SharePoint's functionality.

Wrapping Up

SharePoint might not be your organization's only content repository, and this might be particularly true if you have a legacy records management product deployed. Many third-party products provide connectors to enable you to integrate SharePoint with the repository. SharePoint also exposes an application programming interface (API) that you can use to develop an integration solution.

In this chapter, I discussed planning considerations for integrating with external systems, including capturing scans of physical documents and developing custom interfaces. This integration fits in the content life cycle I discussed in Chapter 1, preserving the records in a different repository. Throughout this book, I have discussed different aspects of the content life cycle, from content creation to discovery, and finally, to managing official records. All these different aspects of enterprise content management (ECM) in SharePoint should help get you started with designing your ECM solution.

Index

■ F, G, H

Get the eBook for only $10!

Now you can take the weightless companion with you anywhere, anytime. Your purchase of this book entitles you to 3 electronic versions for only $10.

This Apress title will prove so indispensible that you'll want to carry it with you everywhere, which is why we are offering the eBook in 3 formats for only $10 if you have already purchased the print book.

Convenient and fully searchable, the PDF version enables you to easily find and copy code—or perform examples by quickly toggling between instructions and applications. The MOBI format is ideal for your Kindle, while the ePUB can be utilized on a variety of mobile devices.

Go to www.apress.com/promo/tendollars to purchase your companion eBook.

Made in the USA
San Bernardino, CA
18 June 2016